# PRAISE FOR PAT JORDAN

"One of the best and truest books about baseball and about coming to maturity in America."                                    —*TIME* on *A False Spring*

"A sports memoir unlike any other."
                —Jonathan Yardley, *The Washington Post*, on *A False Spring*

"The best nonfiction sports book we've seen to date. Do Pat Jordan a favor. Don't call him a sportswriter."
                                        —Paul Hemphill on *A False Spring*

"Tight and true, and lingers in the mind and heart. His is a wonderful prose. There is not an ounce of fat anywhere in this narrative. This is a valuable book for the library of any family who admires the written word."
                —Harry Crews, author of *Blood and Grits*, on *A Nice Tuesday*

"Who is the best sportswriter (ever)? The names that are mentioned most often are W.C. Heinz and Pat Jordan. I concur, but I'll take Jordan in a split-decision."
                —*The Wall Street Journal* on *The Best Sports Writing of Pat Jordan*

"The incisiveness of some of Pat Jordan's stories is scary. They lay bare the sporting life in all its mystery, banality, beauty, sadness, and they do it with a gimlet eye, an exquisite ear, wide curiosity, and timing so sharp it can make you gasp. He is a master portraitist."
                —William Finnegan, staff writer, the *New Yorker*, on
                                *The Best Sports Writing of Pat Jordan*

"Definitely one of the year's best books, sports or otherwise."
                —*Philadelphia Bulletin* on *Black Coach*

# OTHER BOOKS BY PAT JORDAN

*Black Coach*

*The Suitors of Spring*

*A False Spring*

*Broken Patterns*

*Chase the Game*

*After the Sundown*

*The Cheat (A Novel)*

*A Nice Tuesday*

*The Best Sports Writing of Pat Jordan*

# MORE BOOKS FROM THE SAGER GROUP

# MY
# FATHER'S
# CON

## A MEMOIR

Published in the United States of America.

Cover and Interior Designed by Siori Kitajima, PatternBased.com

Cataloging-in-Publication data for this book is available from the Library of Congress


ISBN-13:
eBook: 978-1-950154-84-5
Paperback: 978-1-950154-85-2
Hardcover: 978-1-950154-86-9


Published by The Sager Group LLC
(TheSagerGroup.net)

# MY FATHER'S CON

## A MEMOIR

# PAT JORDAN

THE SAGER GROUP

Artifex Te Adiuva

*This memoir is dedicated to my father.*
*And my mother and my brother.*
*And, as always, to Susan.*

"The past is baggage. It makes you miss the next train out."
—Patsy Jordan

"Only a fool, or a child, believes in perfect justice."
—Patsy Jordan

*Dad was adjusting my tie, one of the few moments he touched me. Ma was looking off furious at the loss of her son, my older brother, to another woman, his new wife, at my brother's wedding. When I was a boy, and I received attention from my parents, I always looked startled. Ma always wore lilac. When I wrote this book, it made me cry. Still does. I miss them all. I am the last one left.*

# CONTENTS

# PART ONE

# CHAPTER ONE

My father's name was Pasquale Giordano. Or Patsy Giordano. Or Patsy Jordan. Or Patrick Michaele Jordan. Like everything about his life, even his name was elusive.

My father's life that he passed down to me over sixty-five years was no well-made novel with expository transitions. It was a collection of slides, like a Raymond Carver short story. A thing happened. Time passed. Another thing happened. The things that happened did not connect, one to another. There was never any attempt to explain the transitions of those things, to string one slide to another to make a coherent narrative for me. The how and why of them. The meaning of them. The point.

My father, in his late teens, on the hustle, sipped a Pink Lady at a table in the Flamingo Lounge at Hialeah Race Track with the beautiful Palm Beach heiress in her twenties. She smoked a cigarette in a silver cigarette holder. She was bored. All the swells were too old, their sons mere boys. She was only there because Daddy insisted. His horse was entered in the Flamingo Derby. After it won, he expected her to be with him in the winner's circle for the photograph that would appear in the *Palm Beach Post*. My father said something. She tilted back her head and laughed, showing him her patrician nose and swan-like neck.

Silly, she said, Daddy's horses always win. That's why he hides them until the Derby.

My father smiled, then excused himself for a moment. The heiress watched him go across the room toward the men's facilities beyond the betting windows. She was distracted by the waiter. Yes, two more Pink Ladies, she said. She waited. The bugle summoned the horses to the starting gate. The flamingoes on the infield grass rose up en masse from their ennui, fluttering their coral-pink wings around a little lake. The heiress looked around for the handsome young man with the blue-gray eyes, but he was gone.

It was a perfect story, but without meaning. Which is why over the years, it dawned on me that all my father's perfect stories might be manufactured, with gears and sprockets and chains, like a perpetual motion machine with eternally moving parts. The machine produced, over and over, all those perfect stories, without a point. Which did not mean there was no point at all, but rather that the point was never in the stories the machine produced. The point was in the machine itself, which was the exquisite perfection of my father's con.

# CHAPTER TWO

My father was a beautiful boy, or so I was told. I know he was a handsome young man once. I could see this for myself when I was a young man, then older, and finally an old man myself, every time I visited my parents' small apartment where they lived the last forty years of their life. We three would be sitting around their small dining room table in my mother's living room-dining room overstuffed with plants and knickknacks and faux Mediterranean furniture. We'd be talking in the late afternoon while eating my mother's lunch of *pasta e fagioli*, with ciabatta bread and pecorino and sweet red roasted peppers in olive oil. Every so often, while they were talking, I would glance up to my left, where, on the wall, looking down on us from a distant past I'd never known, were two large sepia-tinted photographs, each in baroque gold gilt frames one would expect to see in a museum of Renaissance masterpieces. And in a way they were masterpieces, if a masterpiece was something valued for its rarity. They were the only photographs of my parents I ever saw from their past before me. My mother was fourteen in her photograph. A child/woman with black, bobbed hair, thick black eyebrows, dark eyes, a broad nose, and dark skin. She had an attractive Anna Magnani face, mannish, that would be described as handsome as she aged.

My father was the pretty one, at seventeen. He already looked like a man. His slicked-back, sandy-colored hair was already receding from his forehead. He had blue-gray eyes, a straight nose, a full, sensuous lower lip, almost lush, like a woman's, and pale skin. Unlike my mother, he did not look Italian. He looked like William Hurt, the actor, a well-born WASP, who would have gone to all the right schools, Phillips Exeter, and then Harvard or Yale, or, as my father used to call it, "Darthmuth," his only tell he could never shake. Then he would have joined the family's white-shoe law firm. He would have liked those white shoes. He never could resist a bit of flash when he was young, before he got his look just right. In his photo on the wall, he wore a cream-colored cashmere jacket with a silk foulard fastened to his high, starched collar with a diamond stick pin. He was a dandy, like Gatsby, the parvenu, the sweat-stained striving always showing through all his expensive clothes. But my father was a lot smarter than Gatsby. Approaching twenty, he realized his look was a tell. So he changed overnight. He affected a manner of dress that never wavered in the sixty-five years I knew him.

He dressed every morning in the same type of clothes, his uniform. That's what it was for him, a distinguishing uniform no matter whether he was going to throw out the garbage, go to a pool hall, shoot craps at the Venice Athletic Club, or take my mother out to a Vaudeville Show at the Majestic Theater and then a late night supper at the fanciest restaurant in Bridgeport, Connecticut, the Ocean Sea Grill. He always wore an Oxford cloth, button-down collared shirt, white or pale blue; a regimentally striped tie, burgundy with navy blue stripes (no stick pin now); a navy wool blazer with brass buttons; charcoal gray slacks, even in summer; and heavy oxblood, wingtip, cordovan leather shoes. In the winter, he wore a double-breasted, full-length, camel hair overcoat and a felt fedora hat.

My father bought his uniforms at J. Press Clothiers on York Street, in New Haven, a few blocks from Yale. Every five years or so, he'd dress into his threadbare old uniform and make the trip in his Volkswagen Beetle to York Street to buy a new version of his uniform, everything the same through the years, even the sizes. My father was an abstemious man.

He stopped first at the Yale bookstore. He perused the classics among all those young students, and bought something from the works of Plato in paperback, or maybe Aristotle or Socrates. He told the girl checking him out, No bag! He carried the book in his hand as he walked down York Street. The students he passed never gave him a second glance. He could have been any classics professor on campus, even when he was an old man in his eighties, shambling down the street, a little absentminded the students thought, but probably still a brilliant mind. They didn't know how right they were.

His gambling cronies gave him the moniker Ivy League.

My father called his look "My con. The suckers bought it."

His look never changed. My father never changed before my eyes. He never aged, partly because he was already forty, fixed in his look, when I was a child. He looked the same to me when I was a teenager, a father myself, a grown man in my forties, and even the last time I saw him when I was an old man myself at sixty-five, and he was in his nineties. He was a little more halt that last time, a little more bent over. But his look was still the same. His uniform. The bald head with a friar's tuft of feathery, silver hair, like a baby wren's down. The brush mustache he'd affected in old age. The pale skin that was now a baby's pink. The blue-gray eyes, not so vivid now, more opaque. But still darting, like a predatory bird.

By his eighties, his cronies had taken to calling him *Il Professore*. The Professor Emeritus of Con, with maybe a chair named after him at Yale where he had taught, or at his alma mater, Darthmuth. If he had actually gone to Darthmuth, or taught at Yale, or his cronies even knew what such an honor was. A chair? But my father would have loved it. Not the chair itself, the chair was a just thing that meant nothing to him. What would have meant something to him was the idea of it, all those brilliant professors paying homage to *Il Professore*'s superior genius without a clue to what it was.

# CHAPTER THREE

My father didn't believe in things. There were no mementoes in our house. No things from the past that had been passed down from one generation to the next. No grandfather's clock from the old country in the living room. No china or silverware that had been transported lovingly across the ocean a century ago and now rested in our breakfront. No steamer trunk in the attic plastered with stickers, "The Cunard Line," and filled with things musty, faded, creased, dried, as fragile as dust, and as mysterious. No packets of envelopes with foreign stamps on them, and inside letters written in a foreign language in a spidery, brown script. No white lace wedding dress now faded a dirty yellow. No sepia-toned tintypes of great-grandfathers, great-grandmothers, grandfathers, grandmothers, all so foreign looking. High stiff collars, extravagant handlebar mustaches, hair swept up in chignons and fastened with ivory combs, all of them posed for formal portraits with their many children. There were no fresher images, either, of a clean-shaven, modern father and his son, both Americans now, my father and me.

My father never took a photograph of me as a baby, a child, a boy, a teenager and pasted those in a leather-bound photo album. We never sat side-by-side on a sofa with that photo album that never existed, spread out on his knees as he pointed out to me stages of my life, adding a little detail to each photo to flesh out my remembrance of that moment it was taken, the way fathers do. He never kept a shoebox with my things in it. My baby teeth. A lock of my golden curls. My baby's rattle. The birthday card I made for him in the first grade. A child's crayon drawing of a stick figure, the word Daddy scrawled across the top, and a brown birthday cake with flaming candles. When I gave him that card, he thanked me with a kiss, and then it vanished. It was never taped to the refrigerator door, or propped up on the fireplace mantle, or tucked away for safekeeping in that shoebox. It had served its purpose for a moment, then it was discarded, another useless thing from the past.

My father didn't believe in things that were a reminder of the past. He'd never had such things. He never really had a past either, that mattered, that should be remembered, that should be passed on to me, his son. For what purpose? To burden me with pity for him? Pity, like guilt, he once told me, was a destructive human emotion. Which was why he never dwelled on the past. It was baggage, he told me. Baggage held you back. It was heavy, cumbersome. It squatted there, ominous, accusing, beside the railroad tracks in the summer heat. The more you struggled with that baggage, the more likely you were to miss the next train out, although he never said to where. For him it didn't matter. It would always be a better place than the one he was leaving. Which was why he always traveled light.

My father never told me stories about his past in the way of fathers imparting to a son a sense of where they came from, their native land, ancestors, childhood, young manhood, the lives they had lived. It was not because he had no real past, because he had a fascinating past, to me anyway. To him his past was just baggage that he let slip to me in bits and pieces at odd moments over sixty-five years.

My father held up those unnumbered slides from his past for only an instant before he snatched them away. They existed, like stills of a moment, complete in themselves, in relation to nothing else, a past, a future, an idea, a moral, a point. I learned at a young age that I had to make the connections. I had to fill in that black space between my father's slides with an imagined slide of my own, which slides my father omitted for reasons of his own. So I created that slide, which may, or may not, have existed, to give his past meaning. And then, there it was! The point! Or not. Maybe it was just my point.

We'd be driving in the country on a lazy summer Sunday afternoon. My father, my mother, myself at six. A family now, one of the few times we were a family on a scenic Sunday drive. We gazed out the windows to marvel at an expanse of lawn that seemed to go on forever up a rise to a spreading chestnut tree with a dog sleeping in its shade. Behind the dog, on the top of the hill, was an old, white colonial farmhouse with a covered front porch. That farmhouse had a past, and the family inside it were a part of that past.

I leaned forward in the back seat, my hands on the front seat, and said, "Daddy, did you have a dog?" He didn't miss a beat. He said, "In the orphanage?" Not even an answer. Just another question he left for me to figure out the answer.

I tried to picture in my mind the slide that was an orphanage. The car began to speed up. My father checked his watch. The leisurely ride was over now. The farmhouses sped past our window in a blur until my father found a pay phone by the side of the road, and stopped. He got out and went into the pay phone booth. My mother and I sat in the car by the side of the road. Speeding cars whizzed past us so closely that our car quivered. My father took out a matchbook and opened it to the names and numbers I'd seen him write down on the inside cover before we left home. Then he poured coins into the pay phone. The noise from the cars whizzing past us was so loud my father had to shout into the phone. "Chickie, give me five dimes on Frisco!" Then he shouted out more names and numbers.

I tried to picture in my mind a slide that was five dimes on Frisco, then I tried to match that slide with the slide that was an orphanage. But I couldn't. Until I was older.

Driving back home from our country ride, the car was quiet. I spoke up, "Daddy, what was it like in an orphanage?" He was silent for a moment. I could see in the front windshield mirror the reflection of my father's eyes as they blinked once, as if seeing for an instant that slide that was an orphanage. Then his eyes blinked a second time to banish that image. He made a little backhand toss of his hand as if to dismiss my question, or maybe just to dismiss the past he'd let slip out. He said, "What difference does it make? It was all baggage."

# CHAPTER FOUR

My father's mother was born in a little village in the south of Italy, or maybe the north, in the mid-1890s. Her name was Rose. She was a beautiful girl at sixteen, more Greek-looking than Italian. She had lustrous, black, wavy hair, Greek blue eyes, a straight Grecian nose, and skin as pearl white as translucent porcelain.

She was unmarried, and pregnant. She refused to marry the man who got her pregnant. He was too old, or already married, or maybe still a teenager like herself. Or, maybe, whoever he was, he refused to marry her. So, to banish that shame from their lives, her parents put Rose on a steamer ship to America.

She arrived at Ellis Island, seven months pregnant in or around 1910. She was processed as Rose Giordano, which may have been her family name, or the name of the man who got her pregnant. She made her way to Bridgeport, Connecticut, forty miles northeast of New York City, where she would stay with relatives, or maybe friends of her parents, until she had her baby. How she got from Ellis Island to Bridgeport, a scared, pregnant teenager who spoke no English, was never made clear to me. Rose arrived at Ellis Island. Time passed. Then she was in Bridgeport.

Rose moved into a tenement in The Hollow, the Italian ghetto at the bottom of two hills, like a hollowed-out melon. It was a perfect metaphor for those Italian immigrants who had neither the means, opportunity, nor aspiration to climb those hills out of The Hollow up to the teeming *Americano* city of Bridgeport. They were *contento* in their tenements in their *Piccolo Italia*, with their vegetable gardens in the backyard; the Catholic Church, the sermons in Italian; the Italian bakery, the importing store, the meat market. They had a little park, too, with grass and a few trees. The women sat on benches there in the sun. Their children played in the grass. Their husbands played bocce under the shade of a tree. Every so often an old man would come into the park with a switch, herding his goats. He squatted down and watched his goats eat the grass, roots and all. Over the years the grass vanished, and the park became nothing but hard, packed dirt known as Nanny Goat Park.

There was also a convenience store in The Hollow. Everyone met there to buy postage stamps, *La Nazione*, Toscano cigars, and sundry items, which, during prohibition, would include bootleg wine. It was owned and run by my mother's mother, Maria DiMenna, already a businesswoman, and so unlike my father's mother, the ineffectual Rose. Maria's three daughters and one son called her The General, but never to her face.

Did they ever meet? My two grandmothers? The pregnant Rose, holding her big belly with both hands, waddles into Maria's store, with her few coins. She asks for a *francobollo* for the letter she is sending back to *Italia*. Did Maria, staring at Rose's big belly, inquire to whom she was sending that letter? Her *marito*, or maybe just her *innamorato*, with all that implied? Maria was that bold. But was Rose? Did she blush in *umiliazione*, and flee the store? Or did she hold her ground and tell Maria, "Grazie, Signora DiMenna, for your *interesse*. But is no matter to you, *si*?" and walk out with her dignity.

Rose had her baby in St. Vincent's Hospital. An administrator brought her some papers. She signed them to put up her son for adoption. Could she read those papers in a strange language? Did someone explain them to her before she signed? It was never made clear to me. Nor was it made clear to me whether she ever held her infant son before she gave him up. If so, did she cry when her son was taken from her? Or whether she was so heartsick she couldn't bear to hold him one time? Or she was so callous she didn't want to hold him even once? She just wanted him out of her life so she could begin her new life. So, she abandoned him. Maybe too harsh a word. Maybe she felt she was doing what was best for her son. And herself. Who knew what her fate would be? Better her beautiful son be adopted quickly into the kind of home she could never give him. At that moment she must have believed she had nothing to give her son, except his name. Pasquale Micheale Giordano. Pasquale? After her son's father, or her father, or a distant grandfather, or maybe she was just a religious girl? So she named him Pasquale, the lamb. But which lamb? The Lamb of Peace, The Lamb of God, or The Sacrificial Lamb? Was Rose that intelligent, that insightful to give her son a sign, his name, from which he would one day divine meaning? Which might give him some small solace that would free him to forgive her? But if he ever did divine the meaning of his name, or forgive his mother, my father kept it to himself.

# CHAPTER FIVE

My father spent the first fifteen years of his life in a state orphanage. He told me it wasn't such a bad place. "They fed you and clothed you and sent you to a school," he said. "There was no affection, but there was none of that molestation crap either." But he craved affection, or at least what he perceived affection to be, recognition. He refused to be faceless like those other boys. He was determined, by a sheer act of will, not to pass through his life unrecognized, unacknowledged. So he studied the women in the orphanage, the Italian cooks and Polish maids and his Irish teachers, and the nuns who came to the orphanage for the Catholic boys' religious studies. He was looking for what they craved, their tell, which he could play to his favor. When he found it he was amazed to realize that all those women, even the nuns, had the same tell. So he put it in play.

He lived in a dormitory with thirty other boys. They all slept on cots. Others left their cots a tangled mess when they left for school. The maids complained in Polish, with scowls on their faces. So, before he left for school, my father made his bed until there was not a wrinkle in the sheets. The maids smiled at him, patted him on the head, told him in Polish he was a considerate boy. When he stood in the cafeteria line to get his food, he smiled at the Italian women ladling it out, and thanked them. After he ate, he cleaned up his place, went back to the cooks and told them their food was *delizioso*. They, too, smiled at him and told him he was a *piccolo gentiluomo*.

But the prejudiced Irish teachers and nuns were the toughest nuts to crack. The other boys gave them fits. They laughed at the Irishers' attempts to teach them things out of books. What could they learn about how to survive in the world in books? But my father knew that it wasn't only what you learned in books that mattered.

It mattered more what people's perception of you was because you read those books. So he read those books, then raised his hand to ask questions about them, even if he had no questions because he understood it all. He listened to his Irish teachers explain things so condescendingly to him, as if he was some ignorant wop just off the boat. But he never let on. He just furrowed his brow as if struggling to grasp their teaching, and then smiled as he got it, and nodded in gratitude. They bought it! His first successful con. Those tough, homely Irish spinsters, with potatoes still in their ears, now fawned over their little guinea student who willingly stayed after class to clap erasers outside, wash the blackboard, empty wastepaper baskets. They tousled his hair, reached into their purse and gave him a few coins.

"Yer a good wee lad, Patsy," they said, unable, or unwilling, to call him by his Italian name. So they gave him his new Irish name. "Now begone wit ya."

"They were like a mother to me," he told me.

My father never spent those coins on himself. He used them to buy candy for the other boys in the orphanage, the older, tougher boys, who now watched over him. A second lesson he learned from those Irish teachers. You give people what they want, they give you what you want. Which led to a third lesson, the most important of all. The Mark should never know he's been conned. Why court his wrath just for your ego gratification? Better to know what the Mark doesn't know, so he'll keep coming back for more. He told me once, "Some Marks, I beat 'em like a drum, and they still loved me. They were like my own personal ATM...before there were ATMs."

In his eighties, my father used to transport stolen jewelry and coins from a pawn shop in New Haven to a fence in Delaware. The fence would pay him a few hundred dollars for his trouble. "It wasn't the money," my father told me. "I just wanted to keep my hand in." But it was a long, tiring drive for an old man in a beat-up Volkswagen Beetle, spewing gray smoke from its exhaust. So he stopped at a McDonald's on the New Jersey Turnpike for lunch. He left the little shoebox with the goods on the back seat and went inside. He sat by the window so he could look out on his little Beetle. "I never even locked the doors," he told me. I said, "Jeezes, Dad, somebody coulda ripped you off." He grinned at me, "Look at me. An old man, for chrissakes, in a beat-up Beetle, eating a Big Mac on the Jersey Turnpike at 11:45 in the morning. An old man killing time, no place to go, pitiful. Who'd think I had two nickels to rub together?"

Even in his eighties, my father still loved his con. Which was why he played his little games, his small cons, over nothing, just to make a point, that he still had it. He didn't need those few C-notes for all that aggravation. Driving the Connecticut Turnpike, and then the New Jersey Turnpike for hours, dodging those 18-wheelers, and then back again, in that rattling old buckboard of a Beetle.

He did it just to sit there in McDonald's, hunched over, eating his Big Mac, his eyes darting left and right, a small smile on his lips at the pitying glances cast his way by those suckers who bought it. This poor old miserable bastard eating his Big Mac alone. Thinking to themselves, Thank God I'm not him! And him thinking, You bet your ass you're not.

I tried to picture the slides of my father in the orphanage on the day a foster couple came to inspect the boys. The boys all in a line, on display. My father, a boy of six, like an anxious puppy in a kennel, determined to make a good impression, smiling, trying so hard to look sincere, smart, worthy. But he looked only desperate.

But as he got older, nine and ten, he learned from those Irish biddies, "like a mother to me," how to be more subtle, clever, secretive, to get what he wanted. By then he was such a handsome boy, smart and agreeable, it was easy for the orphanage to place him in a foster home. He called his foster women his mother, too. But there were so many different foster homes, so many different mothers, I'd get confused. He would say, "No, that was my first mother. The other one was my third mother."

One time he told me that when he was twelve, he discovered that his mother lived down the street from the orphanage. I thought he meant one of his foster mothers, or Irish teachers. But something about the way he said it, wistfully, made me think he meant his birth mother. "She was married then," he said, "and she didn't want me."

How did he know "she didn't want me"? He must have seen her. At least once. On the street, in Grandma DiMenna's store, at Nanny Goat Park. Did he ever talk to her? I began making slides to fill in the black spaces.

My father, his heart beating in his chest, walked down to her house. He loitered outside on the sidewalk. A door opened. He flattened himself behind a tree. She stepped outside, a beautiful, respectably dressed woman now. He waited for her to walk near him, then he stepped out from behind the tree. "I'm your son," he said. She gasped, put her hand to her cheek as if slapped. She looked at the boy, as if for a sign, and then... What? Threw her arms around him, crushed him to her bosom, weeping tears of joy? I think not... She pulled herself together, her chin up, and brushed past this strange street urchin on toward her rounds... Or maybe she did cry, rushed back into her house, and bolted the door? Or maybe she did none of those things because the story never happened, and if it did, that woman was one of his foster mothers, not the elusive Rose.

My father's foster mothers all had in common, he told me, that "They loved me." I wondered, if they did, why did he have so many? He never did last very long in those foster homes before he was shunted back to the orphanage. Then a few months later he would go to another foster home and a new mother. Why did none of his mothers adopt him? He must have wondered that, too, but never to me.

# CHAPTER SIX

My father was a child of six sleeping on his cot one early morning in the orphanage when a nun poked her finger into his shoulder. "Wake up, Patsy," she whispered, so as not to wake the other boys. "Get dressed." He did as he was told.

She took him by the hand and led him out into the early morning darkness. She pointed at an old automobile with big, skinny tires and told him to get in. He got in the backseat because the only time he was ever in an automobile was when someone from the orphanage was driving him to a foster home.

He rubbed sleep from his eyes. She went to the front of the car, bent over, and did something to the car that made a grinding sound. Then she hurried into the driver's seat and started the car. She turned in her seat to look at him. "We have to hurry," she said. "We don't have much time."

He said, "Are we going to a new foster home, sister?"

"Not this time, Patsy."

"Then where are we going?"

She pushed at a metal lever on the floor and the car jumped forward. She steered carefully, her two hands gripping the wheel as the car lurched down the pebble driveway to the street in darkness. There were no other cars on the road so early. She turned left and went past Nanny Goat Park and then the car struggled up the hill.

Finally, she said, "You're going to visit your mother."

"But I don't have a mother, sister."

"Don't be silly, boy. Everyone has a mother."

When they reached a hospital, she stopped the car and turned off the engine. She got out and waited under the light of the hospital entrance for him. She waved her hand at him to come to her. "We must hurry."

The nun held his hand tightly and hurried down a hallway past doctors and nurses in white, half dragging him behind her. Her black habit billowed up like a sail in his face. When she came to a door, she stopped, leaned toward three numbers on the door, pinched her eyes until they were slits, then nodded. "This is it."

She opened the door and pushed him through it. He turned back toward her. "Go on," she said. "I'll wait here."

"But what do I do, sister?" he said, tears in his eyes.

"Go talk to your mother. She doesn't have much time left." She flapped her hand at him. "Go on now."

He turned and saw a shape lying on a cot. A white sheet was pulled up to the shape's neck so he could see only thick, wild, black hair spread out over a white pillow. He moved closer to see its face. It was a beautiful woman's face with black eyebrows, a straight nose, and fat lips. But the face was thin, the skin stretched over bones, the skin the color of a storm cloud. Her eyes fluttered open. They were blue, like his, only without the gray in them. Her face turned toward him as if with great effort. She studied him with her blue eyes for a long moment, then her purplish lips turned up into a smile.

"*Pasquale, mio figlio,*" she said, then gasped for a breath. When her gasping stopped, she reached out her hand and touched his cheek with cold fingers. "*Quanta bella di faccia,*" she said. "*Ti amo.*" Then she raised her head a bit, her eyes opened in terror, and her hand gripped his shoulder so tightly it hurt. He wanted to pull away, but he didn't. She said loudly, "*Pasquale, mi dispiace! Mi dispiace!*" She began gasping for breath again, and her head fell back on the pillow. Her hand fell from his shoulder, and dangled by the side of the cot.

He heard the nun's harsh voice from the doorway. "That's enough, Patsy. Don't tire the poor girl. Come."

Driving back to the orphanage, he sat behind the nun and said, "Who was that, sister?"

"Your mother. Who else?"

He was quiet for a while as the car moved past Nanny Goat Park in the early morning light. A few young mothers were sitting on the benches in the park, their babies pressed to their chests. They were talking to one another, laughing, while their babies drank their milk.

Finally, he said, "But I thought I didn't have a mother, sister."

"Don't be foolish. I told you everyone has a mother."

"Then if she's my mother, why didn't she want me?"

He saw the nun's face in the rearview mirror glaring at him. "Don't you ever say that, boy, you understand. Never! Of course, she wanted you. But what could she do, a girl, a child herself, sixteen, with no husband? She had no choice but to give you to the orphanage where you could be taken care of."

He was quiet again as the car turned the corner to the orphanage. Then he said, "What's my mother's name, sister?"

"Rose."

He said his mother's name out loud. "Rose." Then he said, "What did my mother say to me, sister?"

"She said that she loved you very much because you were her beautiful son. Then she said she hoped you would forgive her." The nun looked at him through the windshield mirror. "You do forgive your mother, Patsy, don't you?"

He looked at her face in the mirror. She looked back at the street now, as she turned the old car into the pebble driveway. He sat back in his seat as the car moved up the pebble driveway.

My father remained in the orphanage for nine more years. For the first time in his young life, he dreamed. It was always the same dream. He dreamed about his mother, her wild, black hair, her beautiful face, and her blue eyes. Her name was Rose, he knew that now, and she had loved him. And that was all he would ever know.

# CHAPTER SEVEN

My father left the orphanage when he was fifteen. He had only a grammar school education. He walked the city streets looking for a job. The Help Wanted signs in store windows had a postscript, "No Italians!" The only job he could find was the kind of work reserved for the *melanzana*. He got a job sweeping out a pool hall. When the owner asked his name, he said, "Patsy. Patsy Jordan."

At night, he slept on the green felt tables. During the early morning hours, before the pool hall opened, he practiced shooting the colored balls into pockets. He learned quickly how to put different spin on the white cue ball, which determined not only whether the colored object ball fell into a pocket, but also where the cue ball came to a stop relative to his next shot. The secret to the game, he learned, was not in making difficult shots all the time. There was no percentage in that. No player could sustain making one difficult shot after another for long. Besides, making such shots called attention to your skill. That was for preening peacocks. My father never wanted to be noticed for anything, certainly not for flamboyance. He wanted to be the only one who knew what his thoughts, motives, machinations, skills were.

So he hid it all, who he really was, beginning with his skills in pool. He positioned his cue ball for easy shots. He played a boringly perfect game. His exceptional skills and intelligence were overlooked, except by those players smarter and more talented than he was. But there weren't any. He perfected his left-handed stroke with the cue stick until it was steady, smooth, maddeningly methodical, stroke after stroke, like the pistons of a perpetual motion machine.

He had great eyes, too, that saw the colored object balls as being clearer, more defined, and larger than other shooters did, as if he was sighting them through a magnifying telescope. And he had ocular block, the ability to block out everything in his vision so that he saw only the object ball, and beyond it, the pocket.

He also had imagination, which passes for brilliance in pool shooting. He saw possibilities where others didn't. He could look at a cluster of object balls so close together it was impossible to pocket any one of those balls. Except he could see the one ball in the cluster that could be ricocheted off two or three other balls in such a way that it would drop into a pocket. And when it did, his opponents called him lucky. He shook his head in shame, then shrugged, "But I'll take it."

My father also had intellectual vision. He could see into the future on a pool table. His eyes clicked like a camera at the fifteen balls spread out over the green felt cloth. In an instant, with only a cursory glance at the spread-out balls, he could process the entire sequence in which each of those balls could most easily be pocketed, one after another. He never made a production of studying those laid-out balls, as if showing off his acuity, like a lot of shooters. He gave the balls a sideways, passing glance, then quickly shot one ball after another. Even the best players could only process their first five or six shots before they had to reprocess their next five or six shots. My father's vision was like Michelangelo's when he looked at that flawed block of marble and saw in it David waiting to be freed. All my father had to do was chip away the excess marble, shot after shot.

By far, my father's greatest gift as a pool shooter, gambler, con man, grifter, and most of all, as a man, was that he had no fear.

"Fear of what?" he said to me once. "Losing? What did I have to lose in this life? I was born into nothing, and I expected to go out the same way." Then he told me a story. He was on the hustle into Canada when he was nineteen. Quebec. He was at a racetrack there. "I never really liked betting the ponies," he said. "Too many variables. Owners. Jockeys. Trainers. Veterinarians giving their horse a shot. But this time I couldn't resist. The bookie was this big, dumb Canuck, with a knife scar down his cheek. So I past posted him. He was too dumb to notice. He paid me my winning bet, and I started to walk away. But one of his buddies, not stupid like the Canuck, whispered something to him. The Canuck came up behind me, whirled me around, and stuck a big hunting knife up against my throat. He said, 'You cheat Pierre. Give money back, or else.' I said, 'Or else what?' He said, 'Or else Pierre cut throat from ears-to-ears.'"

I interrupted my old man's story. "You gave it back quick, huh?"

He looked at me as if I'd insulted him. "Didn't I teach you anything? You get the lettuce, you never give it up. I stole it fair and square."

"You cheated him."

"Yeah. So? That's fair and square. Cheating is the game. The winner is the guy who knows something the other guy doesn't. No self-respecting con gambles without the vig. Honest gamblers are life's losers."

The old man exhausted me, as he often did all those years, with his impeccable logic. I said, "So. You talked your way out of it?"

"In a way. I looked that dumb Canuck in the eyes and said, 'Go ahead. You don't have the moxie.'"

"Jesus Christ! What'd he do?"

"I'm here, aren't I?"

It wasn't long before the older gamblers in that Bridgeport pool hall were backing my father in games of nine ball or straight pool for hundreds of dollars a game. He was Fast Eddie Felson before there was a Fast Eddie Felson, although my father always admired Minnesota Fats more than the flashier Fast Eddie.

It was not uncommon for my father to shoot pool all night long. When the sun was coming up, he went to the men's room to freshen up. Then he hit the city streets, shot his cuffs, in his cashmere suit, his spectator shoes, with his slicked-back, sandy-colored hair, and as much as a thousand dollars in his pocket. He spent that money in the only way he knew how. He bought his older pool hall cronies a big breakfast. Ex-pugs with scar tissue, dopers, drunks, degenerate gamblers, all twenty years or more older than him. They called him The Kid. He lent them money for their fixes, knowing he'd never get it back. He didn't care. Money's value came from giving it away.

Late in the afternoon, he walked up a hill to Central High School, which overlooked the city. He climbed the front steps to the school's big double front doors, but he never went inside. He just hung back in the shadows alongside those doors, waiting for the bell to ring. His contemporaries burst through the doors, laughing and shouting, as they ran down the steps. They stopped, looked around, until someone saw him and pointed above toward the big double doors. "Patsy! There's Patsy!" He came down the stairs, smiling. They flocked to him as they would the Pied Piper. They followed him downtown where he bought them things. A Big City Dude with patent leather hair trailed by laughing, shouting, jostling boys in T-shirts and worn hand-me-down pants, who were two and three years older than this baby-faced slickster.

One afternoon, my father went to my grandmother's variety store in The Hollow. He saw a beautiful girl sitting on the bench outside the store. He had seen her before in a fancy hotel in the city, having dinner with a small, tough-looking, old man with thick, white hair. He asked around about that girl. She was the daughter of that little, white-haired man, who liked to show off his daughter's beauty at the best hotel in the city. The man's wife had been a beauty, too, but now she had no time for such *frivolezza*. She was known in The Hollow as the *Commerciante*. Which was how my father ended up at my grandmother's store that day.

When he passed that girl on that bench, he saw she wasn't a girl. She was a woman, maybe twenty to his sixteen.

He went inside and busied himself looking at the many things Maria DiMenna had for sale in the store: Toscano cigars, *La Nazione*, pears, candies, milk, eggs. My father had also heard she sold bootleg red wine in gallon jugs out of the back room during Prohibition.

She didn't notice him. She was flirting with a florid-faced Irisher *polizia*. The Irisher picked out a pear from a bushel basket and handed it to her. He reached into his pants for change. Maria, mock frowning, said, "*Non importa, Signor Murphy*." She smiled at him and made a little production of polishing the pear between her ample bosoms. Then she turned her back, withdrew a five-dollar bill from her bosom and wrapped it around the pear. She turned back to the grinning *polizia* and handed it to him. He thanked her and went toward the door and opened it. Her smile vanished. He was no sooner through the door onto the sidewalk when she spat on the floor, "*Figlio di puttana!*"

My father brought a few things up to the counter and smiled at her. She was still glaring at the Irish cop walking up the sidewalk. "*Signora,*" my father said. She turned on him with fury, "*Quale! Quale!*" He gestured toward his items on the counter. Her fury subsided. He paid from a thick roll of bills and inquired offhandedly of the girl sitting outside. An employee perhaps on her break? Maria looked at him with her riveting blue eyes. This fair-haired, blue-gray-eyed, handsome boy in his flashy cashmere suit and stickpin and his earnest smile. An *uomo scivoloso*. She said, "That is Firenze, my oldest daughter." My father nodded and said, "*Bella. Bella.*" He made a humble shrug, a slight dip of his head, and asked if she might introduce him to her beautiful daughter. "My name is Pasquale Giordano," he said. "I don't live in The Hollow. I have an apartment in the city." He was no fool. His new Irisher name, Patsy Jordan, wouldn't play with this Italian *matrona*. He gestured with his hand, up the hill, as if to another world. He wanted her to know he was no Old World ignorant wop intimidated by the white Americans in the big city.

But she didn't introduce him to her daughter that day. She told him her daughter already had a *fidanzato*. An older man, a businessman, *rispettabile*. She did not tell the boy that this older man was also a bully, with the easy, false charm of a *grande amatore*.

But my father was persistent. Firenze DiMenna was the first person, and, quite possibly, the only person he ever wanted to share his life with. He began to spend his free time in The Hollow now, ingratiating himself with the DiMenna family. The weak and ineffectual son, Benjamin, so like my father's own mother, Rose. The two young, impressionable daughters, Josephina and Marie. Their older sister, Firenze, not so impressionable, more practical, hardeyed, and tough like her mother. Except when it came to handsome men. And then there was Sam, the padrone, a peacock of a little man. His women catered to him when he was sitting at the kitchen table, sipping his espresso with a lemon peel in a delicate cup. But when he was gone, laying bricks, gambling at the Venice A.C., or boxing some big Irisher in a club fight on Saturday night, Maria DiMenna, The General, ruled the house.

She tolerated no feminine weakness from her daughters. She taught them how to rule their men, how to keep their own bank account, and, if necessary, to keep their legs in the air. And then after sex, she told them to take a bath in warm water and vinegar. She told them never fall for superficial charm, but find a good, practical man who would support them. Marie listened, and married a stockbroker. Josephina listened and married a lawyer who became a Judge. My mother listened, then married a womanizer with money the first time. The second time, she married a gambler, con man and grifter, who would be faithful to her for 70 years. But when she first met my father, she played him off for years. Firenze wanted a man of substance, dependable, not a gambling peacock like her father.

My father mooned around the DiMenna family. He tried to ingratiate himself with the family with a kind of sweet obsequiousness he always thought, to the day he died, was irresistible. He bought the younger sisters sweets and trinkets. He ran errands for Maria. He went to Sam's club fights, worked his corner, booked bets around the auditorium, and shared his winnings with Sam. He didn't care if his con took years before it bore fruit. Besides, it was a good lesson, patience, perseverance. Everything that happened to him in his life he learned from and found a way to use it in his con. This pursuit of Firenze DiMenna taught him a lot about the long con verses the short con. Which was why it was the first and last time my father ever played the long con. He'd always thought the long con wasn't worth the time and energy and money and danger for either a big score, or nothing. And maybe a beating, too, or worse. There were too many variables, too many people involved he had to trust. He preferred the short con, on his own, the quick hit and out. On the next train to anywhere. But with Firenze DiMenna he was willing to play it out as long as it took.

My father was 17 when my mother married the *rispettible* businessman and, soon after, became pregnant. My father was heartsick, but not broken. He regrouped, made plans. He knew he needed seasoning.

At the time, he was renowned as the best pool shooter in the city. Another lesson. His renown was a detriment to his business. No one would play him anymore, not even if he spotted them the seven, eight, and nine in nine-ball. There was no future for him in Bridgeport now. "The suckers had dried up," he told me. "Your mother was married. It was time."

So he hit the road on "The Hustle." He was gone for six years, traveling the rails first throughout the Northeast, then the Midwest, then the Far West, California, the land of fake dreams. He never settled long enough in any city or small town for his con to be discovered. Familiarity breeds, not contempt, but recognition, a kind of death for a con man. He learned that lesson and many others during those years. "It was my Ivy League education," he used to say. "My PhD in Con from Darthmuth."

During those years he made periodic trips back to Bridgeport. He checked in with his cronies, and off-handedly inquired about Firenze DiMenna.

# CHAPTER EIGHT

At the age of 17, my father left Bridgeport with a carnival heading for the little farm towns in upstate New York. He signed on as a roustabout, a laborer. He put up and folded the carnie's tents at each town. He unloaded the heavy wooden boxes of bootleg whiskey that would be sold out of a backroom of a tent as medicine that cured all ailments. He fed the two-headed calves. Carted garbage. Ran with the other roustabouts to the call of "Hey, Rube!" when the farmers were spoiling for a fight after they'd been fleeced in a crooked card game or a game of craps with shaved dice. He ran errands for the fortune teller in her flowing robes and the trapeze artists in their risqué, sequined costumes. He stood guard outside of a tent set far off from the other tents where farmers and teenaged boys waited in line, jostling each other and giggling in anticipation of seeing the women inside in their flimsy costumes, nothing more than a gauzy covering that revealed the outline of their naked bodies as they performed exotic dances. And, for a nominal fee, other exotic acts behind a curtain at the back of the tent.

After a few weeks, he was elevated to a more important assignment. When the carnival entered a town and began putting up tents, it was his job to drive the old, dilapidated truck into town with Max the Patch sitting beside him. Max the Patch was a small, soft, hairless man shaped like a pear, like a *castrato*, but with a steel-trap mind. My father parked the truck in front of the local police station and went inside with Max the Patch. They sat outside the police chief's office for long moments before they were summoned inside. The Chief made them stand in front of him as if supplicants, while Max the Patch presented his proposition. He told the Chief he wanted to make sure the carnival had his approval to conduct certain sporting games in one of their tents and to sell the carnival's medicines that would be so beneficial to the farmers' aches and pains. Max assured the Chief that he understood that certain permits must be paid for those games and medicines, and he was more than willing to comply. He pulled out a role of bills. The Chief eyed the roll and told him how much those permits would cost. Max peeled off the bills and added an extra bill to those he handed to the Chief. "One more request, Chief," Max the Patch said. "If it becomes necessary for you and your officers to visit our business, we would appreciate being given advance notice." The Chief smiled, and said, "Of course."

Driving back to the carnival, Max the Patch said to my father, "Everyone has a price, kid. And a weakness. You just gotta find it, is all, and then figure out how to exploit it."

It didn't take long for Max the Patch to realize that the kid from Bridgeport had a lot on the ball. He was good-looking and smart and quick on the uptake. So he taught him how to be a shill. My father stood on a platform in front of a tent, the rubes clustered around him below, suspicious at first, until he enticed them to pay a quarter to come inside and see the Wonders of the World, which included a two-headed calf, the Bearded Lady, the midget, and the Geek.

The Geek took a liking to my father. Maybe it was because he admired my father's beauty in contrast to his own monstrosity. He was a hunchbacked man with hair all over his body and his face. He looked like a stone-age savage and acted like one, too, behind the bars of his cage. He growled like a rabid animal and held up a live chicken for the rubes to see. Then he bit off its head, blood spurting all over him, to the horrified screams of the female rubes, and the laughter of their husbands. The Geek tossed the chicken on the sawdust floor, the chicken racing around with its head cut off, drenching the sawdust with its blood until it finally keeled over dead.

One night, the carnival closed up early after the weekly police raid, always on a Wednesday. When the police arrived in their squad cars, announced by their sirens and blinking lights, the medicines and games of sport and exotic dancers were all nowhere to be seen.

My father and the Geek stood in front of a tent watching the police spread out to search the tents. The Geek, his ragged clothes drenched in blood, laughed at the police's futile efforts. Then he looked at my father and said, "Come to dinner tonight, kid. I could use the company. My old lady don't talk much." He held up the headless chicken in his hand and said, "She's roasting a chicken."

My father went to his tent to clean up and change his clothes. A few hours later, he sat with the Geek at a table in his tent. He saw the Geek's wife, her back to them, bent over, pulling out a platter of roasted chicken and potatoes from a makeshift stove. She looked like the housewives my father had seen only in magazine advertisements. The pretty housewife cooking at her stove while her perfect family, her husband, their son and daughter, smiled expectantly at the kitchen table. My father wondered if such families truly existed, and if so, where?

The Geek's wife wore a simple print shift with flowers on it and a white apron over it. She had quilted mittens on her hands so she wouldn't burn them on the platter. She put the hot platter on top of the stove, took off her mittens, then turned toward my father and smiled. She had pretty eyes and a cute nose. My father stared at her as she stared at him as if unaccustomed to seeing such a beautiful young man in her tent. Then, absentmindedly, with a languid gesture so sensual, she began stroking the long, silky, luxuriant beard on her face that settled in a tangle on top of her breasts.

They ate a silent dinner, my father mute, working so hard not to stare at the Bearded Lady across from him. He kept his eyes on the Geek, all the while my father thinking to himself, I'm in one of those pictures in magazine advertisements. The husband and wife eating dinner with their guest. It was a scene played out in millions of homes every night, except for one minor detail.

After dinner, the Geek and my father sat at the table, talking and drinking bootleg whiskey while the Bearded Lady washed the dishes at the sink. My father finally glanced at her, his eyes fixed for a long moment on her luxuriant beard, hypnotized. He heard the Geek's harsh voice, "Don't get any ideas about my wife, kid."

Late at night, after the police left, all the carnies, men and wom-
en, went to a small tent to drink whiskey and play poker and shoot
craps. My father had not played those games much in Bridgeport.
They were too complicated for him, and besides, he didn't need
them. He thought of them, then, as games of chance. He didn't like
chance. He liked pool, which he controlled with his talent. But he
joined in those games this night, and every night afterwards. He
bet only small amounts because he learned quickly that everyone
cheated in those games. The secret to cheating, he learned, was to
spot the other guy's tell. Then use that tell to cheat him right back
in a way he couldn't detect. The games weren't about chance after
all. They were about perception and deception, intelligence and skill.
They were about illusion. He could see the skill in Fingers Brown's
long slim fingers as he dealt the cards. But it was a different kind of
skill than my father's pool shooting skill. That skill was visible to
everyone, his smooth stroke and unerring accuracy. His talent was
his "tell." The best cheaters in cards and dice, or any con, had no tell,
which gave him a feeling of infinite power over all.

It took a few years for my father to realize he had great skills for
these games of chance, dice and cards. He was smarter than most,
more fearless, ruthless. He also had a physical skill, as in pool. It was
in his hands, fat-fingered, puffy. Perfect hands to conceal shaved dice
in his palm and to cover an entire deck of cards as he dealt them from
the bottom of the deck. His hands had dexterity, too, so that when
he shot cards around the table with only one hand, he spit them out
like bullets spitting out of a gun, quicker than the eye could see.

It also wasn't long before Max the Patch noticed the dexterity of
my father's hands. He gave him the pea in the pod scam. He set up
a table most visible on the fairgrounds. The rubes clustered around
it in front of my father, just a kid with sandy hair. He lined up the
three pods, like walnut shells, and put a pea under one. Then he
exhorted the rubes to follow the shell with the pea under it. His fat
hands began shifting those pods on the table, moving them around
each other in figure eights. When he stopped, he raised his hands,
palms out, as if to surrender. "Can anyone tell me where the pea
is?" he said. One of the rubes shouted out, "Under the middle pod."

My father lifted up the pod to reveal the pea. The rube grinned like a retard, and the others laughed and hooted at the hapless kid behind the table. My father shook his head in embarrassment. He said, "Give me another shot, OK. This time for a small wager." The rubes slapped down their bills on the table. My father began shifting the pods around again, more quickly, his hands covering the pods, moving so swiftly, smoothly, that when he stopped this time, the rubes were silent, staring.

# CHAPTER NINE

In the late summer, the carnival set up tent at a fairgrounds a few miles from Saratoga Race Track. One afternoon, my father put on his tan cashmere suit and spectator shoes and went to the track with some other roustabouts. He was curious about the ponies. The roustabouts kidded him about his fancy dress, "the kid thinks he's a big shot," compared to their own work clothes. They bought tickets for the cheapest viewing, standing room only, up against the fence closest to the track. My father bought them all beers. They slapped him on the back, "You're a good kid, Patsy." When they turned their attention to the first race, he slipped away from them and went upstairs to the Private Clubhouse where the swells congregated. The maître d' at the door looked him up and down. A slick kid, trying to con his way into someplace he doesn't belong. But he could be the son of a wealthy businessman? My father turned the maître d's momentary hesitation to his advantage. He gave him a guileless smile and reached out to shake his hand. The man shook his hand, and when he released it, there was a neatly folded tiny square of paper in his palm. A sawbuck.

My father stood at the bar, sipping his scotch, and watched the swells behind him through the bar's big mirror. The men sat around tables with their women. They smoked big cigars, drank scotch, and laughed with a careless ease as if they were in their private, exclusive club. They were tanned, with tousled hair. They wore the same costume, black cashmere sports jackets, white slacks, and white suede shoes. A few of them wore captain's yachting caps.

The swells' women wore long, chiffony, pastel-colored dresses, pink, mint green, pale peach, with matching wide, floppy-brimmed hats tilted just so over one eye. They were drinking champagne out of long flutes, and smoking cigarettes through long mother of pearl

holders encrusted with diamonds. He had seen the same kind of cigarette holder a few months ago when he had taken a train to Miami
for the Flamingo Derby, and had drinks with the Palm Beach heiress
in the Flamingo Lounge. The swells had no imagination. They bought
their clothes and toys and cars all from the same places. They lived
in their mansions in the same places, too. Their entire world was a
series of small, expensive, exclusive clubs. They vacationed with the
same swells at the same times at the same resorts in Newport, Monte
Carlo, Palm Beach. The husbands and wives had affairs, but only with
the other husbands and wives from their group of swells. Their children married into the families of other swells they had known since
infancy. All that inbreeding, my father thought. It made them dumb,
like that Palm Beach heiress, all patrician beauty, without a brain.
Daddy's horses always win, silly. He wondered if she was still waiting for him to return from the men's facilities. The swells didn't have
to be smart. They had the money. They lived in their little cloistered
worlds, like convents, surrounded by moats. Nothing ever changed
in their worlds, not the people, the parties, the conversations, the
life. Nothing new ever entered that world to confuse their dimness.
But more importantly, to them, nothing bad ever entered that world.
The sameness of it, my father thought, would drive him mad.

After a few minutes, one of the swells got up and went over to
a gentleman sitting alone at a banquette against the wall. He looked
different than the other men. His skin had a grayish pallor, as if his
life was spent in dark rooms. His hair was greased back. He had a
hooked nose and bad teeth, like most of the *morto Christo* shylocks in
Bridgeport. They hung around the pool halls looking to loan money
to the losers. This man was dressed differently than the swells, in a
gray, pin-striped business suit, with a vest, like a banker. The swell
standing over him was not so carefree now, trying to force a smile.
He reached out a hand. The man ignored it. The swell cleared his
throat and asked the man something. The man looked up without
interest, and shook his head, no. The swell nodded, thank you, and
backed off. He returned to his table, wiping perspiration from his
forehead.

My father ordered another scotch and soda. When the bartender put it down in front of him, my father pushed a fin across the bar. The bartender pocketed it and said, "Can I be of assistance, sir?" My father tossed a head fake toward the lone man against the wall. The bartender looked up and said, "Mr. Rothstein, sir. Mr. Arnold Rothstein, from New York City. His friends call him A.R."

My father knew who the man was. He said, "That name sounds familiar?"

The bartender leaned over the bar and said, "You might have heard of him, sir. He's very famous. Some people call him Mr. Big, others, The Brain or The Banker." He glanced left and right, then whispered. "The Fixer, too, but never to his face."

"What does he 'fix'?"

"He's a sporting man."

"Yeah. What sport does he play?"

"Oh, no, he doesn't PLAY sporting contests. He fixes them. So he has a certain advantage. The rumor is he fixed the 1919 World Series and won a million dollars. But it was never proven." A man at the end of the bar signaled the bartender. "Excuse me, sir."

When the bartender returned, my father said, "What does Mr. Rothstein drink?"

"Oh, only scotch. The best. Single malt."

"Send him a bottle, on me." He took out a neatly folded square of paper from his jacket pocket and put it in the bartender's palm. A C-note.

"Right away, sir."

My father sipped his drink, his back to the room, his eyes on the bar as if contemplating the odds on the next race. A few minutes passed before he sensed someone standing behind him. Without looking behind him, my father said, "Can I help you?"

The man with the bad teeth said, "Yeah, you can help me. Why's a kid like you flashing a C-note on someone he don't know?"

"I know who you are, Mr. Rothstein."

"Then why waste a C-note?"

"I didn't waste it. It was an investment. And here you are, Mr. Rothstein." My father turned to face the man. The man was smiling as if it pained him.

"How old are you, kid?"

"Seventeen, Mr. Rothstein."

Rothstein shook his head. "You got balls, kid. Who are you?"

"Nobody now. But I could be someone useful to you."

"I don't talk to nobodies. You got a name?"

"I got names."

Rothstein stared at him, waiting.

"Sometimes I'm Patsy Jordan. Sometimes Pasquale Giordano."

"So, which are you? A wop or a mick?"

My father shrugged, made a gesture with his hands. "Depends. I was born a wop, but sometimes it's to my advantage to be a mick."

"You look like a mick, kid. But you're dressed like a wop in that cheap suit."

"It wasn't cheap when I bought it. But I figure working for you I'll learn how to dress, and be able to afford it, too."

Rothstein made a mirthless laugh, two short breaths. He studied the handsome kid for a moment, with his sandy hair and blue-gray eyes. A Waspy-looking college kid could be useful. But there was something about him older than his years. Wiser, too. He didn't seem to fear the man he was talking to. That could be useful, too. Or it could be a threat. Maybe both.

"What's your scam, kid?"

"I'm a carnie shill. Pea in the pod. I shoot some pool on the side."

"Cards, dice?"

My father shook his head, no. "I don't like chance. I like things I can control."

"You can control dice and cards, the nags, too."

"So I'm told." He paused, then added, "But I don't know how yet. That's why I'm talking to you."

The Jew nodded, "Smart kid," then withdrew his leather wallet from the inside of his coat pocket and counted out ten crisp C-notes from it. He handed them to my father. Then he handed him a slip of paper with the name of a horse on it. "The seventh race. You think you can lay this down for me?"

My father looked at the C-notes in his hand. "Why take a chance? I could take your C-notes and walk out of the track."

"You could. It's a gamble. How'd you put it? Oh, yeah, 'an investment.' Maybe it's worth the risk to me."

"Why?"

"I cause attention."

My father nodded.

"And put a sawbuck on the nag for yourself... But no more."

My father nodded again and left the clubhouse.

# CHAPTER TEN

For the next week, my father spent his afternoons at the track. The maître d' greeted him with a smile now and directed him to Mr. Rothstein's table.

He ran errands for the Jew. Placed bets, delivered fat envelopes to men spread out in the stands, or more often, received fat envelopes from those men and brought them to Mr. Rothstein. What my father found strange was that the Jew never studied a racing form, never left the Swell's Clubhouse to watch a race, and was never affected by a winning wager, or, more importantly, a losing wager. When he got up the nerve to ask him about these things, the Jew said, "I'm a businessman, not a sportsman. I take no pleasure in a poor nag running in circles, only in the result. And you can't do anything about losing. It's in the past. The Mark can outsmart you once in a while. Give him credit. Besides it's good for business. He wins, he comes back. He loses all the time," he made a slight dip of his head, "he gets tapped out, or, if he's got a brain, he quits." He looked up at my father. "Just don't let him win too often."

After a few days, Rothstein told him he had another job for him. "More important," he said. He looked my father up and down, and said, "But not in that wop suit. It's a tell. You need another look. Respectable."

"Like you? A banker."

The Jew snapped at him, "Don't be a fucking smart ass. You know what I mean. You could be a college kid with your looks. One of those Ivy brats, like at Darthmuth."

The next morning, my father went to the library. He looked for magazines about Ivy League life. All the boys in their fedoras, their raccoon coats, the girls, too, waving pennants amid autumn leaves, stopping to swig from a silver flask, laughing, then continuing on to the stadium for the Big Game. A life he'd never know. So he kept looking, flipping the pages, until he found it. Then he got a Saratoga telephone book and looked through it for a men's clothier.

That afternoon in the Swells' Clubhouse, he stood before the Jew in his new clothes. The Jew looked up at him and said, "You lost, kid? Darthmuth's a coupla hundred miles east of here." Then he studied the kid. Finally, he said, "You got it right. But it's too old for you right now. In a few years maybe. Take off the fedora, and the sport coat." My father did as he was told. He laid them on a chair. "Now roll up the sleeves of that white shirt, just below your elbows." He did as he was told. The Jew nodded. "One other thing. No more wop grease in your hair. You leave here, go to the men's and wash your hair. Dry it real good then just toss it a little bit with your hands, so it looks like you just run all the way from class."

"I understand, Mr. Rothstein. Now what is it you have for me?"

"From now on, every morning before the sun comes up, I want you to go to the stables," he said. "Just hang around. Talk to people. Pick up things. The nag is off its feed. Or hyped up. Got a slight limp. The trainer's on the sauce again. The owner's short cash. The jockey hasn't been paid." He handed my father a leather-bound notebook and a fountain pen. My father handed the notebook and pen back to him.

"Good," Rothstein said.

That week, my father had the most fun he'd ever had in his life— a life that by any measure had been devoid of much fun of any kind. He went down to the stables in the cool early morning just as the sun was coming up. It was always a little misty, damp, so he bought one of those heavy Ivy League cable-knit, V-neck sweaters, with his school colors in a stripe around the V-neck, green for Darthmuth.

It was quiet in the stables. Just the horses snorting in their stalls and the small birds chirping as they pecked for worms in the grass. The stables smelled of coffee brewing, fresh hay, and horse shit, not an unpleasant odor that steamed up from the stalls. The stable boys were pitchforking up the shit and heaving it into a wheelbarrow. Then they tossed down some hay, spread it out evenly, and finally attached a little bucket of feed to the horses' long noses so they could eat. The stable boys didn't acknowledge him, not even when he said good morning to them. Maybe it was because they were not boys. They were old men, bent over from a lifetime of backbreaking work, melanzanas who grew up picking cotton.

A little beyond the stables, the horses' walkers were hunched over an empty metal oil drum with a fire in it. They were warming their hands over the fire and sipping coffee. White boys, and girls, his age, a little older maybe. They could have been college students, like him, working odd jobs in the summer to pay for college. But he knew they weren't because of the way they treated the horses. They were like those monks in the orange robes who had given up the world to devote their lives to something most people would never understand.

The walkers couldn't keep their hands off the horses. They rubbed their hands over the horses' wide flanks, their barrel chests, whispered in their ears as if to a lover. He'd never before seen a person have affection like that for an animal. He hung around outside the stables just watching for a few minutes. Then he got up the nerve to ask one of the walkers if he could pet the horse to see how it felt. It was a girl walker. She laughed. "Sure, college boy. But be gentle. They might look big and powerful, but they're delicate, sensitive creatures." She showed him how to rub his hand gently down the horse's long nose. He could feel the downy fur, like on a baby's head, and the delicate bones and cartilage that made up the long nose. When he petted the noses of those big-bellied, majestic, self-contained beasts, he realized what a contradiction they were. Delicate and powerful. It seemed a miracle they could walk on their skinny, bony legs, much less run like the wind.

The girl walker gave him an apple and told him how to offer it to the horse, "On the palm of your hand so's he don't bite your fingers off." He fed the horse the apple. The horse munched the apple with his big teeth, his lips peeled back. After the horse finished it, he nudged his nose against my father's hand. "He wants another," the girl said. "But only one."

My father felt like he was in one of those pictures he'd seen in magazines. The country squire with his horses, a rich man's pets.

He'd never had a pet. There was no percentage in a pet if you travel light. He'd never thought much about the country, either. All those trees and distance and solitude, with no action. He smiled to himself. The closest he'd ever been to the country in Bridgeport was Nanny Goat Park. A few spindly trees and hard-packed dirt without grass.

The walkers saw how much pleasure he took in the horses, so they kidded him, "Hey, Ivy League, take one back to your dorm as a pet." He grinned sheepishly. Then they said, "Hey, Ivy League, you want some Joe?" He nodded, and accepted their coffee. He stood around the blazing drum now, too, listening to their chatter—a horse off his feed, a little cough, a slight limp you could barely notice. He never asked any questions about the horses they talked about. He just listened and remembered.

Some of the girl walkers flirted with him. They invited him out dancing with them at night. He told them he didn't dance. They grinned lasciviously, "Not to worry, college boy. We'll teach you." He blushed, stuttered, "I have to study for next term." It was only half a con, the bashful college boy. It wasn't good business to get too close to a Mark. He might let it slip that at night he worked the pea under the pod scam at the carnie and stood guard outside the exotic dancers' tent while they performed for the farmers behind a curtain. He wondered if the girl walkers knew how to do the things the dancers did with the farmers. Maybe they did, and with enthusiasm, too. But he never found out. The true part of his con was that he really was bashful around women with knowing smiles. He didn't know women. He moved in a world of men. Older men, like the Jew. He knew them. Pretty soon the girls got the hint and stopped flirting.

At mid-morning, the walkers slipped a lead over their horses and took them out of their stalls. They walked them around the stables on a dirt path, the horses clumping along stiff-legged. My father thought they were lame. When he said something to the walkers, they laughed at him. One of the girls said, "They weren't meant to walk, college boy."

Then the trainers and owners and jockeys showed up. The walkers ignored him now. The trainers were sour, suspicious men. The owners were arrogant, dismissive. The jockeys were fidgety little hop heads. My father left before they could throw him out.

He told Rothstein the carnival was leaving at the end of next week. Rothstein said, "I heard. You going with them?"

"Maybe."

"There's no future in the carnie, kid. It's small time. A trap. It's fun when you're young. But you stay, you get old, bitter, an alky, a hop head, maybe a pederast." It wasn't the first time the Jew used a word my father didn't know, and he didn't let on he didn't know until he went back to the local library and looked up the word in a dictionary. He looked up a lot of words with the Jew. So he bought himself a little dictionary. He carried it with him for years.

"I'm going back to the city in a few weeks. You could come, too. I'd put you on the payroll. No more nickel and dime handouts." My father thanked him for his confidence in him. He'd think about it and let him know. The Jew nodded, "Of course."

My father had never questioned the money the Jew gave him at the end of a day. He just took it, whatever it was. He felt like he was going to one of those fancy colleges now, like Darthmuth, that parents paid a lot of money to teach their sons and daughters things in books. Except his college wasn't Darthmuth. His college paid him for teaching him things he could never learn in books. The Jew called it the "the college of hard knocks." At Darthmuth you learned the surface of things in books. At his college he learned the substance of things. He could see those things, feel them, smell them, touch them, breathe them in until they became a part of him, not just in his head, his heart, his veins, but in his entire self. Like those horses in their stalls. They weren't just ponies to him now, or nags with a number on their back you bet on. He KNEW them now. They were noble, majestic beasts to him, living, breathing, eating, shitting, with fragile, spindly legs and a heart as big as a locomotive engine. He felt things in his own heart for them. It was painful. But now he had no choice. Before, he had avoided betting on the ponies because he thought it was a fool's bet on chance. Now, he avoided betting on the horses because he knew them. Once you know something it changes you. You can never go back.

One morning, he woke before the sun. He went to the track and down to the stables. It was dark and cold and eerily silent. He shivered as he walked past the horses' stalls until he came to a horse with his head poked out of his stall. He looked alert, inquisitive. My father stopped and reached up his hand. The horse's eyes opened wide, and he pulled his head away from Dad's hand. Dad held his hand in the air for a moment until the horse calmed. Then he put his palm on the horse's nose and ran it gently down to his nostrils. The horse snorffled at his touch. My father looked around. There was no one. He opened the horse's gate and went into his stall. He shut the gate behind him. It was only him and this big, majestic beast. It surprised him that he was not afraid. He went close to the horse and ran his hand along his flanks. He felt the animal's heat and hard muscles. Then he rubbed the horse's massive chest and felt the horse's big heart beating. The horse rotated his neck and swished his tail. My father got closer to the horse and put his hand on the horse's neck. The horse's long mane felt like silk threads. Dad stayed like that for a few moments, staring into the horse's big, wide-opened eye. Then he patted the horse on his neck. The horse leaned his head toward my father. My father pressed his cheek against the horse's cheek, felt his warm, soft flesh covered with silky hairs, smelled his musky horse odor.

My father slipped out of the stall. He latched the gate. As my father walked away, the horse whinnied.

Quite by accident, his professor had taught him something profound that my father had never felt before. An emotion for a living thing. My father smiled. His professor? Not some tweedy old fool smoking a pipe, scurrying down a hallway, his long, black robes billowing behind him, swooping into his classroom like a crazed bird, fluttering and flapping, dropping his books on his desk, turning to face his class, all those blank minds, to whom he began expounding as if he was a god, above it all, clueless.

I know nothing compared to my professor, my father thought. His professor knew things about living things, man and beast, what went on in their minds and hearts. It didn't matter that his professor only used that knowledge for his own purposes. It mattered only to my father that he'd taught him about such things. It was up to my father, now, to use those things for his purposes, whatever they might be someday.

Imagine! A little Jew with bad teeth, in a banker's suit, who had never graduated from grammar school, who was on the hustle when he was 14, in the biggest city in the world. And now he was one of the most famous people in the world. Respected. Feared. But not loved. Still, if he could make himself such a thing then what could my father become? That thought made him feel as light as air, as if he could fly. He could be something, too. But what?

# CHAPTER ELEVEN

My father never went with Arnold Rothstein. He worked at the carnie until it broke camp, then he quit. He was ready now, he thought, to hustle on his own. He had learned many things from the Jew, and he was grateful. He told him so. The Jew nodded, and said, "It works both ways, kid."

The Jew taught him how to avoid those hard knocks. Never go on a con without a plan. The plan always begins with an Exit. If your con starts to go south, be open to mystery to right it. A con is more than a blueprint. It's an art form. At some point your instinct has to take over for your brain, and so you make it up on the fly. If the con really goes bad, point of no return bad, go to your Exit. Never chase a con to keep it alive. A great con artist is never desperate. Admit it's as dead as Kelsey's nuts and save yourself. Greed kills.

A con can go bad for many reasons. It's not clearly thought out, or not executed properly. Maybe something unexpected pops up, and you don't have the instincts to adjust. Time to go back to the carnie. In mid-con, sometimes it's necessary to reimagine a new con out of your faithful dog. A fantastical hybrid. A pig that can fly, a horse that breathes fire.

Cons begin to smell, like *pesci*, when you stay in one place too long. A few days at most. Longer, even the dumbest Mark will get a whiff. Don't be cocky with Marks. They can surprise you.

Stay in the shadows. Don't talk too much. Let the Mark read into your silences what's in his mind, not yours. He knows he's smarter than you, that's why he's a Mark. Don't disabuse him of that. He knows when you win it's because you're lucky. Admit it, be ashamed. He knows when he wins it's because he's brilliant and you're over-matched. He'll tell you as much. Agree. What's the harm? A con is not about ego, winning or losing. It's about who walks out with the lettuce. The Mark loses, he pays. That's why he's a Mark. He lives there. People know him. He doesn't pay up, word gets out, he'll get no more action. You're a stranger, the train schedule in your pocket. You lose, you never pay. See rule one: The Exit.

The most important thing he learned from the Jew was something the Jew taught him inadvertently. He was subservient with the Jew. Yes, Mr. Rothstein, No, Mr. Rothstein, I'm sorry, Mr. Rothstein. It stuck in his craw, but he never let it show. He learned from the Jew that he didn't like working for anyone, not the Jew, nor the carnie, nor his cronies who backed him in pool in Bridgeport, nor the nuns and Irish spinsters who controlled his life in the orphanage. Working for people could be useful, you learn things, but then move on. Everybody needs a consigliere at some point in their life. But not for too long. You get to rely on them. They become baggage. You're afraid to leave them. It's a trap. You miss the last train out. Rule one.

My father decided at the age of 17 that he never again wanted to answer to anyone. Good or bad, win or lose, he would pay his own way. And something else the Jew taught him. Trust no one. "It made sense to me," my father told me once. "I was never a part of a pack. I was born a lone wolf. So, I became a freelance."

He left the carnie and began hustling in small farm towns throughout upstate New York. He went into a pool hall, sat at the bar, and ordered a beer. The farmers in bib overalls glanced at him, a college kid on summer break, and dismissed him. He sipped his beer and looked around. Two farmers were banging the balls around on a pool table in the center of the room. A deserted poker table in the back of the room near two doors. A big door marked Exit, and a small one. He asked the bartender where the men's was. The bartender tossed a head fake toward the two doors. My father walked behind the men shooting pool to the doors. He opened the one marked Exit and looked out into an alley. One end of the alley was the wall of a tenement. The other end led to the street. He heard the bartender's voice, "The other door, college boy!" My father waved a 'thanks' and went into the bathroom. Two stalls, a sink, a urinal, a cast iron radiator, and, above it, a small window. He put one foot on the radiator, grabbed the window overhang, and pulled himself up. He stood a little wobbly on the radiator. When he steadied himself, he tried to push open the window. It was stuck from years of grime. He took out his folding knife and cut around the windowsill until finally he could open it. He stuck his head out the window and saw the alley that led to the street. He closed the window, but not all the way.

He hung around the pool hall most of the afternoon, sipping beers, not speaking, glancing at the pool game, waiting, until the two farmers asked if he wanted to jump into their nine-ball game. "Four bits on the nine," one said. My father said, "Excuse me, sir?" The farmer smiled, "A half dollar, kid." My father hesitated, "I'm not much for billiards. I only played a few times in my dorm." The farmer smiled, "Billiards? Don't worry kid, we'll take it easy on ya."

He played nine-ball for a few hours, with his unsteady, open bridge and his herky jerky stroke. When the game broke up, he'd lost a few sawbucks. One of the farmers slapped him on the back, "You're a good sport, kid. Come back tonight. There's a poker game. Maybe your luck will change." My father dug into his pants pocket and pulled out a white envelope with crisp, new twenty-dollar bills in it. He flipped through the bills, the farmers watching, and said, "It's for my tuition. But I'd like to make up for what I lost." He smiled at the farmer. "Maybe I just might."

That night, my father's luck wasn't much better in the poker game than it was shooting nine-ball. He won a hand here and there, but only when he had great cards, three kings, a pair of aces and jacks. When he held mediocre cards, or worse, he folded early. A beginner's game.

After midnight, the pots got heavier and heavier, four, five, six C-notes a pot. Around 1 a.m., the pot reached over a G-note. My father kept raising the bet until the pot was $1500 strong. Finally, the last farmer folded his hand. "The kid must have the goods," he said, shaking his head.

My father laid his cards face down, hugged his winnings to him, pocketed the bills, and stood up. One of the men reached out a hand and turned over my father's cards. The farmers stared at the cards. A two, six, jack, five, nine, all of various suits. They looked at each other. One of them got up and walked back to the Exit door. Another went to the front door. My father said, "Going to the men's. I'll be back in a jiff to give you a chance to win your money back. Only fair, right?"

The farmers waited for him to return. After fifteen minutes, the farmer by the Exit door opened the bathroom door just about the time my father was boarding the last train out.

In early November 1928, my father crossed over into Canada. He was 18 years old, with five Gs in his kick. He past posted the Canuck in Quebec and escaped with his life, and the lettuce. He resisted the urge to call the Jew and tell him. But he didn't want to push his luck. It was time to take a little break, treat himself. He booked a room in the swankiest hotel in Quebec, the Château Frontenac. He had room service that first night. The waiter who carried his food into the room was a kid, too, a few years older than my father. He gave my father a look, dismissive, and looked around for an adult. My father said, "By the window." The waiter did as he was told. He made a little fuss opening the bottle of scotch, taking the metal covers off the food with a flourish. He picked up the bottle of scotch and said, "Shall I pour, sir?" My father nodded. The waiter said, "Water and ice?" My father said, "Neat." The waiter poured two fingers, then turned to leave. My father reached out his hand and put a folded square of paper in the waiter's hand. The waiter nodded, thank you, with barely a smile. As he walked toward the door he unfolded the square, stopped a moment, turned back to my father with a big smile, "Thank you, sir, very much. Any further assistance, just summon me . . . A companion, maybe?" My father said, "Not necessary."

He ate his steak and drank his scotch by the window. He looked out at the falling snow in darkness illuminated by the lights of a big city.

The next morning, he sat in the ornate lobby, on a plush, burgundy velvet chair with the elaborate chandelier over his head. He read all the newspapers and watched the swells come down for breakfast. He studied them, the air they had about them, superiority. The world was their oyster, and everyone else was in it to shuck it for them. Nothing bad could happen to them. The fatal flaw of a Mark.

At noon, he went shopping in the falling snow. He bought conservative Ivy League clothes, a navy sports jacket, gray, flannel slacks, a few white dress shirts, a rep tie, and an extravagance, a full-length, double-breasted, camel's hair overcoat. He studied himself in the store's full-length mirror. He put on his fedora hat. The Jew was right. He'd grow into his look someday. Only he'd grown into it much sooner than the Jew had expected. Too bad he wasn't here to see it. He'd appreciate it.

A few days later, already bored, ready to take off again on the hustle, he sat in the lobby one morning and opened a newspaper. There was a photograph of the Jew on the front page under a bold headline, "Arnold Rothstein, Fabled Sportsman, Shot Dead." He read the story carefully. The Jew had got into a fixed poker game in a New York City hotel room. Nothing out of the ordinary for the Jew. Except in this game, he was the Mark. After three days and nights of poker, he had been fleeced of over 300 Gs. He refused to pay up. My father smiled. One of the Jew's rules. The con never pays when he loses. Only the Mark pays. But the Jew couldn't wrap his mind around the fact that this time, he was the Mark. So he refused, and some mick called Hump shot him in the stomach with a .38 police special. It took the Jew a few days to die in his hospital bed. When the police questioned him as he was dying, the Jew said, "Me mudder did it," and died.

My father put the paper down. The Jew was a stand-up guy to the last. My father admired that. But he had no emotional attachment to the Jew. It had been business for both of them. Still, he felt something for the Jew. Not affection. But something he didn't yet understand. Gratitude? Maybe loyalty? Rispetto? My father smiled to himself. A wop value, respect. The Jew might even smile over that one. "So, you are a wop after all, eh, Pasquale?"

But the more my father thought about the Jew, the angrier he got. What a waste! The Jew knew better. He let his ego get in the way. Like those swells. They were so sure they were too big to have bad things happen to them. But bad things did happen to them. They boarded the biggest, most luxurious ocean liner in the world, and then drowned in icy Atlantic waters when the ship that "even God couldn't sink," sank like a stone.

But those swells hadn't caused their own demise like the Jew had. His ego wouldn't let him admit that he was the Mark this time.

He rationalized that it would ruin his reputation and his business if the word got out. A.R. was supposed to be invincible. So he had to turn it all around, prove to everyone that A.R. never had to pay, even when he lost. Which meant he wasn't a Mark. So he went against his own cardinal rule. Don't let your pride affect your con. Never get desperate. Give up a failed con. Greed kills.

# CHAPTER TWELVE

My father left Canada in 1929 when he was still 18. He crossed the border into Vermont, moved east into New Hampshire, then farther east into Maine. He stayed in flop houses, ate in cheap diners, did nothing to call attention to himself. Waitresses flirted with him. He let them know he had no interest. The Jew had told him, "Dames you don't know could be lethal." He hustled a little pool, but that was self-defeating. He had to work too hard not to show his hand.

Sometimes, in the middle of a nine-ball game, he'd be so bored he'd lose his concentration. When he got it back, he realized he'd just run the rack, 1-to-9. His Marks would be looking at him in disbelief. He'd try to laugh it off, "just lucky," but they weren't that stupid. So he concentrated more and more on cards and craps. He played poker in seedy hotel rooms with a men's down the hall, a knotted rope hanging out the window with a sign over it, Fire Escape. Like Tarzan, my father thought. The fucking rope would be the first thing to catch fire. He never played cards in someone's house. Too many rooms. The guy whose house it was knew where things were. A piece in the breakfront. Two thugs sitting in the upstairs bedroom, sawed-offs laying across their legs, waiting for a signal.

He shot craps in darkened alleys. He gave a kid a sawbuck to stand on the sidewalk, leaning against the wall at the end of the alley, smoking a cigarette, keeping his eyes open for the *polizia*, or rip-off artists. He liked such illicit gambling the most, the danger of it. It made him feel more alive than anything else he did. It added to his sense of invincibility, his worth. It began to dawn on him why he gambled. He needed something from it that was more than the lettuce.

Then he moved south into Massachusetts, all the while avoiding big cities, as he gained in confidence. He went through Rhode Island, avoided the small wop towns like Knightsbridge, where it was dangerous to be a stranger, especially one who looked like a mick. He turned west like the Pilgrims and hustled his way through Connecticut until he came to Bridgeport.

He was 20 years old now. He stopped at the Venice A.C. to touch base and play poker with his cronies. He made a point of not showing them what he'd learned the last three years. Besides, he wanted to repay them for financing him in pool games when he started out. He let them win a few C-notes, big money for them, and still he bought them a fancy dinner after the game. But first he slipped a C-note to the old Mustache Pete, who sat on a milk crate outside the door, smoking a Toscano cigar, reading *La Nazione*, while keeping an eye out for the *polizia*. The old man's eyes got wide, and he smiled up at my father, "*Grazie, Signor Giordano, mille grazie.*"

Patsy Jordan wasn't a kid anymore. He was a man worthy of rispetto. My father realized how strange it was for him to get such *soddisfazione* from giving people what they wanted, and, on the other hand, how *esilarante* he felt when he ruthlessly took from Marks what they had. Even if it was something they needed to feed their family, he showed no mercy. "They wouldn't show you mercy," the Jew told him. "Fuck 'em. They want to be a Player, they gotta pay the price. You're doing them a favor." Maybe for the Jew, but not for him, my father thought. There was something in him that needed to be both, dominating and loved. So he took their money ruthlessly and then gave it away generously.

Over a big dinner, my father told his cronies about his adventures, the Geek and the bearded lady, the Canuck with the hunting knife, the Hialeah Heiress, and lastly he told them about the Jew. They nodded silently, with rispetto, at the mention of the Jew's name. Like he was a star baseball player, my father thought, like that Ruth, a *bastardo* like himself.

When they finished dinner and got up to leave, my father asked, off-handedly, about the DiMenna family in The Hollow. They told him the DiMennas had changed their name to Diamond, like Jews, which they were, going back centuries to diamond merchants in Italy, especially the *Commerciante*. Then he dutifully asked them about the *Commerciante's* children, going first from the youngest, Marie, then Benjamin, then Josephine, and finally, trying to conceal the beating of his heart, the oldest, Firenze. They told him Firenze now went by her *'mericano* name, Florence. She was still married, with a little boy, two years old, named George after his *cafone* of a father.

My father left Bridgeport that night on a train and headed west across the vast country he had never seen before. Through Pennsylvania and Ohio, then the Midwest, the prairie states, the small towns one hundred miles from each other, the flat limitless plains, nothing but wheat and horizons, until he got to the mountains of Colorado. Then he caught a train over and through the mountains to the Great Salt Lake of Utah, the land of religious gangsters and perverts, who took many wives, most of them young girls. He was disgusted by such sexual perversion of young girls. He didn't stay there long.

Soon he was into the deserts of Nevada. A Godforsaken land on which nothing could live under the scorching sun. He was twenty-two when he reached Vegas, but he didn't stop there. There was no point. It was controlled by those Mormon gangsters and their partners in evil, the Black Hand. White and Black, they were both heartless and cowardly, especially the *mezzo-melanzana-siciliano*. They were feared by the weak and the helpless because of their cruelty and the power of their numbers. My father hated them, even then. Jackals, scavengers. They had no honor, no courage. Together, the Mormon perverts and the Black Hand institutionalized prostitution and gambling in casinos. The Jew had told him never to play in casinos, "You can't beat the iron." The casinos had floor men looking over your shoulder at the poker table. There was no chance to cheat, unless you were *pazzo*. And then the floor men would summon their thugs who would drag you out into an alley and beat you methodically with brass knuckles. "Always private games," the Jew told him. "Games you can use your wits and balls, and then get the last train out."

When he reached California, he went straight to Los Angeles. Fake Spanish buildings and faded, dying palm trees. Everyone had automobiles, but no one had water. An arid land being methodically built up year after year to look like a lush oasis. It was where people fled to reinvent themselves into selves which had nothing in common with what they once were. *Finocchios* with girls' voices became *forte pistolero* cowboys in the silent moving pictures. Which was why he was here in this make-believe place. He had been told, over the years, by so many men and women, how handsome he was, like that spic film star, Valentino, who passed himself off as an Italian. Why him and not me? What was acting? Just a different kind of con. So he used the Jew's name to get a meeting with morto Christo film producers. They were nothing like Rothstein. A man with style and brains and balls. They were coarse, vulgar men with guttural accents. They sat behind big desks, eating a pastrami sandwich with their mouths opened. They told him to stand up, turn around, eyeballing him like he was a side of beef.

He left the fake city two days later and went north to San Francisco. A real city, more to his liking. Small *immigrante* neighborhoods of wops and micks like in Bridgeport, but some neighborhoods, too, of the Chinamen he'd never seen before. He learned they were the most degenerate of gamblers. They were ruthless. Small, yellow, timid men, and women, too, the first serious women gamblers he'd ever met. They bowed and scraped with humility, but with hard, slanted eyes, too, like the Black Hand assassins. Only scarier. You couldn't read them. *Inscrutable* was the word people used out west. Those narrow eyes that showed nothing. They were assassins on a poker or craps table. They killed, took no prisoners, gambled until they busted the bank, or themselves. They went two, three days without sleep, barely eating, until either they, or the house, went bust. Watching them, he learned what ruthless really was. The first gamblers he'd met, other than the Jew, he admired. He made a mental note. "Never gamble with little people with yellow skin," and moved north to Seattle. A city of white breads who smiled at him on the street and said, Hello, a beautiful day today, isn't it? The one day in two weeks it didn't rain. They were *idiota*. Not worth his time to con. It was beneath him. Like taking a kid's milk money.

The rain began to depress him, so he headed east looking for the sun. He found it in a little town in Idaho a few miles from the Canadian border by a clear blue lake surrounded by mountains green with fir trees. The town called itself America's Bavaria. It looked like it should be on a postcard.

So he took a room in a boarding house and found a pool hall. He was banging the balls around a table, waiting for a Mark to come over to him, when he saw a calendar on the wall. He reached into his back pocket and pulled out a worn, folded piece of paper he always carried with him. He unfolded it, an official looking document from The State of Connecticut. The first line was written in ink in an elaborate yet fading script: Pasquale Michaele Giordano. Born September 8, 1910. At the bottom it was stamped with an official looking seal, an eagle, and a shield. Proof, at least in the eyes of a State, and himself, if to no one else, that he was *legittimo*.

He was twenty-three years old this day. Alone as usual. But for some reason, maybe Fate, it depressed him. He'd had a few birthday parties in the orphanage, but they'd meant nothing to him. Childish celebrations for what? Being born? It made no sense to him. A birthday party without family? What was the point? To remind him what he was in this world?

So, on a whim, he called the Venice A.C. He asked for one of his cronies, Tommy the Blond, who was not really blond. He was just not so dark as his cronies. My father thought talking to someone he knew, more importantly, someone who knew him, would cheer him up. He stood against the wall in the darkened pool hall in Idaho and talked to his crony for a few minutes. When his crony said he had to go, there was a crap game forming, my father panicked. He blurted out, "*Uno momento, Tomas! Come va con Firenze? La ragazza DiMenna?*"

And Tomas said, in *Inglese*, "She got smart finally, Patsy. She divorced that *cafone*. She's living in her mother's tenement in The Hollow with her kid."

# CHAPTER THIRTEEN

Four days later, my father appeared in The Hollow, and presented himself to my mother, as if a Knight in Armor on a horse, with a lance, come to sweep her up into his arms, and ride off with her to his castle where he would protect her forever. She looked at him with a jaundiced eye. My mother, not then, and not ever, saw herself as a fragile heroine weeping for a savior.

She saw that my father was still handsome, but no longer boyish. His hair was thinning, and there was an air about him of weariness as befits a man. He was dressed more conservatively, less flash, in the kind of clothes she'd seen on Yale boys in restaurants in Bridgeport with their blonde Greenwich girlfriends. She admitted to herself, but not to him, that Patsy Jordan had more weight than when he'd left. How much more was the question.

My older brother, George, who was six at that time, told me once, "Oh, Patty, it was a long wooing! Dad mooned around Ma for more than two years before she gave him a tumble."

My father never had the patience for the long con, too much trouble for a questionable return. But this time, the return would be worth it, he thought, although still highly questionable. So he worked around Florence for a year, seducing her family one by one. Her homely sisters were easy Marks, her ineffectual brother, too. Sam, the father, would have been his most stalwart defender in his quest, if he hadn't died a few years before my father began the siege of his oldest daughter.

Sam Diamond had been a tough little man with a shock of white hair. He was a bricklayer and a club fighter, who held his own against the big Irishers. In one fight, a big Irisher knocked him to the canvas. The dumb mick stood over my grandfather and taunted him. Sam rolled over on the canvas and sank his teeth into the mick's ankle until blood spurted out, and even then, like a muscular little pit bull, Sam wouldn't let go. It took four men to pull Sam off the screaming mick, who was awarded the fight on a technical disqualification of his opponent. He had to accept his victory sitting on his stool, while his handlers stanched his bleeding ankle. Sam was cheered by the crowd as he was led out of the club.

Sam was also a gambler, but not like my father. Sam was a Mark. My father tried to keep him out of fixed poker games. But Sam wouldn't listen to him. He had that arrogance of most Italian pa-drones who had been pampered by their women. Besides, Sam was a Mark even in poker games that weren't crooked. So my father joined him at the poker table as a beard. Sam was clueless as my father ruthlessly forced the other players to fold game after game until only he and Sam were left at the table. Then my father folded his hand, giving the pot to Sam. While Sam hugged his winnings to him like an eager child, my father buried his three aces and two jacks into the deck before anyone could see them.

Now, without Sam as his champion, my father needed to seduce the matriarch DiMenna, now Mary Diamond. A formidable obstacle, he thought. Mary ruled her household with an iron hand. She was not a frivolous woman easily seduced by a *faccia bello*. But she surprised him. One night at her house, Mary heard her daughter rebuff my father's offer to take her to dinner. Mary turned on her daughter and snapped, "*Basta*, Firenze! Take a meal with Pasquale. He's a good boy." Which did not sit well with my mother. She had no intentions of surrendering her life, and her son's, to a *reggazo con faccia bello* who was a *speculatore*. She wanted a *uomo forte*. My mother's weakness. Her stubbornness clouded her perceptions. My father may have been a pretty boy then, but he was never weak.

Her mother already knew this about my father. Mary Diamond was a smart woman who saw through my father's façade to the man he was. In fact, Mary was The Godmother of The Hollow. Women sought her advice about family problems. A wandering husband. Lazy sons. Flirtatious daughters. Mary dispensed advice, and the women followed it. Weeks later they brought her a small gift as *reconoscenza*.

But her strong-willed oldest daughter gave her fits. Crossed her at every turn. Told her she had no intention of going out to dinner with Patsy Jordan. My mother's two sisters were horrified. They looked at her, shook their heads no, in silent warning. Don't cross The General! Mary spoke deliberately to her oldest daughter, "You will go to dinner with Pasquale as your mother wishes if for no other reason than to show your mother rispetto." She left unsaid the fact that she had taken Firenze and her son into her house after her divorce. So my mother went out to dinner with my father. He took her to the fanciest restaurant in the city in the Hotel St. George. It was an expensive dinner, the best money could buy, but a silent one, at first. Then not so silent. Mary Diamond was pleased.

My grandmother had her own reasons for wanting her oldest daughter to be married off again. It would be a good match. She knew Pasquale was moonstruck over her daughter and would make her a good husband. Pasquale was smart enough to know he could never control the combustible Firenze. But he was self-assured enough not to care. So he gave Firenze her reins and let her run.

Firenze would be a good wife for him. Pasquale had been on his own too long. Like a *cavallo* born in the wild, always running with the wind without reins. Mary Diamond knew he needed to become *domesticare*. He needed someone to put a saddle on him, rein him in, make demands, force him to do things he had never thought he would. They would make each other better.

Mary also had a selfish reason for wanting her daughter married off. She wanted a little peace in her life. She had four adult children and a grandson living in her house. Marie was mercurial, Josephine phlegmatic, and Benjamin pampered and compliant. As for my mother, she was a prickly woman, combative, quick to see a slight, especially when it concerned her son.

One cold winter night, Marie and my mother got into a furious argument over their apartment's heat. My mother had jacked up the heat to protect her son from the feared influenza. It had already claimed her younger brother, Peter, when he was six. But the mercurial Marie wanted the apartment cooler. My mother grabbed her purse and her son's hand and stormed out of the apartment. As

she walked along a darkened alley in the cold, she passed the kitch-
en window where she saw Marie, illuminated at the sink, washing
dishes. My mother flung her handbag at the window, shattering the
glass. The terrified Marie screamed. My mother shouted through the
broken window, "Is that cold enough for you?"

Finally, to everyone's relief, my mother consented to marry my
father. But she had conditions. My father had to give up gambling and
get a respectable job, like an American. Secondly, he had to promise
to raise her son as his own son. My father had no problem with the
latter. He already liked little George, a respectful, serious boy for his
age. His mother said he was "a little man already." Besides, my father
wanted a family. He had spent so much time around the passionate yet tight-knit DiMennas, the first time he'd ever been close to a
family, that he found it comforting after twenty-five years of being
alone. The fact that it was a ready-made family pleased him even
more. They already knew about families. He didn't. So all he had to
do was slide into the DiMenna family, pay attention, and become a
part of it. In this way he would avoid disruption to his life, and his
gambling. A family he made on his own, a child, would have been
inconvenient. It would have cramped his style. My father didn't have
to change little George's diapers, feed him from a bottle, walk him
in a stroller, talk gibberish to him, getting nothing in return. Little
George was eight years old. He was intelligent. He had a personality.
He was close enough in age to my father that they both thought of
each other as fellow running mates. Which brought my father back
to Firenze's first condition. He told her he would raise her son better
than any father could raise his natural son. But she must never ask
him to give up gambling. She fumed, not used to being denied. But
for one of the first times in her life she overcame her stubbornness,
and agreed, reluctantly.

Both my father and my mother got what they wanted. So, in The
Hollow, years ago, they each signed off on their spoken unusual pre-
nuptial agreement and were married in a civil ceremony at City Hall
in 1935. My father was twenty-five, and my mother was twenty-
nine. My brother, eight years old, attended the ceremony in what he
called "the monkey suit Ma insisted I wear."

Over the next five years, they lived in relative harmony in Bridgeport. My father no longer went on the hustle for more than a few days. He confined his gambling to Bridgeport and the Fairfield County area, and only occasionally on hustles farther north and east throughout New England. Often, he took my brother with him. My brother grew up with my father in dingy hotel rooms, among strange men smoking and drinking while they played poker all night long. George brought the men their drinks from a makeshift bar. They tipped him loose change and told my father he had a good son. My father nodded.

After the games ended and the men left, George helped my father clean up the room. Then he jumped on the bed for his favorite part of the night. My father dumped all the bills he'd won that night in a pile on the bed. George stacked the bills according to their denomination. Then he added them up and told my father how much he'd won.

# CHAPTER FOURTEEN

By the time my brother turned eleven, he had lost interest in going with Dad on his gambling trips. He had a new interest, sports, especially baseball and basketball. Such interests would have been squashed by any other Italian father from The Hollow as *frivolo*. In his free time, the proper son of an Old World wop was expected to work with his father gutting fish in his market. But my brother had been blessed with his new father, who encouraged his interest in sports. My father also liked having George go with him on his gambling trips, especially those he felt would be interesting to his son. When Dad was about to go with a traveling carnival for a few days, he tried to get George to show some enthusiasm for such a trip. He described to George all the exciting wonders he would see, the bearded lady, the two-headed calf. George pouted, refused to go. He wanted to stay home and play baseball. So Dad offered to buy him a new baseball glove and play catch with him every day if he went with him. Finally, George relented.

They left town with a carnie couple Dad knew, Locks and Margaret. Locks, his nickname because of his beautiful hair, was in charge of the carnie's gambling. Margaret, his wife, was the carnie's fortune teller. She darkened her skin with chimney soot and wore gypsy clothes and a turban. She spoke with an indecipherable foreign accent, which, strangely enough, vanished when she took off her turban.

George was expected to be Margaret's shill to earn his keep. He stood outside her tent exhorting the rubes to step inside where The World-Renowned Mademoiselle Margareet would foretell their future. Margaret told George the trick of enticing the rubes was to make personal contact with them. So George hit on the idea of asking each of the rubes their first names and then repeating their names loudly so

Margaret would hear them. When the rubes sat across from Margaret and she called them by their names, they would be astonished. But they weren't sitting across from Margaret. They were outside the tent having conversations with this charming boy. The conversations lasted so long the rubes forgot to go into the tent with the fortune teller. Finally, The World-Renowned Mademoiselle Margareet swooped out of the tent, her long, gypsy skirt flowing behind her, and snapped at George, "Enough already with the first name shit!"

George sulked with Dad on their way back to their hotel. So Dad offered to have a catch with him in the hallway outside of their room. Dad, a southpaw, had bought himself a left-handed glove for their catches. But it wasn't much use to him. I doubt that Dad had ever had a baseball glove on his hand until then. As they threw the ball back and forth in the narrow hallway, the balls rattled off the walls, bounced down the hallway, a comedy of errors. The other guests stuck their heads out of their doorways and complained about the noise. The manager was called up to their floor. The catches ceased.

When I first heard that story of George and the fortune teller, and Dad and the balls bouncing off the hotel walls, I thought it was a funny story. I thought that was the point of the story. But there were other points. Dad wanted George to come with him because he liked his company. So Dad bribed his son by buying him what he wanted, a new glove. Dad's modus operandi. Then I realized there was another point. George, the once dutiful son, was now disagreeing with Dad as any boy would as he developed interests of his own. George was growing into a mind of his own.

But there was still another point. *The* Point, actually. The story was about Dad's and George's relationship. My father had raised George so naturally as his son that George thought of Dad as his natural father. Which was why it never occurred to George not to be a spoiled brat when his father asked him to do something he didn't want to do. So he sulked. Wouldn't every son?

Seven years after their marriage, my parents were living in a three-story house in the suburbs north of Bridgeport. There were trees along the street and grassy lawns. There were other single-family homes whose families inside those homes were not Italian. My mother, father, and brother were settled into a tightly-knit, content-ed family, maybe the first nuclear family. They circled the wagons, protected each other from threats.

Then, my mother discovered she was pregnant again, after four-teen years. She was thirty-six, my father was thirty-two. She took baths in vinegar, but to no avail.

A few days before I was born, back in The Hollow, my father changed his name legally so I could have an American name. I would be a new generation Italian-American, more American than Italian. On April 22, 1941, I was born Patrick Michele Jordan Jr. My father's son. The only blood relative he'd ever known.

My father held his son for the first time in the hospital room where my mother lay in bed. My mother watched him, the look on his face, and was overcome with fear. What if, now that my father had a son of his own, he would lavish all his attention on him, and ignore her son? And why not? In those days, nothing was more sacred to Italians than family blood. But my father knew nothing about such blood. As far as he was concerned, such beliefs were Old World superstitions from the Dark Ages. They kept Italians from becoming Americans. Closed, distrustful, clannish. Afraid. The greatest curse of his life, and at the same time its greatest blessing, was that, as a child and young man, he had no family blood. No materno who emasculated him by pampering him like A Guinea Prince. No padrone at the head of the table under whose thumb he would spend his life. An ignorant wop dispensing orders to his son. "Don't disrespect the family. Remember your blood. Don't rise above your *stazione*. Put out of your head childish ideas of going to a *scuola 'mericana*. You'll work with me in the *mercato*. Then one day you, too, will be a fishmonger, like my father and his father before him."

To my father, then a young man, such a life was worse than death. My father had made his own life out of a blank slate. Nothing of that life resembled the lives lived by those Italian immigrants in The Hollow. He'd made his own choices. What he learned from those choices he passed on to his sons. Which profoundly affected their lives.

All my life, until the day he died, my father was my consigliere. Even after he died and I lived on, I would think, when confronted with a problem, what would Dad do? Among the many lessons he taught me, the greatest, and the most painful, was one he repeated over and over to me through the years.

"Remember, Patty," he said. "Love is more important than blood."

# PART
# TWO

# CHAPTER FIFTEEN

I spent the first four-and-a-half years of my life with my parents and my brother in that three-story house with grassy lawns on a tree-lined street. I remember little about those years except what I had been told by my parents and my brother. They held up to me slides of those years – The Boy and the Cat, The Bottle of Coke, The Cut-Glass Ashtray, The Scene in the Grocery Store, The Girlfriend and the Crib – which all had in common one point. What a demon I had been as a child.

We had a pussycat. My mother told me pussycats had nine lives. I loved the pussycat. I held him in my arms on the floor and smothered his fur with kisses. One day, I threw him out of the second-floor window. The pussycat landed on all four paws and walked away. The next day, I threw the pussycat out of the window again. My mother was in the kitchen washing dishes when the pussycat flew past her window.

My Uncle Ben parked his shiny new 1943 Ford Super Deluxe automobile in our driveway. He sat at the kitchen table with my parents and brother. My mother brought Uncle Ben a glass of scotch. I whined and cried. My mother gave me a bottle of Coca Cola. Uncle Ben told my parents he had no more ration stamps to buy gasoline for his new car. So I went outside to his shiny new 1943 Ford Super Deluxe automobile. I pried open his gas cap and poured my coke into it. On his drive home, his engine seized up.

The little boy who lived next door was two years older than me. He was not Italian. But still, my mother let him come over to play with me. We sat on the living room floor with my toys. My mother was in the kitchen. I gave him my favorite toy. He played with it for a few moments, then broke it. I gave him another toy. He broke that one too. My mother heard a scream. She ran into the living room to see blood gushing from my playmate's head. I was holding her cut-glass ashtray.

My mother took me to the grocery store. We walked down the aisles. My mother picked up colorful boxes and cans from the shelves and put them in her cart. I picked out a colorful box and put it in her cart. She put it back. I took it again and put it in the cart. She put it back. I grabbed it again. She tried to take it from me. I held on tight. We both pulled, back and forth, until she wrenched it out of my hand. I threw myself on my back on the floor, shrieking and kicking my legs in the air like an upended turtle. Other mothers stared at me and frowned. My mother gave me back the box. I stopped shrieking and put it in her cart.

One night, my brother brought his girlfriend to our house to meet his parents and me. My father was ingratiating. My mother cool. I was upstairs in my crib. My brother led his girlfriend upstairs. He opened my bedroom door. His girlfriend hesitated. She'd heard stories. He allayed her fears, "He's harmless when he's sleeping." She approached my crib as if maneuvering around landmines on Normandy Beach. My crib had slatted fencelike sides. And another slatted fence on top. I was boxed in. She stared at me sleeping. I looked like a cherub from a Renaissance painting, sans wings. Luxuriant, wild, blond curls. Fat pink cheeks. Cupid bow lips. She knelt down and put her face close to the slats. She said, "But...he's an Angel."

There were other slides, too. According to those slides, when I was a baby my brother changed my diapers. He fed me from a bottle and burped me. He gave me sponge baths in the sink, then dressed me and put me to sleep. He babysat for me when our parents went out at night. On warm days, my brother took me for walks in my stroller. He passed mothers with their babies in strollers, too. They looked into my stroller, smiled at my shoulder-length blond curls, and said, "What a beautiful little girl!" My brother, at fifteen, was humiliated. One day, he'd had enough. He took me to a barber shop and had all my curls cut off. When we got home my mother made George go back to the barber shop and sweep up my curls and bring them back to her.

When I was old enough, I slept in bed with my brother. He told me stories about Jimmy and the Ghost, but only if I scratched his head. The stories about Jimmy and the Ghost went on and on until I fell asleep. When I woke in the morning, I asked my brother, what happened to Jimmy and the Ghost? He said, "I'll tell you tonight, Patty." But those stories never came to an end.

When I was four, my brother told me not to call our mother "Mommy" anymore. "That's for babies," he said. "Call her Mom, or Ma." Then he taught me how to shake hands, "like a man," he said. "Firmly, like this." He squeezed my hand until it hurt. "Not like a girl."

Then he was gone. He went off to college, Georgetown University in Washington, DC, then Georgetown Law School. I saw him now only sporadically over the next six years. During those years, it was left to my father to hold up to me slides of my brother's life I never saw, or, if I did, I never remembered because I was a child. Which is not to say, again, I ever doubted their veracity. Which is also not to say, that, as I got older, I saw the same point in those slides that my brother and father did.

My brother, tall and rangy, stood beside the Bridgeport railroad tracks waiting for a train that would take him to Georgetown for his first day of college. He felt a tug on his wallet in his rear pocket. Without looking, he whirled around and punched the pickpocket in the jaw. He fell to the platform, blood gushing from his nose. A filthy old bum, emaciated, hungry. My brother was overcome with guilt. He helped that old man up, stanched his bleeding nose with his own handkerchief. Then he gave him most of the money in his wallet.

During my brother's first year at Georgetown, he wrote Dad a letter on Georgetown University stationery. At the top of the letter was a seal, an American eagle on a shield, surrounded by the words Collegium Georgiopolitanum 1789. Dad must have loved that seal. It was not much different than his alma mater's seal at Darthmuth.

George wrote:

Dear Dad,

I got your letter this morning and was very glad to hear from you. I don't think you should have sent me all that money tho dad. I really don't need that much ever but I think I can put it to good use. I've got to get Mom something for Mother's Day and I can use the rest for train fare when I come home the twenty-sixth so don't send anymore and tell mom not to either. Tell her to send some food tho, o.k? Well dad the work has been getting a lot harder but I get it all done without too much trouble so if it keeps up like this I don't think I'll have much trouble.

How did you do on The Derby, dad? I said a little prayer that whoever you have would come in. I hope it was Jet Pilot. I'm looking forward to the day when I'm rich enough to take care of you and mom for the rest of your lives. I'd like to have enough money so you could take it easy and bet on the horses and all just for enjoyment and not because you have to support a family. If I ever do get rich you'll never have to worry about a thing. I know I owe you just about everything I have or ever will have and I'm never going to forget it. I know I don't act very grateful most of the time but I hope you know how I feel dad and I think you do because I think you're about the same way. I know I couldn't have a better father ever dad and I mean that.

I've got to go to class now dad so I'll close for now – after all this is what's going to make me rich. Tell mom I'll write tomorrow.

Your son, George

If not for Dad, George would not have gone to Georgetown, or law school, or become a rich and successful lawyer.

In the eighth grade, George worked in a fish market with his friends. He liked the independence of it, the money in his pocket each week, his co-workers. He told Dad that he'd found the job he wanted for the rest of his life. How that must have broken Dad's heart! His son, like an Old World wop, gutting fish all day and coming home stinking of fish. But he said nothing, until it was time for George to go to high school.

George wanted to go to the public high school, Central, up the hill from The Hollow, with his friends. But Dad had greater aspirations for his son, aspirations denied him. He told George that a new private Catholic Prep school had opened its doors in the wealthy, leafy suburb of Fairfield. It was to be run by Jesuits, those fiercely intellectual priests who had a reputation for their mental, moral, and physical rigor that turned boys into men. Yet, despite their close relationship, George fought Dad's wishes. Still, Dad insisted. He told his son he had too many gifts to waste his life as a fishmonger. He could be anything he wanted to in life, a doctor, lawyer, professor. "Not like me," Dad said. "A wasted life." One of the few times in his life Dad ever resorted to self-pity to get what he wanted.

Backed against a wall, Dad was a street fighter. He'd use whatever was at hand, a brick, a broken beer bottle, self-pity. It was worth it to save his son's future. It was always about the bottom line with Dad. Despite his romantic infatuation with the intellectual life, all those dead Greek philosophers on the meaning of existence, Dad was at heart a hard, cold pragmatist. Fuck the meaning! Get it done. Any way you can, and don't get caught.

In his early eighties, Dad took Mom out to dinner at a little trattoria in The Hollow. They were walking to the restaurant when a young man, maybe twenty, burst out of an alley, ripped Mom's purse off her shoulder, knocking her to the sidewalk, and took off running. Dad ran after him. Down the sidewalk, into an alley, gone. Mom did not scream. She pulled herself up and waited for Dad to return with her purse. When he finally did return to her, out of breath, she said, "Where's my purse?" Dad flung his hand in the air, and said, "I almost had him, Flo, until he jumped over a wall."

I was fifty when Dad told me that story. I said, "Are you fucking crazy, Dad? What were you gonna do if you caught the kid?" He shrugged, and said, "I wasn't thinking about that. When I caught him, I'd know what to do."

But even that was not the point of that story, an old man chasing a kid into an alley over a woman's purse with a few bucks in it. The point of that story, in *my* family at least, was that Ma expected Dad to chase that kid, and to get back her purse. When he didn't, she was furious with him.

George never understood Dad's hardness, refused to believe it even when it was obvious. Which was why he was a sucker for Dad's con, especially his self-pity.

"What do you mean, 'A wasted life,' Dad? You're the greatest."

So, my brother relented. Prep it would be. George told me, years later, "Dad had never pressured me to do anything in my life up to then, so I realized how important this was to him. I didn't want to hurt his feelings, after all he'd done for me. So I went to the Prep." George nodded. "Dad was right, like always. He changed my life."

I said, "Brother, admit it. You fell for the old man's con."

My brother shrugged, with a small smile. "There is that, too."

# CHAPTER SIXTEEN

I had always wondered how Dad was able to change my brother's life by paying for his education at Georgetown and Georgetown Law School when our own finances at home were so precarious. I found out in my late thirties when Dad told me.

When Dad married Ma, he'd extracted a promise from George Senior that he would never interfere with Dad's upbringing of George Junior. George's birth father was only too willing to oblige. He told Dad he had no interest in being involved in George's life. And he wasn't for years. Until it was time for George to go to college. Dad didn't have the money to pay for that education, so he drove up to Eastover, Massachusetts, where George Senior had a thriving business as an owner of an exclusive resort, which had made him a wealthy man by then. Dad stood before George Senior, seated at his desk, and pleaded his case. Then silence. George Senior thought for a long moment, then agreed to finance his son's college and law school education with one stipulation. He didn't want Dad to think that this meant he wanted a place in his son's life now. He had a new family now, a young wife and three daughters, none of whom knew about his son.

Dad said, "I understand."

When Dad told George his father would finance his Georgetown and law school education, George was thrilled. Not only for the education, but because this showed him that the father who had given him up actually cared enough about him to change his life.

Dad said, "I'm happy for you, son."

One day, in my seventies, I asked George about his childhood years with Ma and his birth father. He told me they had all three lived briefly in Stamford, Connecticut, on a ranch, with horses. "Ma used to love riding horses," my brother said.

"Ma!" I said. "A wop Dale Evans?" I couldn't believe it. The city girl from The Hollow. This was one of the many stories about Ma and Dad and George and their early life before me that no one ever told me.

George said his father was embarrassed by the divorce. In those days, divorce was *umiliazione* in the Italian community. So George Senior tried never to acknowledge his first wife, his divorce, or his son to anyone. "I didn't hold that against my father," George told me once. "That's the way things were in those days."

When George's birth father died, he received a call from his three daughters. George Senior had told them in his later years about his son, George Junior. So now, they called their half-brother and invited him to walk down the church aisle with them at his father's funeral.

"I walked down the aisle arm-in-arm with my sisters," he told me. "It was very moving for me."

It infuriated me.

A few weeks after George's first letter to Dad in his first year at Georgetown, my brother wrote Dad another letter, which I never saw. Dad recounted the contents of that second letter to me many times over the years. In that letter, George told Dad he would take over "the burden of raising Patty" to repay Dad for being such a terrific father to him. Dad told me that letter showed how much George loved me, and him. "Your brother and I have a special relationship," he said.

But George didn't raise me. I rarely saw my brother when he was at Georgetown and Georgetown Law School. By the time George graduated from law school, I was nine, and he was twenty-three. When he returned home, he was married, with a child. He no longer lived with us. He was a struggling young lawyer for a few years, with three children now, then after a few more years, he was a successful young lawyer with six children. I seldom saw him except on his occasional lunchtime visits, when he stopped by to have a catch with me on the sidewalk in front of our house.

My brother did things with me that Dad didn't. He took me to a basketball game, had a catch with me on the sidewalk or, on rare occasions, at the baseball diamond at the nearby park. Dad had no interest in, or concept of, such fatherly bonding as it would be called today. The important things Dad learned in his life he learned from experience, on his own. Dad always felt his responsibility to me and my brother was not to amuse us, but to prepare us for the real world of hard knocks.

I got in a car accident when I was sixteen. Just a fender bender. But it was Dad's only car. I nursed the dented car home and told Dad, "It wasn't my fault, Dad. The other guy ran the red light."

Dad looked at me with disgust. "You should have known," he said. "The other guy always runs the red light. An accident is always your fault. Only a fool or a child believes in perfect justice."

Dad knew a lot about justice. If there was justice in this life, he would have had a mother and a father.

So, it was left to my brother to do boyish things with me. Like those catches on the sidewalk. George would appear in his Lincoln Continental, late, in a rush. The busy lawyer in his gray flannel suit and blue Oxford cloth button-down collared shirt. I'd run out of the house to greet him. He'd say, "No time for the park today, brother. I only have a few minutes. I have to get back to the office." And my heart would skip a beat, oh, no! George saw the look on my face and smiled, "Don't worry, brother. We'll catch here." I'd had my two gloves and a ball with me. I gave a glove to my brother, and we began our catch on the sidewalk in front of my house. Ma and Dad sat on the concrete front steps and applauded my throws. When I'd throw a particularly fast pitch, my brother would yank his hand out of the glove and blow on it as if to alleviate the hot pain. Ma would laugh at George's antics, and call out, "Patty, don't you hurt your brother now." My heart soared! I threw the ball to George as quickly as I could, to get in as many throws as possible, because those catches didn't last long. In my rush, I threw a wild pitch. George walked after the ball rolling down the street. My heart sank! George walked back with the ball, so slowly it seemed to me then, that I called out, "Hurry, brother!" And then George was back in his car again.

Dad would say, "Did you thank your brother?" I nodded. And then my brother was gone, and I was left with Mom and Dad to raise me.

# CHAPTER SEVENTEEN

I remember the first slide from my childhood that I saw with my own eyes. I was four-and-a-half years old. What made that slide so important to me was that it was my first sentient awareness of my life.

My parents were arguing in the kitchen, over me. It was a cold, wintery Saturday morning. My mother was putting me in my little powder blue snowsuit with the fur-lined hood and the mittens attached to the sleeves with safety pins.

"You're taking him," she said.

"I'll be working," my father said.

My mother looked at him. "Work? You call it work?"

"What am I gonna do with him?"

"Find something."

My father put me on the front seat of his old, black Ford, and we drove to downtown Bridgeport in silence. He parked the car off Main Street. We walked up State Street in a cold wind that stung my cheeks. I followed behind him in his brown fedora hat and double-breasted camel hair overcoat. The wind caught the insides of Dad's overcoat, and it flapped up behind him like the wings of a giant bird. We passed women shoppers going into the Mohican Market, with the painting of a big Indian chief on the sign. I stopped and stared in the window at all the cakes and pastries lined up on trays. When I turned back up the sidewalk, my father was ahead of me. I hurried to catch up to him. When we reached the Waldorf Cafeteria, with its big plate-glass front windows that were steamed up from the heat inside, my father took my hand and led me inside. There was a big, empty, barren room except for dozens of small tables with red Formica tops and aluminum legs. The chairs had aluminum legs, too, with red plastic seats. A few old men were sitting at the tables, alone. Most of the tables didn't have an old man.

My father led me to a wall of small glass doors with plates of food on shelves behind the glass. He gave me a handful of quarters and showed me how to put them in a slot. "Put in four," he said. I put one quarter after another into the slot. They made a metal sound when they settled.

"Now point to what you want, Patty," he said. I looked at all the different kinds of food behind the glass. Scrambled eggs. Toast. Orange juice. Donuts. Then I pointed. He said, "See that little shiny handle in front of the pancakes? Pull it towards you." I took off one mitten and pulled the handle. Miraculously, the plate of pancakes was pushed toward the glass door, which swung open. "Now take your pancakes and go find a table near the window so you can keep your eyes on me. I'll be outside for a while."

I found a table near the plate-glass window and sat down with my pancakes. Dad went outside. I looked around me. Some of the old men seated alone were staring into their cups of coffee. One of them was looking at me in a strange way. He smiled at me. I looked away from him at some of the other old men who had laid their heads on their tabletop and were sleeping. I watched one old man look down at the floor, bend over, and scrape up a crushed cigarette stub with his fingernails. He straightened the tiny stub in his hands and lighted it with a match. He inhaled deeply and then blew out smoke.

I turned back to my pancakes and poured syrup on them from a glass bottle on the table. Then I cut them into pieces with my knife and began eating them with my fork.

While I was eating my pancakes, I noticed my father through the fogged-up window. I put on a mitten and made swirls against the window with it until I could see Daddy clearly now. He was standing on the sidewalk with other men dressed like him, except their hats and overcoats were black. They were smoking cigarettes, talking, laughing, rubbing their hands together and stomping their feet to warm them while they waited.

I wondered what Daddy and the men were saying. I wished I was outside with them so I could listen to them talk. Maybe they were telling funny stories. If I was out there with them, I could tell them funny stories, too. Like the time I threw our cat out of the second-story window. Then they would laugh, and I could laugh with them. I could stamp my feet, too, in the cold. It was hot in the room I was in. The iron radiators against the walls rattled and hissed out steam that billowed up. I wished I could take off my snowsuit, but I didn't know how.

A long, shiny, black car pulled up to the curb. One of the men went over to the front driver's side window. The window rolled down. The man leaned his head close to the window and said something to the man in the car. Then he took a white envelope out of his inside overcoat pocket and handed it through the window. The window went up, and the car drove away.

I finished my pancakes and watched my father and the other men outside for the next two hours. A lot of different cars pulled up to the curb, one after the other, all of them black. Different men went over to the cars when it was their turn. I wondered how they knew it was their turn. When would it be Daddy's turn? All of the men handed their envelopes to the driver. None of them received an envelope from the driver.

Finally, it was Daddy's turn. He went over to a car, and a hand reached out the window with a white envelope in it. Daddy took the envelope, nodded to the driver, and he drove away. I wondered why he got to get an envelope, and the other men had to give up their envelopes to the men in the cars. I saw Daddy open the envelope, finger something inside it, then close it again. He put it in his inside overcoat pocket. Then he went up close to the window where he could see me. He tapped on the window to get my attention. I waved at him and said, "Hi, Daddy." Then he signaled with his hands for me to come outside.

Driving home, Daddy talked to me. So I asked him why the other men had to give up their envelopes to the men in the cars, but he got an envelope from a man in a car. He said because he was smarter than the other men.

"Was there a prize in the envelope?" I asked.

"Yes."

"What was the prize, Daddy?"

Daddy looked at me. "You ask too many questions, Patty. Sta da zitt."

Before we got home, Daddy told me what to say to Mommy.

When we were back home in the kitchen, Mommy knelt down and started to take off my snowsuit. She asked Daddy something. He said, "Sure, he did, Flo. Ask him."

Mommy looked at me and said, "Patty, did you have fun with your father?"

I glanced at Daddy, then back to Mommy. I smiled at her and said, "I had lots of fun, Mommy."

It was my first con. And my first Mark was my mother.

# CHAPTER EIGHTEEN

That first slide from the Waldorf Cafeteria is still clear in my mind even as I write this in my late seventies. Other slides from my later childhood come rushing after it, so fast and clear, that I remember them, too. Those slides were minted into my consciousness because they were not imagined. I saw them. I know what they meant, the story they told, the points they made, because I was now the final arbiter of my experiences. It was my life I was living from the moment I entered the Waldorf Cafeteria when I was four-and-a-half years old.

The second slide I remember from my childhood was of my brother's wedding in the late spring after my fifth birthday. I was standing on the steps of a cathedral, staring straight ahead, expressionless, my hands at my sides as if at attention. My parents were standing to either side of me. My mother, wearing a flowered hat, a summer dress, and white gloves, was looking away from me and my father with a pained look in her eyes. My father, dressed in a tan gabardine suit with a white carnation in his lapel, was looking down at me with just a hint of the faintest smile. He has reached out his hand to adjust his son's tie. My tie, like his, was navy, and my suit jacket, like his, was tan. He seemed to me then, and now, to be expressing with that gesture of his hand, and that faintest of smiles, his pride in his small son, while my mother, with her pained and distant look, seemed to be expressing what she felt over the loss of her son to another woman.

We moved from Bridgeport to Fairfield in the summer after I turned five. It was the wrong end of Fairfield, closer to the Bridgeport city line, and The Hollow, than it was to Fairfield's quaint faux Revolutionary War town center. It was, in fact, the immigrant section of Fairfield.

A little enclave where the Polacks, Czechs, krauts, Swedes, wops, micks, Hunkies, Jews made their first tentative step out of the comfort and security of their immigrant ghettos in Bridgeport into that thrilling yet dangerous foreign world of "real" Americans.

But still, our neighborhood was in Fairfield, that wealthy, Waspy little town with not many names in the phone book that ended in a vowel. We lived on a tree-lined street of 1930s Dutch Colonial houses, all alike. We had a two-car garage and a small back yard with a big stone barbecue that looked like a fireplace with a chimney. There was a spreading maple tree in our front yard. It blocked out the sun and killed all the grass, which was fine with Dad. He was not a suburban, mow-the-lawn kind of dad. His mantra to Ma, whenever any small thing in the house broke, was, "Call the man."

There was a woods across the street, with a river running through it for the entire length of our neighborhood. Dad bought me a cap pistol, and I roamed those woods shooting Indians from behind bushes like Hopalong Casa Dice, as my mother, the wop Dale Evans, called him. Which was an odd name for an American cowboy, but a more appropriate name for an Apache Indian. Hopalong Talking House.

I made a fishing pole out of a branch from a tree, with a safety pin tied to a piece of string at the end of the branch. I stuck a poor squiggling worm on the pin. Brown gushy stuff seeped out of him. I sat by the bank of the river for hours but never caught anything, except one time. I felt a tug on my string and yanked up the branch. A twisting eel flew at me, smacked me in the face, then wrapped himself around my neck. I pulled him off and threw him and my fishing pole back into the river and never fished again.

I gave up trying to be Tom Sawyer and concentrated on my new-found interest, baseball. There was a park a mile from my house. It had jungle gyms, shootie chutes, swings, a tennis court, a rancid pond, and two baseball diamonds at either end. A Little League sized diamond and a major league sized diamond. That's where my brother took me to have a catch. He insisted I throw the ball from the major league pitcher's mound to him at home plate, rather than from the Little League mound much closer to home plate. "That's for babies," he said. "You can do it." The first few times I threw off that mound it seemed a mile away from my brother. The ball bounced halfway to the plate and rolled to George. But after a few days I finally was able to throw the ball all the way to his glove, sixty feet, six inches away.

Most of the families on my street had children my age. After I overcame my initial shyness, I joined them in their games on the street, in the woods, their backyards, and in their houses. I even went to their birthday parties. Which was why I was so excited when my sixth birthday approached.

My mother planned my party. Antipasto, lasagna, and a Cassata cake. I helped her in the kitchen that night. I put the Cassata on the table and asked her why I couldn't have a birthday cake like my new friends. Whipped cream frosting, strawberry jam filling, and blue, hard-sugar flowers on top with the words in blue, "Happy Birthday, Patty."

"Because your aunts and uncles like Cassata," she said. She meant her sisters and brother and their *sposato*, the only people she invited to my party. My brother was away at law school. But he'd made a point of sending me a present, a baseball glove.

I had already asked Ma why I couldn't have my new friends to my birthday party, with hot dogs and cokes and balloons. She said that balloons were a waste of money, and my new friends were too noisy. "You can't expect your aunts and uncles to eat that Irisher food," she added.

But hot dogs were an American food, and my new friends were not all Irishers. They were immigrants like us. But they weren't like us, my mother said, "They're white."

We were the only Italians in that neighborhood of Northern Europeans. And we were certainly the only family whose breadwinner slept all day and gambled all night at the Venice Athletic Club. That was the real reason my mother didn't want my new friends to come to our house. They would discover our otherness. A breadwinner who wakes at five in the afternoon and sits in our little breakfast nook sipping an espresso from a delicate cup with a lemon peel while shuffling a deck of cards. He fans the cards out, makes them into a pyramid, collapses the pyramid, and folds the cards into the deck, all with only one hand.

When he's ready he calls my mother, "Flo!" She sits across from him. He holds up the deck of cards in one hand so she can see them. Then, with his pudgy fingers, he manipulates the cards. He splits the deck open, slips a card out of the middle of the deck, deposits that card on top of the deck while simultaneously pulling out the bottom card in the deck and sliding it into the middle of the deck.

"Ready?" he says. My mother nods.

For the next hour, my father deals cards to my mother. She disregards them. Her eyes are riveted only on his pudgy fingers firing cards at her. He talks to her to distract her, but she ignores him. When he gets to the last card in the deck, he holds it up for her to see, the ace of spades. He sticks the ace between his first two fingers, holds his hand out to her so that she can only see the back of the ace. Then he walks the ace down between his fingers to his pinkie and then back again to his thumb, and then again and again until he stops. He turns the ace toward Ma. It's now a three of hearts.

Then he shuffles the cards and begins dealing again. When he finally stops dealing, he lays the cards on the table, fans them out with one hand, turns up the last card, which then flips over the entire fan until all the faces are showing. Then he collapses the fan between both hands until it becomes a deck again. He lays it gently on the table, raises both hands to Ma, and washes his hands of the whole thing. Finally, he holds up his hands again to Ma, palms out, as if to surrender, and says to her, "Well?"

Ma shakes her head, "Nothing."

After Dad's little magic show, he left for work at 7 p.m. As soon as he was out the door, Ma always turned to me to remind me, "If your friends ever ask why he's home all day and gone all night, what do you say?" I told her. She said, "Good boy, now go to bed."

My new friends did ask me. "Why doesn't your daddy go to work in the morning like ours?" With a smile, and without hesitation, I said, "Oh, my daddy works the night shift at the Brass Factory. He made bombs during the war." They bought it. My second con. And my second Marks were my friends. It didn't bother me in the least.

Actually, it was only half a con. Dad did work for a munitions factory during the war. It was his way of avoiding the draft. He was the timekeeper on the factory floor. When the workers punched in on the night shift, they booked their sports bets with Dad. When they punched out in the morning, they paid him his winnings, or, on rare occasions, collected their winnings from Dad.

My new friends never came to my house, but I went to theirs a lot. My mother said, "Good. You'll be out of my hair."

My new friends' houses are an exotic new world for me. They have dogs and cats and little sisters and freckled moms and smiling dads, who never speak loudly, in Italian, or gesture with their hands. Their dads are never too busy to go outside to toss a baseball with their sons and their friends. Their moms are never too busy to make us all peanut butter and jelly sandwiches on fluffy white bread for lunch. Those sandwiches are so exotic to me! My lunch at home is always *pizza fritta*, dough fried in olive oil and dusted with confectioners' sugar. But only after my mother says first, "I suppose I have to make you lunch."

My friends play wildly in their houses. They shout and laugh, throw things and break them. I watch in horror, then glance at their parents. Amazing! Their parents are smiling at their rambunctious children. Then they sweep up the broken vase.

I did not know such things existed in this world. Children my age who never worry about pleasing adults, and adults who only worry about pleasing children.

When I talk too much or laugh too loudly in our house, my mother snaps at me, "Shoosh, your father is sleeping." And when he wakes late in the afternoon in a foul mood over last night's losses, my mother tosses me a look. "Go to your room, Patty. Color in your book."

When my aunts and uncles arrive for my birthday party, my aunts kiss me on the lips and tell me I'm beautiful. My uncles pinch my cheeks, then fish in their pockets and pull out some wrinkled bills for me. I thank them and am forgotten. My father already gave me his present, a wrinkled twenty-dollar bill dusted with powder blue pool chalk.

My uncles and my father pour themselves scotch and go into the living room to listen to a Yankee game on our big mahogany radio. We are all Yankee fans because they have so many Italians on their team. Crosetti, Lazzeri, Berra, Raschi, Rizzuto, DiMaggio. The conversation in my family is always about Italians we knew who had become doctors or lawyers, or famous Italians like Joe D, who became America's first Italian hero.

The women loved Joe D because he was handsome, graceful, and dignified. "Sooo American," they would say. My mother called Joe D "a white Italian. Not like the other one." She meant Sinatra. He was a *melanzana* Italian. "A real guinea," she said. I piped up, "What's a guinea, Ma?" She said, "You'll know one when you meet one." The self-loathing of immigrants in America in those days knew no bounds.

But the men loved Yogi Berra, the Yankees' catcher, because he was squat, homely, and hard working. They loved the Dodgers' catcher Roy Campanella, too, because he was Italian, but not always. They argued over who was a better catcher. My father said, "What's the difference? They're both Italian." The men still argued. Berra was always a paisano. Campanella was only a paisano sometimes, when he hit a home run. When he struck out, he was a *melanzana*.

I can still see my father sitting, hunched forward, listening to those games on the radio with my real uncles. Their lives and their natures were nothing like Dad's. They were nothing like Dad. Uncle Ben, a draftsman, was prissy like a spinster; Uncle Pat, a stockbroker, had the sly smile of a cynic, watching but rarely speaking; Uncle Ken, the lawyer, then the Judge, was loud, pompous, opinionated, and stupid. A motley crew to hang with for a man like Dad.

Years later, when Dad was an old man, I asked him how he put up with my uncles he had nothing in common with. He said, "Whatever they were, they were my family."

I stay in the kitchen with the women who drink scotch, too, and smoke cigarettes while they help my mother. Aunt Marie holds up a sausage link she is about to drop into the spaghetti sauce and says something in Italian. The only word I recognize is DiMaggio. The women laugh.

My mother holds up her hands a foot apart and says something in Italian. More laughter, and oohing and aahing. Finally, Aunt Joe says, "What a big bat!"

After we eat, my mother passes around little plates for the Cassata. She picks up a knife and is about to cut the Cassata into pieces. I say, "Put candles in it first, Ma."

"Candles?" She cuts the cake in pieces and hands them around. She gives me the biggest piece and says, "Eat your cake and go to bed." I do as I am told.

I say good night to everyone, but I am already forgotten. They are smoking Camel cigarettes, drinking scotch, and talking in Italian. I go up the stairs, but I do not go to bed. I sit on the top step. I can see my aunts and uncles and my parents as shadows illuminated on the living room wall. I hear their voices, their laughter. I hug myself and rock on the top step in the darkness. I think of my new friends. How different I am from them. The loss of their privileged childhood one day will be so painful for them. But not for me. I understand it all at that moment. My parents are not raising me to be a child. They are raising me to be an adult. That realization excites me. I cannot wait for that moment when I will step out of the shadows of my silent, solitary childhood and become an adult. It is what I would have wished for if my mother had lighted candles on my cake and I blew them out.

# CHAPTER NINETEEN

In the summer after my sixth birthday party, my father invited my aunts and uncles to a barbecue cookout in our backyard. These were not my aunts and uncles from my mother's family. They were my aunts and uncles from my father's side. His gambling cronies and their *sposato*. They did not have real names and jobs like my Uncle Ken, the lawyer; Uncle Pat, the stockbroker; and Uncle Ben, the draftsman. Their names were Uncle Chick, short for chickenass; Uncle Sciamo, the jabbering one who seldom spoke; Uncle Gaspipe, his weapon of choice for deadbeats; Uncle Freddy the Welsh, short for welsher, which was not his real last name; and my favorite, Uncle Joe, a jovial man of many last names, depending on his outstanding warrants. Their jobs were fluid, based on their circumstances, their whim, the heat. Debt collector, shylock, card sharp, bookie, carnie shill, horse tout, white collar fraudster, or, like my father, a general contractor sort of con man.

They were not like my real uncles who had no interest in me, or the uncles of my friends, tall, smiling, blond uncles who taught them how to toss a baseball. They were short, swarthy, somber men with fastidious manicures, in their shimmering silver sharkskin suits. They smoked Toscano cigars and always spoke in muffled voices as if to foil a wiretap. But they always had time for me. They taught me things. How to palm the ace of spades, how to spot shaved dice, how to past post a bookie, how to read a racing form, how to figure the odds on a baseball game.

The Sunday afternoon of my father's cookout was hot and sunny. My uncles stood around the barbecue fireplace under the shade of a tree while their *sposato* and *goomahs* sat around a picnic table shaded by a fringed umbrella and played penny ante poker. They all sipped scotch and made nervous small talk while listening to the

Yankees-Red Sox game on the radio propped in the open kitchen window overlooking the yard. I stood under the window and listened to the game, too.

I saw my father bent over the briquettes in the fireplace, lighting match after match. He cursed the briquettes' ancestry, the day they were born, they should die from a rainstorm. Still, they refused to light. My uncles laughed at his discomfort, then fell silent as a crucial play unfolded on the radio. They resumed their small talk.

One of my uncles, with exaggerated politeness, asked my father for permission to light a cigar. Of course, my father said, why not? My uncle shrugged his shoulders. He was a gruff little man I'd never before seen in daylight. I knew him only as a voice on the telephone when I answered it. "Is Patsy dere, kid?" Now, in this Waspy, bucolic setting he made a sweeping gesture with one arm as if reminding my father of our serene surroundings. Like all my uncles on my father's side, he still lived in The Hollow, where he spent most of his waking hours behind the heavy, bolted door of the Venice A.C. Finally, he lighted his cigar.

I went over to the circular table where the women were playing poker, deuces and one-eyed jacks wild. My mother, a dark, fierce, little birdlike woman, passed around a bottle of scotch. The women poured the scotch into their glasses. My mother said, "Water? *Con gassata?*" Hands went up, palms out, imperceptible shakes of the head. "Just rocks, hon." They smoked Camels and chatted like magpies. I stood behind them, a child in short pants, and followed their play. Every so often, one of them would show me their cards. I'd point to one of the cards and shake my head, no. She discarded that card.

The warm air was heavy with the scent of peroxide and cheap perfume and cigarette smoke. The women blew the smoke out of the side of their mouth with one eye pinched shut.

One of my aunts, a gaunt, nervous woman, began to cough. A forced cough it seemed to me even then. She cleared her throat. "A summer cold," she said. The others commiserated with her. She reached into her handbag and withdrew a bottle of Cheracol codeine cough medicine. The others looked away, busied themselves with their cards. My aunt unscrewed the top and raised the bottle to her lips. The back of her skeletal hand quivered like a dying sparrow. She threw back her head and took a gulp.

I stood behind my aunt my mother called the Braciola, but never to her face. She was a big-boned, red-haired Irisher with translucent white skin like parchment filigreed with blue veins and dotted with freckles. A cigarette dangled from her painted lips. She wore a low-cut summer dress of orange polka dots on a field of white. Standing behind her, I was hypnotized by the heaving of her freckled breasts. She studied her cards through wisps of smoke, one eye shut, then looked over her shoulder at me. She showed me her cards and whispered in my ear, "Whaddaya tink, kid? Should I stick with Kinks?" Caught in the cleavage of her huge breasts was a residue of talcum powder. "Well, kid?" I nodded seriously. Her shrill laughter rang through the neighborhood. From the barbecue, her husband glanced at her through narrowed eyes. But she didn't notice him. She turned back to her cards and stuck with her "Kinks."

When she won that hand, she reached out with both hands and hugged her winnings to her breasts. The loose flesh under her arms quivered. She stubbed out her cigarette, turned around to me, grabbed my face in both hands and kissed me hard on the lips with her greasy lips. She laughed again, "Flosy, da kid's a doozy." My mother gave her a smile as thin as a blade.

The Braciola turned back to her next hand. She absentmindedly ran her tongue over her upper teeth to suck off the excess lipstick. I wiped her lipstick off my face with the back of my hand and went over to the kitchen window to listen to the game. The adults were oblivious to me now. My aunts chattering gaily at the table. My uncles huddled, like crows, in a dark cluster at the barbecue, watching the pieces of chicken and pork and sausage sizzling over the flames. My father poked at the meat with a long-handled fork and nodded. The Country Squire in his navy blazer with brass buttons.

I lost myself in the Yankee-Red Sox game for a few innings. The score was tied in the bottom of the eighth when Joe DiMaggio hit a go-ahead home run for the Yanks. I shouted out "Yeah!" and clapped my hands.

Suddenly, I was aware of everyone looking at me. My uncles' muffled voices and my aunts' gay chatter were stilled. My father's face was flushed. My mother's stern face caught my eye. Her lips were pursed into a threatening smile. She called out sweetly to me, "We mustn't root for the Yankees today, Patty. Uncle Gaspipe is down on the Red Sox."

A lesson learned. We defer to our guests. But there was a more shocking point that my mother's words revealed to me. It turned the question of our priorities upside down. No matter how much we worshipped the Yankees, our fellow Italians, gambling was our true god.

But there was a third point, too, in her admonition to me. A subtle point I almost missed. My mother took it for granted that her six-year-old son knew precisely what the words "down on the Red Sox" meant.

# CHAPTER TWENTY

It was exhausting being a con man's son. There were so many things I had to remember, most of them lies. Dad's mythical job at the Brass Shop. His name in the *Bridgeport Post* when the vice squad arrested him and his cronies in a gambling raid at the Venice A.C. There it was, on the front page the following morning, Patsy Jordan, or Pasquale Jordan, or Pasquale Giordano, arrested for illicit gambling. My mother told me, "If anyone asks, you tell them it wasn't your father, his name is Patrick Jordan."

Gambling was the evil stepson in our house. We had to feed its grossness even as it tried to smother us. But we weren't the only family on our street cursed with an evil stepson. The Irisher family had one, too. They called him, The Curse. Tall, pale Mr. Brown, who lived three houses down from us, came staggering up the sidewalk, red-faced, babbling. The older kids laughed at him. Mr. Brown swatted at them, almost falling over. His daughter, Patty, appeared. A pale, serene girl of twelve, with green eyes and Irisher red hair. She came to her father, said something softly in his ear, then entwined her arm with his arm as she would again the day she married. The older boys were stilled now as she led him, docile as a lamb, back home.

My father bought me my first bicycle on a Friday. I pedaled it on the sidewalk, shakily, that Friday, and less shakily on Saturday. By Sunday, I was pedaling it up and down the sidewalk, much steadier. I kept it in our garage at night. By Monday morning, it was gone. "Somebody stole my bike!" I wailed to my mother. She didn't seem surprised, "It'll turn up."

That afternoon, real estate women knocked on our door. They wandered through the house looking behind curtains, inquiring about heating costs, taxes, the roof. That night, my mother told me we might have to sell the house to cover Dad's gambling losses over the weekend. I cried out, "But where will we live?" She said, "We'll find something. Maybe in The Hollow." I cried, "But I like it here!" She said, "Don't worry, your father will figure something out. Now go to bed like a good boy."

So, I went upstairs. But before I got in bed Monday night, I knelt down on the floor and said my prayers. I asked God to *please* let the Celtics beat the Knicks by at least a point and a half tonight so my father could cover the spread. I told God if He granted my wish, I would see to it that Dad never gambled again. God bought it! The third con of my young life. And this time my Mark was the most powerful all-knowing Being in the Universe. The following night in bed I wondered, if He did know everything, even before it happened, why did He fall for my con?

My bike magically reappeared in the garage. My mother put her fingers to her lips, "Sssshhh. Not a word." The real estate ladies didn't return, until a few weekends later when the whole cycle repeated itself, as it did all the years of my childhood. This second time I hesitated asking God again for a favor, not after the last time I conned Him. He was probably really mad at me. But I was so desperate, the real estate ladies bustling about, my bike gone again, The Hollow looming in my future, Nanny Goat Park replacing my green baseball paradise only a mile from my house. So, to assuage my despair, I overcame my fear and asked God for another favor. But I promised, double promised, that this time I'd *definitely* make Dad give up gambling, if God would only let the Bruins beat the Rangers tonight by a puck, puck and a half. But God was no fool. Fool Me once, shame on you. Fool Me twice, shame on Me. The Rangers blanked the Bruins, 3-0.

But we didn't lose the house. Dad found the money, somehow. He borrowed it, or cheated someone out of it, or conned some poor Mark. We escaped the precipice again. After a few more precipices, and escapes, it began to dawn on my six-year-old mind that Dad liked living on the edge. But I didn't know why until I got older. He told me once, when I was a grown man, "Sometimes I was so beat up, I didn't want to get out of bed in the morning. I didn't even have loose change. I'd tapped out everyone. I was without hope. But I found a way." He liked standing over the abyss, I realized then. It made him feel more alive than anything else in his life.

My father always told me, "Hell, for a gambler, is a game he can never lose. The possibility of loss is the juice, not winning."

This whole reoccurring scenario was actually a little drama my parents played out every month or so. They had the script, knew how the drama would end, not with destruction, but with redemption. But I didn't know! I didn't have the script! I didn't know it was some adult drama they played out! I thought it was real! It was real to *me!*

But I learned, adjusted, realized I was in on it with them. I had bills to pay, too, in this family. Children's bills, but with adult consequences. I was forbidden to play with matches, forbidden to look inside their bedroom dresser's top drawer, forbidden to listen to *The Lone Ranger* on the radio on certain days.

So naturally, my curiosity got the best of me. I was a con man's son, but I was a child, too. While they slept in late one morning, I was downstairs in the kitchen eating my Cheerios. I saw a book of Dad's matches on the table. He kept a box of them in the kitchen drawer. Matchbooks were strewn throughout the house, in every room, with a stubby pencil beside them all. I always wondered, why? Dad didn't smoke. Maybe there was something about matches and fire that was mysterious. So that morning I took a book of matches, lit one, and the whole pack flamed up. I tossed the flaming matches into the plastic garbage pail. It caught fire, the flames licking the wall, melting the garbage pail. I panicked, then remembered something I'd heard somewhere. I got Mom's jar of flour and threw it all over the garbage pail. The flames died out. Just then, Mom and Dad came downstairs into the kitchen. They saw me with flour all over my face, the singed wall, the melted garbage pail now a puddle of plastic.

They didn't spank me. In fact, my parents never hit me or manhandled me once in my lifetime. But they did punish me. A double punishment. No baseball at the park with my brother. No listening to the radio at night in bed. Any other boy my age would have asked, why a double punishment for one transgression? But I already knew the answer to that question at six.

My first punishment was for disobeying my parents' order to never play with matches that could burn down our house. The second punishment was for incinerating Dad's betting line for that night's action, which he always wrote on the inside cover of matchbooks for a very good reason. When the vice squad raided the Venice A.C., as they did regularly, my father was put in the back of a police car with two mick cops in front. He always asked one, "*Per favore*, Detective Ford, a cigarette?" He was now on a first name basis with those cops, who, in fact, liked the easygoing wop with the Irish name. He was not like my hard-assed uncles, like Uncle Gaspipe, who treated those cops with derision even as they arrested them. Which naturally incited those mick cops to slap Gaspipe around a little before they got him to the precinct. "Foolish," my father said to Mom one morning. "Taking a beating you can avoid? There's no percentage in that. Proving you're a tough guy?" He shook his head in disgust. The curse of Italians, *Salvare la faccia.*

I never forgot that expression. It saved me a stretch in the can when I was in my mid-twenties, hotheaded, angry. I was driving around Bridgeport one Saturday morning looking for a parking space. They were all taken. After fifteen minutes, I found one. I began backing my car into it when a Volkswagen Beetle behind me scooted into that space. I stopped my car, got out, and went to the Beetle's driver's side window. The guy inside rolled up the window and locked the doors. I screamed at him. He just stared ahead. So I opened the trunk of my car, took out the tire iron, and went back to the Volkswagen. I was just about to smash it into his windshield when I heard Dad's voice, "The curse of Italians, *Salvare la faccia.*" I threw the tire iron back in the trunk and left.

The mick cops driving Dad to the police station always gave Dad a cigarette when he asked for one. They even offered him a light. He held up his own book of matches, and said, "*Molto grazie*, Detective Ford." He lighted his cigarette, then so off-handedly, an absentminded gesture really, so natural to him, it seemed, without a thought, he tossed the matchbook out the window with the only incriminating evidence against him written inside it.

One late afternoon, Dad was in the kitchen dealing cards to Mom at the breakfast nook table before he left for work. I was upstairs in my bedroom, coloring in a book when I got an idea. I went into their bedroom, reached up on my tiptoes to their top dresser drawer, and pulled it open. Tucked in between my father's socks were three white boxes with numbers written on each. One, two, and three. I took them out and opened them. There were pairs of red, shiny dice with white dots on them in each box. They all looked the same, so I emptied them onto the bed and started rattling two of them in my hand the way Dad did at the breakfast nook table with Ma. I tossed them onto the bed. "Craps," I whispered. Shook them again, "Baby needs a new pair of shoes." I rattled them bones for a few minutes until I heard Dad say to Mom downstairs, "Time to go, Flo. I need my dice." I quickly stuffed the dice into the three boxes, put them back in the drawer, closed it, and hurried back to my bedroom as Dad came upstairs.

That night, at two in the morning, I heard Dad screaming at Mom downstairs. "I'm gonna kill that kid!" Mom said, "You're not gonna touch him. He's a kid. He didn't know." Dad said, "He's supposed to know."

Sometimes, at night, I listened to *The Lone Ranger* on our big mahogany radio in the living room while Ma and Dad talked in the kitchen. I tried to see, in my mind's eye, the Lone Ranger and Tonto riding across a rocky landscape, the reddish-orange mountains around them in setting red sun, and, up ahead, a fleeing band of outlaws. I marveled at how, from such a distance, on bouncing horses, Silver and Scout, they managed to shoot those outlaws out of the saddle.

One night, Dad came into the living room and said, "I have to get the results at Hialeah, son." He turned the station to Harvey Pack at the Track. I whined to him, "But I was listening to *The Lone Ranger*. That's not fair." He said, "Just the fifth race, son." I yelled out, "Ma, Dad won't let me listen to *The Lone Ranger*!" She came into the room and began arguing with Dad, too. The both of us arguing with him now over the voice of Harvey Pack reading the results. Dad tried to listen, but the sound of our voices drowned out Harvey Pack's voice. "For chrissakes, Florence, gimme a break!" But she wouldn't shut up, and neither would I.

Finally, Dad ripped the radio's plug out of the wall, lifted that big radio in his arms, and struggled with it to the kitchen stairs that led down to the cellar. He propped the radio precariously on the top step. Ma and I stared at him. Ma put her fists on her hips and said, "Go ahead!" Dad took a step back, then kicked his foot into the radio. It tumbled, head over heels, down the stairs. When it hit the cement floor, it shattered into bits. The curse of Italians, *Salvare la faccia*.

Mom and I were stunned to silence. Dad stormed out of the house.

When I was thirty years old, I lived a few miles from my parents' apartment in Bridgeport in their old Dutch Colonial where I was raised. I had bought it from them a few years after I got married at nineteen. I had a wife and five children now, and a job writing for *Sports Illustrated* and other magazines, which kept me on the road a lot. Other than my large family, my life was a lot like Dad's when he was on the hustle in his late teens and early twenties. Cheap hotels alongside a highway. Greasy spoon diners. Waitresses with tats and a knife scar. He gave me advice on how to eat and drink on the road. "Never soup or stew. Who knows what's in it? If you're in doubt, order eggs, sunny side up. They can't fuck them up, and you can see what you're eating. If you're on the balls of your ass, like I was, you can always make hobo stew. Ask the waitress for a cup of hot water. Pour in some ketchup, crush in some crackers, salt and pepper, stir it up, delicious."

He added, "As for booze, before you go drinking take a glass of milk or some bread to coat your stomach. It'll soak up the booze. And only drink your booze straight. It's the crap you mix it with that gets you sick."

He even gave me advice on how to approach the temptations of the road. "There's only three vices in this world, kid," he said, "broads, booze, and gambling. If you're gonna do it right, pick one and stick to it." Dad was never a committed drinker, and he never cheated on Mom. I told him I wasn't much of a drinker either, and I never gambled. He laughed at me, and said, "You never gamble? You're a freelance like me." He was right, as always. I was a freelance like him, except for the broads thing.

I didn't see Mom and Dad much in those days. They saw my brother mostly. He drove over from his law practice in Fairfield every Tuesday and Friday for lunch. Ma made him tuna fish sandwiches on white bread. After George had eaten, my mother stood behind his chair and scratched his head. Whenever I drove past their apartment and thought of stopping, and then saw George's Lincoln Continental in the parking lot, I kept on driving.

One afternoon, I drove to their apartment and saw George's Lincoln wasn't there. I parked and climbed the stairs to their second-floor apartment and knocked. No answer. I opened the door and went in. Ma was at the kitchen counter, talking into the telephone while bent over, scribbling something on a napkin. She looked up at me and put a finger to her lips. Finally, she said into the phone, "I'll tell him, Sciamo. *Un momento.*" She called out, "Pat, Sciamo says the Cubs are plus-150 and the Cards minus-200."

Dad called out in a scratchy voice from their bedroom, "Five dimes on the Cubs, Flo!" Then he coughed and added, "Get the line on the Yanks-Red Sox, too."

My mother said, "Sciamo, he'll take the Cubs, five dimes...now..."

I went around the corner to their bedroom. Dad was in bed in his pajamas, propped up on pillows, blowing his nose into Kleenex. The bed was littered with used Kleenex. "Pop," I said, "what's wrong?"

"Oh, Patty. Good to see you, son. Aw, it's nothing. Summer cold." He got out of bed and put on his bathrobe. "Ma should be finished by now."

"She's booking your bets these days?"

He gave me his little con man's smile — he called it "kidding on the sly" — and said, "After forty years, son, I wore her down." I gave him a doubter's look. He shrugged, "OK, I gotta pay her 10 percent every bet." I nodded. He said, "The vig's worth it. Keeps the peace."

We went into their tiny kitchen, and all three of us sat around their little table. Ma had put the wine, ciabatta bread, some olives in oil, and a chunk of Asiago on the table. We sat close together and picked at the olives, cheese, and bread and drank our wine out of small grape jelly glasses as we talked. I told them about my latest story, and they were happy I was working so steadily. Then, as always, we began talking about the past, the distant past when I was a child. We laughed over the melted garbage pail and the mixed-up dice and the time I broke Dad's finger.

I was ten, a star pitcher in Little League. My fastball was explosive, the speed of boys five years older than me. George could still catch me on the sidewalk in front of my house, but Dad had trouble with my fastball. When George didn't show for our catch one day, I harassed Dad into catching me. He put the right-handed catcher's mitt on his right hand, the wrong hand for a lefty, his pinky finger in the mitt's thumb.

I warmed up slowly for Dad. He lunged at my throws with both hands like a boxer. I said, "Let the ball come to you, Dad." When I was loose, I said, "A fastball, Dad." He got down in his crouch. I began my windup, he tensed, I threw, he stabbed both hands at the speeding ball, and caught it on his bare hand. He screamed, blood spurted into the air, Ma came running out of the house. Dad ran into the house holding his bleeding hand.

I stayed outside for a few minutes, terrified at what I'd done. Not because I broke Dad's finger, but because I broke Dad's finger on the night I knew he was dealing cards at the Venice A.C. When I finally did go in, Dad and Mom were sitting at the breakfast nook table. Dad, with a bloody handkerchief wrapped around his fingers, was trying to deal from a deck of cards. Each card slipped in his bloody fingers, fell to the floor. Dad cursed their ancestry, picked the cards up, and tried to deal again.

And so it went, for an hour, while I watched. Curses and blood-stained kings.

When I finished that story, my mother and father were laughing. I said, "Did you deal that night, Dad?"

"I managed." He gave me a look. "But nothing fancy, mind you."

"The first time you ever dealt from the top of the deck," I said. "It musta broke your heart."

He shrugged, "I had no choice." Then he said, "I told everyone what happened, your uncles, Tomas, Freddy, Gaspipe, Sciamo. 'My son broke my finger with his pitch. Imagine! Ten years old and he could throw that fast.' They all nodded, impressed." I tried to picture that clutch of dark crows nodding and clucking together over a ten-year-old kid's fastball. They did it for Dad. He was so proud of me. The point of that story for Dad, but not for me. I remembered the point being the fear in my throat. The house sold, a tenement in The Hollow if Dad didn't deal cards that night. Which made me think of *The Lone Ranger* and Harvey Pack at the Track. The radio in pieces at the bottom of the stairs.

They caught my silence. Ma said, "What's the matter, Patty? Something bothering you?"

I faked a smile. Ma bought it. I don't know about Dad. I reminded them of *The Lone Ranger* story, the radio, Harvey Pack. I left out the cellar stairs, the radio smashed, see if they'd fill in the blanks. They knew.

They looked at each other, then back at me. Ma said, "That didn't happen, son. Your imagination."

Dad said, "He's a writer, Flo. He makes things up."

I smiled and said, "Yeah, that's it. You caught me, pop. I can never slip anything past you." I laughed, Dad looking at me. He knew a con when he saw one.

# CHAPTER TWENTY-ONE

Every Saturday night of my childhood, Mom and Dad got dressed into their finest clothes and went back to Bridgeport for dinner at the Ocean Sea Grill, across Main Street from two Vaudeville theaters, the Loews Poli, and the Majestic. Once I turned six, they always took me with them. I was dressed in my best clothes, too, like Dad. A navy blazer with brass buttons. A button-down collared shirt, a rep tie, gray flannel pants, only mine were short pants to the knee.

It was dark when we arrived outside the Sea Grill. Across the street, lines had formed for tickets to the Vaudeville Shows. Lousy was selling newspapers in front of the Sea Grill. A hunched-over man in his fifties, wearing a dirty trench coat, summer or winter. He nodded to my father.

"Good evening, Lousy," my father said. He reached out his hand. Lousy put a newspaper in it. My father handed him a fin for the five-cent paper. Lousy nodded again. My father said, "You're welcome, Lousy. You doing all right?" Lousy nodded. My father said, "If you need anything, let me know." Lousy nodded.

We went inside to a narrow foyer that led to the coat-check girl. If it was summer, and we had no coats, Dad put a fin in her tip bowl. If it was winter, and he checked our coats, he put a sawbuck in her tip bowl.

Near the coat check girl was the cash register with a beautiful blonde sitting behind it on a high stool. Her legs were crossed in her slit skirt, revealing a hint of white flesh above the tops of her stockings. "Mr. and Mrs. Jordan," she said. "A pleasure to see you... And young Master Jordan." She smiled at me. I said, "Good evening, Kay." My father handed Kay the early edition of the newspaper, and she dropped it into the waste basket behind her.

The two dining rooms were spread out before us. The big, open dining room was in back, separated from the front dining room by a half wall and glass. It was illuminated by harsh overhead lights. Families with children ate there on plain tables with white tablecloths. It was a noisy room, with adults talking loudly, children squalling, the clatter of dishes and silverware.

The more luxurious and intimate dining room was up front. It was dark and quiet with only the sound of hushed voices. A few dark mahogany wood tables were in the middle of the room. The curved burgundy leather banquettes were against the walls and the front windows.

Tommy the maître d' appeared. He looked like a second-rate guinea crooner who played Vegas when Vic Damone was not available. Wavy, swept-back, black hair shimmering with pomade. He wore a ruffled, white tuxedo shirt, and a black tuxedo with slim, pointy-toed, black, patent leather shoes. He greeted my father effusively, "Mr. Jordan, always a pleasure," and my mother by kissing the back of her hand. "You look exquisite tonight, Mrs. J, as always."

"Thank you, Tommy," my mother said, without a smile. She was dressed entirely in lilac chiffon. A loose-fitting dress, off the shoulder, and a floppy brimmed hat tilted to one side almost concealing one eye.

Tommy said, "The usual, Mr. J?" Dad nodded. The two men walked ahead of us toward a banquette against the front window, my mother and I following. I saw Tommy lean toward my father's ear, and whisper. My father whispered something to him, and Tommy nodded.

I slid into the banquette first, as always, my back to the front glass window so I could face the room. My mother slid into one side of the banquette and my father the other side so they could face each other, and see through the window outside to the lights of the theaters, and inside the room, too. Just as my father slid into the banquette, he reached out his hand behind him, like a basketball guard slipping a pass off his hip. Tommy, faking a look around the room, reached out his hand to my father's, took something, and slipped it into his pants pocket.

He turned back to my parents with a gleaming smile of piano keys, and said, "Enjoy. I'm at your service." And like an apparition he was gone, melting into the darkness.

My mother took out her gold cigarette holder, put a cigarette into it, held it at her lips while my father lighted it with a gold lighter. She took one puff and then put one hand under her elbow, raised the other to the side of her head, limp-wristed with her cigarette, and posed. These were the only times in my childhood when I remembered my stern mother as a sexy, beautiful, sophisticated woman.

The waiter appeared. He asked for our drink order. My father said, "Three Manhattans." The waiter looked at me. My father said, "Just tell Tony at the bar it's for Patsy."

The waiter handed my father three elaborate menus, bound in burgundy leather, and left. Dad put them to one side without looking at them. I looked around the room while my father and mother talked. I saw my Uncle Sciamo with his much younger, peroxide-blond *sposato*, Betty. And Uncle Freddy at another table with his *sposato*, the redhead, Irish Braciola, Aunt Helen.

The waiter returned with our darkly-colored Manhattans in inverted pyramid-shaped glasses. One of them had four long-stemmed maraschino cherries in the glass, their long stems hanging over the side of the glass. He set that one in front of me, and the others with one cherry in front of Dad and Mom.

We sipped our Manhattans. Mine was *con gassata*, a Coca-Cola.

The waiter returned and asked for our order. My father ordered for all of us. The waiter said, "A child's portion for the young man, sir?"

My father shook his head, no. "Adult portion," he said.

Uncle Sciamo and Uncle Freddy stopped at our table to pay their respects. They talked to my parents for a few minutes while I sipped my Manhattan, ate one of the cherries, and looked around the dark room and beyond it, to the harshly-lighted back room, like the Waldorf Cafeteria. I could see other children my age and older laughing loudly and fidgeting in their chairs. They kept getting up and walking around the room, bumping into waiters, until their parents rounded them up and brought them back to the tables, where the children now sat petulantly, bored.

I was never bored at the Ocean Sea Grill. It was one of the most exciting times of my childhood with my parents.

Before my uncles left, each, in turn, leaned close to my father's ear and whispered.

The waiter returned with three big trays with our food on them. He deposited my mother's steak Florentine in front of her, and my father's plate of aglio e olio in front of him. A peasant dish. Cheap, plain, white. Even the poorest wops in the old country could put together spaghetti aglio e olio for a meal. But it was a delicacy for Dad when he was a kid, with nothing.

Then the waiter deposited a huge plate with a two-pound lobster, in its shell, in front of me, with a little cut-glass bowl filled with warm, melted butter. He laid beside the platter a small three-pronged fork, a slim metal pliers, and a thin metal rod with a metal hook at one end, like a question mark. It looked like the tool dentists used to clean your teeth. Then he took from his arm a large white paper napkin in the shape of a person's chest with a red lobster drawn on it. The napkin had a scooped-out neck with a string that could be tied around the neck.

Before the waiter could hand it to me, my father said, "He doesn't need it."

I picked up the pliers and began cracking open the lobster's claws. Sometimes they were so hard I had to use both hands on the pliers for strength. If my father ever saw me struggling with those pliers, he never made an attempt to help me. And I never asked. It was my lobster. If I couldn't handle it, I shouldn't have ordered it.

My parents ate their food while they talked. My father twirled his pasta on his fork, while I ate my lobster. When the claws were cracked open, exposing the lobster's white flesh tinged with coral, I took the little dentist's tool and pried out the meat. Then I used the tiny fork to spear the meat, dip it into the warm butter, and put it in my mouth.

I worked my way through the meat in the claws, scraping out every bit of meat until the claws were spotless. I operated very slowly, very seriously, my brows furrowed in concentration. Then I used the little fork to scoop out all the green, gushy stuff close to the lobster's head. It was spicy and delicious. Finally, I pulled out the meat from the lobster's tail. This was the most tender, most flavorful of the lobster's meat. I always saved it for last. I cut it in pieces, speared each piece, dipped it in butter and ate it slowly.

When I finished my lobster, its shell was spotless, without a crumb of meat left. I sipped my Manhattan and sat back. I heard noise outside. I turned in my seat and looked out the window at all the people exiting the Vaudeville shows. Some of them crossed the street to Lousy. They bought a late-night edition of the paper with the late sports results in them and entered the restaurant.

The waiter removed our dishes. My father ordered two espressos with anisette and lemon peels. The waiter said, "And for the young man?" My father shook his head, no.

The men and women from the theaters stood in a line that began at the cash register and snaked out the door to the street. Some of them saw my father and came over to our table. Ex-pugs, like Billy Bones, a small bald man with cauliflower ears and thick scar tissue in his eyebrows. Baggy pants Yiddish comics with hooked noses and bulging round eyes. Peroxide-blond exotic dancers in skintight dresses that showed the top half of their pillowy, white breasts. The men who danced on stage with the exotic dancers were slim, dark, exotic-looking men who moved gracefully. My father called them *finocchios*.

The men and women waiting to talk to my father formed a small, single-file line in the dining room. Other diners, couples, who didn't know my parents, stared at us. Each person in line waited their turn to talk to my parents. Then they stood over us talking respectfully to my mother and father, whom they always called Mrs. Jordan and Mr. J. The exotic dancers admired my mother's hat, "so chic," they said, and her gold cigarette holder. Then they leaned over close to me, their breasts spilling out of their dress almost in my face, and pinched my cheeks with both hands. "Oh, your son is such a gorgeous little man, Mrs. Jordan," they said. "If only he was older." I said, "I'm going to be seven years old." The exotic dancers laughed, too loud, caught my mother's look, and went silent. I don't think my mother's aspiration for me then was that when I became a young man, I would have a Vaudeville stripper on each arm.

Before they left, each of the men leaned over close to my father's ear and whispered. He whispered something back. The men smiled at him, and said, "Thank you, Mr. J." Then they glanced at me, sitting there, silent, and said, "Your son's quite the young man, Mr. J." Dad nodded, and looked at me for the first time this night. I could see he was proud of me. I felt as if my heart would burst through my chest.

Then, one after the other, the men and women peeled away from us, the men half bowing, before they turned and went back to the line waiting for a table. I saw one of the comics say something to the maître d'. A few moments later, a waiter appeared with a bottle of champagne, "Compliments of Mr. Kleinman."

The one reoccurring image I have of my childhood, besides those pillowy, white, strippers' breasts in my face, is of my father, standing, or sitting, while various strange men, mysterious and furtive, leaned close to his ear and whispered.

When I was a young boy, four and five years old, I used to imagine what those strange men whispered to my father. Some magical secret about unicorns and mermaids with a fish's tail they'd seen, or dragons breathing fire and beautiful princesses with delicate, pink wings you could see through. By the time I was six, sitting in that banquette in the Ocean Sea Grill, I had put those fantastical childish imaginings out of my head. I knew now what those men were whispering to my father.

"Who do you like in the series, Mr. J?"

# CHAPTER TWENTY-TWO

Every birthday since I turned five years old, I asked my father to take me on a fishing trip into the Maine woods. We'd set up camp in the woods by a rocky stream. First, we'd put up the tent where we'd sleep the night. Then we'd put on our rubber boots and go wading into the stream with our fishing poles. We'd cast our fly hooks into the rushing waters and pull out squiggling rainbow trout, one after another. We'd put them in the little wicker baskets at our hip until we had enough for dinner. Then we'd go back to camp where Dad would gut and clean the fish while I foraged in the woods for smooth stones. I'd see deer staring at me with their big, innocent eyes and hear black bears grunting and thrashing through the brush. When I'd get back to camp with the stones, I'd arrange them in a little circle on the ground. I'd get dried twigs and crisscross them in the center of that circle. I'd put our black metal grate over the twigs, and Dad would light a fire under it. When it was hot enough, he'd put the trout in a black frying pan coated with sizzling olive oil and fry them until they were crispy brown. We'd eat them by the fire and then put a little tin coffee pot over the fire with water and chocolatey-smelling ground coffee in it.

At night in the tent, by the light of an oil lamp, and to the hoots and caws and growls from the woods, Dad and I would lie side-by-side in our sleeping bags, while he told me scary stories that never scared me because I was with him. Then I'd fall asleep.

On my seventh birthday, Dad bought me a bamboo fishing pole with a white line and a hook. He said, "Tomorrow morning I'm going to take you fishing, son." I was so excited that night I couldn't sleep. So I got up and packed my suitcase with what I thought I would need in the Maine woods. Dungarees, heavy flannel shirt, flannel pajamas, and rubber boots.

I fidgeted all morning until Dad woke up at noon. An hour later, after his espresso, he said, "Let's go fishing, Patty." I grabbed my suitcase. He looked at it and said, "You won't need that."

We drove three miles from our house until we reached the Brooklawn Country Club on our right. Across the street on our left were a few stores, a drugstore, beauty parlor, and a bar, the 19th Hole.

The Brooklawn Country Club was set back from the street, high up on a hill. It looked like an old, white colonial mansion with black shutters that the early WASP settlers in Fairfield built for themselves in the 1700s. My father hated that country club. It was the last bastion of a fading elite that had ruled Fairfield for 300 years. Pinched WASP bankers and factory owners and stockbrokers who retired up to that hill to their clubhouse library where liveried waiters served them drinks, and they reminisced among themselves about their world that was fast disappearing. The latest reminder of this indignity was the recent arrival of their first wop member, a doctor named Dimarco. My father hated him, too, for throwing his lot in with those withered old WASPs, as dry as dust that would soon blow away. That doctor named his first son Brian.

The hill the white mansion was on was part of the club's golf course that sloped down to the street we were on. The 18th hole was close to the street. In the middle of the 18th fairway, a few yards from the street, was a small pond.

Dad dropped me off at the pond with my rod and a can of kernel corn for bait. He said, "When you're finished, I'll be at the 19th Hole."

"But...I thought we were going to the Maine woods," I said.

"Don't be foolish," he said. "There are no telephones in the woods. Now go on."

I watched him park his car across the street in front of the 19th Hole and go inside. I walked to the edge of the pond and looked in it for fish. It was only a few feet deep. The bottom was covered with dark brown mud. I couldn't see any fish. The only thing I could see on that muddy floor were dozens of white, round eyeballs staring up at me. Each of the eyeballs had a name in black on it, Spalding Kro-Flite, Wilson 4, Starfire 2, Pro 100.

For my eighth birthday, Dad bought me a new bicycle and a dog. A Schwinn and a delicately beautiful collie with wavy sable and white fur and an aristocratic, pointy nose. I named her Lady. She was the first living thing I loved more than myself. I fed her twice a day, took her into the woods with me to play cowboys and Indians, then brushed the tangles out of her fur. I let her out at night by herself to go to the bathroom, and then called her in after a few minutes. If she didn't return right away, I felt a catch in my breath and a panic until she appeared at the door.

I was old enough now to ride my bicycle to the park to play baseball. Lady ran alongside me all the way. She stood panting beside me in right field during those pickup games with boys older than me, at ten, eleven, and twelve. Those boys always put me in right field where I couldn't do much damage, because I was the youngest, and because I wasn't a very good outfielder or hitter. Lady jumped and danced around me in right field, while I assumed my fielder's stance waiting for a fly ball. She bit the cuff of my blue jeans and yanked them just as a ball went flying over my head. We both raced after it while my teammates screamed at me to throw it home. Lady got to it first, grabbed it in her mouth, and ran to the small pond off the right field line. She jumped in the water with the ball in her mouth. My teammates and I screamed at her to bring the ball back. She looked at us, then dropped it into the deepest part of the pond.

One day, I was in right field with Lady when a car pulled up and parked behind the home plate screen. A tall, lean man with freckled skin and sandy-colored hair got out. Our game stopped, the players stared at him, then began running toward him. One of them called back to me, "Come on, stupid. It's the Little League coach."

We all stood around him while he asked for each of our names, and ages, and what position we wanted to try out for. He wrote everything down on a clipboard. When he pointed to me, I said, "Pitcher!"

We practiced three nights a week. The older boys did most of the hitting while I shagged fly balls in right field with Lady. Finally, one night after practice, the coach told me to stay behind. After the other boys left, he put me on the pitcher's mound, and he got behind the plate with his catcher's mitt. We threw the ball for a while, his eyes studying me, then he got down in a crouch. "All right, you can cut loose now."

I began my motion and threw a fastball. He caught it and held it in his glove. Then he got up and walked to the mound. "How old are you?" he said. I told him, eight. "Who taught you how to pitch?" I said my older brother. He said, "How many times did he have you throw off this mound?" I said, "He never let me throw off this mound." The man looked at me, then said, "Then where did you learn to throw?" I turned my back to him and faced the big-league diamond at the other corner of the park. I pointed to the pitcher's mound and said, "He always made me throw from that mound."

When I turned back to the man, he was nodding his head. He said, "Do you want to be on the team?" I said yes. He said, "You might not get in a game all year. But you'll get a uniform and you can pitch batting practice to the older boys during practices and before each game. Do you think you'd like that?" I nodded again. He said, "Good. Because next year you'll be our starting pitcher."

Before our first game, the local newspaper ran a story about each team. The paper mentioned my name as the youngest boy ever to make a 12-year-old Little League team in the state of Connecticut. But that notoriety didn't get me in a game that year.

One of the boys in our neighborhood saw my name in the paper, and he began to bully me because he was jealous. He was a big, fat twelve-year-old who never played sports. He just picked on all the younger kids. But that summer he confined his bullying to me. One day he pushed me in the chest and I fell backward, hitting my head on the grass with a thud. I was dazed for a few seconds. Then I got up and staggered home. By the time I got into the kitchen where my mother was cooking, I was crying softly. She asked me what happened. I told her what Pauly had done.

"Well, are you all right?" she said. I nodded. "Good. Now get back outside and get even with that *bracaccio*."

"But he's bigger than me, Ma."

"You want him to keep bullying you all summer?" I shook my head, no. "Then stop him now, once and for all." I hesitated. She glared at me. "What are you, a baby? You're old enough. Be a man. Get out there. And don't come back to this house until you get vendetta. Do you hear me?"

I nodded and went outside. I went up the street until I saw Pauly. I got as close to him as I dared before he recognized me. Then I hid behind the big trunk of an oak tree and waited. When he walked past me on the sidewalk, I jumped on his back like a monkey. He fell face down on the sidewalk, his nose gushing blood. I got up and ran home before he got to his senses.

In the kitchen, I told my mother what I had done. "Good boy," she said.

There was a knock on the door. A voice called out, "Mrs. Jordan!" My mother put her finger to her lips and went to the door. She opened it to Pauly, crying, his nose bleeding. He wailed, "Patty pushed me to the sidewalk and gave me a bloody nose!"

I heard my mother's voice. "Poor boy, Pauly. You wait right here. I'll fix him good."

She came into the kitchen and whispered to me, "When I clap my hands you make believe you're crying." I nodded. She began clapping her hands, "Take that, you little brat!" I wailed crocodile tears.

Pauly left smiling. My mother and I waited until he was far enough away before we began laughing. My mother was not a woman to laugh much with me. When I did something funny, I could see her trying not to laugh. I was a burden to her. "I suppose you want lunch?" Then she made me the simplest lunch she could, *pizza fritta*. When I got a winter cold, she snapped at me, "I told you to wear a sweater. Now you expect me to baby you. Go to your room and draw your pictures."

Which is why I remember that moment so clearly. My mother and I, co-conspirators, sitting at the breakfast nook table laughing so hard together. It was one of the few times in my life my mother allowed herself to laugh with me.

Before we married, I told my soon-to-be second wife, Susan, that story of my mother throwing me out of the house to get even with the bully when I was eight. A few days later, Susan met my parents at their apartment for the first time.

I knocked on the door. My mother's voice called out, "Who is it?"

I winked at Susan and called back, "It's your favorite son, Ma."

She said, "Oh, Dad, it's George!"

I whispered to Susan, "Told ya."

Dad opened the door, "It's Patty, Flo. And a pretty young girl."

He flashed Susie one of his obsequious smiles, with a little bow, and took her hand, gently, with his fingertips. Jesus! I thought, he's going to kiss Susan's hand. But he didn't.

Susie said, smiling, "Not so young, Mr. Jordan. But thank you just the same."

Ma came to the door and saw me. I said, "Disappointed, Ma?"

She flapped a hand at me. "I knew it was you all the time." I introduced her to Susan. Susie smiled. My mother didn't. She cast an appraising look at Susie as if she was casting her for a role in a melodrama. The Irisher *puttana* daughter-in-law to be.

All my teenaged years, my mother waited for me to bring home a nice Italian girl. But I never did. I'd spent too many years of my childhood in the kitchen with my mother and her two sisters. Tough, hard women with dark skin and black hair. I brought home demure, pale, blond Czechs and sweet, dumb Polacks, and occasionally, a wild, red-haired Irisher. Ma would say, "You do it on purpose, to torment your poor mother. Look at your brother. He has a nice Italian wife." (What Ma did not say was that she sustained a war with George's poor wife until the day my mother died.)

I said, "An Italian wife like you, Ma?"

She said, "Of course."

"Ma, if I want a man in bed, I'll become a *finocchio*."

She flung the back of her hand in the air and said, "Better than an Irisher *puttana*."

We sat outside on their little patio shaded by trees. Ma brought out the ciabatta and Asiago and a cluster of black grapes. Dad poured the red wine. We sat there, making small talk. Susan reached for the grapes. Dad said, "No, dear. Use these." He handed her grape scissors.

My mother glared at him. Then she said to Susan, "Ryan! Is that Irish?" Susan said yes. My mother gave her a blank look I knew only too well. I had the insane thought that, at this moment, my mother wished I'd have brought home one of those Vaudeville strippers with pillowy breasts from the Sea Grill, instead of this tall, lean, blond "hated Irisher" with blue eyes.

After we left the apartment, I said to Susan, "I told you. Thank God she never had daughters."

Susan said, "Maybe. But she sure knew how to raise sons."

# CHAPTER TWENTY-THREE

My brother graduated from law school in the late spring the year I turned nine. He returned to Fairfield with his new wife, Mildred, and their baby daughter and rented a house. Then he took the Connecticut State Bar Exam. While he waited for the results, he worked for Uncle Ken's law firm in Bridgeport as a paralegal.

Every day that George went to work, Uncle Ken asked him if he'd got his bar exam results yet. He seemed anxious to hear if George passed, or not. At first, George thought Uncle Ken was eager for George to become a lawyer so he could integrate him into his firm. But after a while, George realized Uncle Ken was hoping George had failed his exam.

"Uncle Ken had failed the exam four times," George told me years later. "It would be an embarrassment to him if I passed it the first try. He was supposed to be the smart one among the men in the family. When I did pass it that first try, he seemed disappointed. Even though I was a lawyer now, he kept giving me the most menial jobs. Title searches in the courthouse basement that paralegals did, not lawyers."

When George told Dad all this, Dad was furious. He could never countenance disrespect to his sons from anyone. But from family? It confused Dad. He had never had a real family of his own. He had only idealized visions of family he'd seen in magazine advertisements when he was a young man. The perfect family, father, mother, children, aunts, uncles, grandparents, all seated around a festive table at Christmas dinner. And then, as a young man, he'd found his own adopted family, the fractious, combative, hot-tempered DiMennas. But they were loyal and supportive of each other, too, which is what Dad thought families were. It didn't matter to Dad that he had little

in common with the men of the family. He suppressed his annoyance with their idiosyncrasies that were so foreign to him because
they were his family now. Uncle Ben was penurious and Dad was
so generous. Uncle Pat was circumspect and Dad was so passionate.
Uncle Ken was a pompous blowhard and Dad was self-effacing. So
what? They were Dad's family now. He was blindly loyal to them.
Just as he expected his two sons to be loyal to each other.

What confused Dad about Uncle Ken's disrespect of Dad's son
was not only because he was family, but also because Uncle Ken was
beholden to Dad for everything he had in life. Without Dad, Uncle
Ken would have been disbarred, maybe even imprisoned.

The story, as told to me, went like this:

Years before George became a lawyer, Uncle Ken was a young,
struggling lawyer himself. Desperate to make money and a name for
himself, Uncle Ken took on a client he never should have. A man
with a shady background and a violent temper. He may, or may not,
have murdered someone. He had been arrested on a lesser charge
involving his restaurant business. He was sitting in a jail cell waiting for his trial. He complained to his *avvocato* that he was being
mistreated in jail because he was *Italiano*. He demanded Uncle Ken do
something about it, or else.

Frightened, and weak, Uncle Ken spoke to one of the guards at
the jail in an attempt to get his client preferential treatment. There
was the question of a gratuity being offered. The guard went to the
judge handling this case. The judge was so furious he threatened to
bring Uncle Ken up on tampering charges that could get him disbarred, even jailed.

Uncle Ken could think of no one to turn to that he trusted, except my father. He confided in my father his problem. Dad said, "Not
to worry, *Fratello*. I'll make it go away."

At the time, Dad had connections in the police department,
namely the cops who had so often arrested him. One of those vice
squad cops was Detective Ford, the man who had ushered Dad out
the back door of the Venice A.C. during a raid. Detective Ford always respected Dad for the way he comported himself. Even in the
backseat of a police car, on the way to the precinct, Dad was always

the gentleman. He treated those Irisher cops in the front seat with rispetto. "It was his job," Dad said of the cop. "It was my job not to get caught." Dad was nothing like my Uncle Gaspipe, that belligerent wop, always ready to belittle those cops. "So I played the good wop to Gaspipe's bad wop," Dad said. He shrugged, "The cops bought it."

True to his promise, Dad made Uncle Ken's problem go away. George told me, "It was murky, how Dad managed it." Then my brother smiled, "You know, brother, the way Dad always did things. You never knew how."

And then, years later, this was how Uncle Ken repaid Dad for saving his livelihood. He disrespected his son. Dad told George, "Fuck that *stronzo*. You don't need him. Go out on your own. You need anything, I'll get it for you."

So George set up a small law practice in Fairfield not too far from my baseball park.

# CHAPTER TWENTY-FOUR

When I was nine in the early spring of 1951, my father would give me a five-dollar bill every Saturday morning. "Here, buy your friends' tickets and popcorn," he said. But I never did. I preferred to go alone to the movies.

Before noon I would take two buses from Fairfield to Bridgeport. I got a transfer on the first bus and got off at Black Rock. I waited on the street corner with old men and old women, who worked as janitors and maids, for the next bus that would take us all into Bridgeport, a factory city of over 100,000 people. That bus dropped me off on Main Street in front of Morrow's Nut House, "Nuts from all over the World." The sidewalk was crowded with shoppers jostling me as I made my way north toward the Globe Theater. I stopped along the way three times. Once at the Yankee Stamp Shop to buy old, canceled United States stamps and a second time at Max's Stamp Shop to buy mint new issues with rocket ships on them from African countries whose natives carried spears and had bones in their noses. I saved my last stop for the New England Stamp Shop, where an old Austrian Jew with swept-back, white hair taught me how to collect stamps. He called me his "little goy" and insisted I buy stamps from Italy and the Vatican because, he said, "You must collect the country and the religion of your ancestors, even if their stamps are worthless." Then he scissored his hands through his hair and said, "Look at me! I collect Israel, worthless pieces of shit printed for stupid collectors, not to stick on a letter." He threw up his hands in surrender. "But what can I do?" he said. "Israel is my history." He gave me a sad smile, "But not my future."

When I came to the Globe Theater, there was a long line of rowdy kids my age waiting to get inside. In the 1920s and 1930s, the Globe had been a bustling Vaudeville theater with leering, popeyed, baggy pants comics and peroxide-blond dancers my father called "ec-dysiasts," whatever that meant. After World War II, the Globe fell on hard times and was now reduced to holding kiddie matinees.

After I got my popcorn and Jujubes in the lobby, I searched for a seat in that dark, crowded, noisy theater that smelled of sweat. I found a frayed burgundy velvet seat and sat down beside a smelly old man in dirty clothes. It was not unusual to find such bums scattered throughout the theater each week, their heads nodding on their chest, snoring. It was cheaper for them to pay twenty-five cents to sleep in the warmth of the theater than it was to spend a buck for a flophouse bed. There were other strange moviegoers at the kiddie matinees, too. Teenaged couples in the balcony, kissing. And an oc-casional woman, my mother's age, in a flowered dress with shoulder pads, staring at the screen without interest, the theater their refuge, from what?

Always before the images flashed on the screen, I looked up at the huge overhead chandelier, like icicles, that I feared might fall on my head at any moment.

For the next four hours, I laughed at the cartoons with Bugs Bunny, Daffy Duck, and fat, pink, stuttering Porky Pig. I laughed, too, at the cowboy serials of the prissy Hopalong *Casa Dice*, as my Italian mother called him. Did he hop-a-long through the sagebrush chasing outlaws on one foot like the girls at my school played hop-scotch? He dressed entirely in black with a ten-gallon cowboy hat, its crown bigger than an upright ostrich egg. He chased outlaws on his white horse named Topper. Hoppy and Topper. Hoppy never shot those outlaws. He just sat stiffly upright in his saddle and shot their guns out of their hands with one shot. He was a gentleman cowboy who didn't like violence. He never cussed or lost his temper. He only got into fights, which never mussed his shellacked, white hair, when he had to frequent saloons in search of desperadoes. Desperadoes always hung out in saloons. Hoppy stood at the bar, ill-at-ease, look-ing around for the culprit. The bartender asked him, "What's your poison, Pahdner? Whiskey?" Hoppy said, "Make mine sarsaparilla." It sounded like an exotic drink to me then. So I asked Dad what it was. Dad said, "Old-time root beer. Ladies drank it instead of whiskey."

But I never laughed at Hopalong's folksier shambling counterpart, Roy Rogers, in his serials. Roy wore dusty, leather chaps and a worn cowboy hat. He looked like a real cowboy who spent his hot, dusty days on his palomino horse Trigger, cutting cattle out of a herd. I booed and hissed at Roy's enemies, marauding Indians with painted faces, and gangs of outlaws with droopy mustaches. But there was no real menace in those serials. Roy, half hanging off of Trigger, fired his six-shooter from under Trigger's neck and shot those outlaws and Indians out of their saddles without spilling a drop of blood.

Not so with the *Flash Gordon* serials. They filled me with a very real menace. Each week, Ming the Merciless, with his oriental robes and Fu Manchu mustache, sat on his golden throne and dispatched his evil minions to capture Flash Gordon in his metallic-silver space suit with his matching metallic-silver hair. Whenever our beleaguered hero, Flash, seemed on the brink of thwarting Ming the Merciless's plan for Galactic domination, the evil Ming captured our hero in the last second with a dirty, deceitful trick. Ming's favorite trick was to capture Flash's beloved girlfriend, Dale Arden, and then threaten to burn her at the stake unless Flash surrendered to Ming. The noble Flash always surrendered himself to Ming the Merciless once he promised to release Roy's beloved Dale. The kids in the audience screamed out, "No, Flash! No! It's another trick!" And it always was. Ming never freed Dale. He planned to marry her and make her his Queen of the Galaxy.

I always wondered why the innocent Flash never saw through Ming's deceit like we did.

Each week's serial usually ended with Dale tied to a wooden stake, the heavy ropes hanging loosely around her body as if Ming's evil minions had forgotten to tie them. Why didn't she run away? I wondered. But she just stared in horror while Ming, cackling evilly, dragged Flash to the brink of a fiery pit. Just as Ming was about to push Flash into the fiery pit, I'd put my hands over my eyes. When I took my hands from my eyes, I saw Flash still standing on the edge of the pit, frozen on the screen, as was Ming, while across the screen these words appeared: "Tune in Next Week for the Further Adventures of Flash Gordon."

The following week, we all cheered Flash in his toy spaceship the shape of a tiny, silver football that was held up by a faintly visible string as it wobbled across a black Galaxy in pursuit of Ming the Merciless. We'd already forgotten last week's fiery pit.

I remember one Saturday at the matinee I was sitting terrified as Ming pushed Flash toward his fiery doom, when I felt a hand land softly on my thigh. It belonged to a bum beside me. He stared straight ahead at the screen as if he didn't realize where his hand had landed. Then it moved more firmly up my thigh. I brushed it off with my hand. A few seconds later, I felt that hand again on my thigh. I flung it away and stood up. I squeezed past other kids down the row of seats to the aisle. I hurried up the aisle, shamefaced. Had I done something wrong? I pushed open the big theater doors and stepped outside into a blinding sunlight. I realized something bad had happened. But I didn't know what it was.

When my eyes adjusted to the sunlight, I hurried up Main Street toward my bus stop. I glanced over my shoulder to see if the bum was following me. But he wasn't. When I got to Morrow's Nut House, I waited for the first of my two buses with the old men and old women returning from their jobs as janitors and maids. I had never noticed them before, as they got on and off the buses with me week after week. But I studied them now. Old ladies wearing babushkas and carrying bags of groceries. Hunched-over old men, with dirty clothes, like that bum in the Globe.

I moved a little away from them, but I kept my eyes on them until my bus arrived.

When I got home, I didn't tell my mother about the bum. I wasn't afraid she'd be mad at me, because I'd done nothing wrong. But she would be annoyed with me, as she often was. She'd fling the back of her hand in the air and say, "*Basta*, Patty! It was nothing. You should have known not to sit next to the *barboni*. When are you gonna grow up?"

Then I ate dinner by myself. My father had already eaten and gone to the Venice Athletic Club, where he would shoot craps and deal hands of poker all night long. My mother always ate much later by herself, in the half light of a small lamp. When she finished, she lighted a Chesterfield cigarette then poured herself a glass of scotch.

After my dinner, Ma sent me to my room so she could eat her dinner alone, without my chatter. I spent an hour there at my draftsman's drawing board putting my new stamps in my albums. Then I sat at my drawing board and drew pictures from memory. Flash and his rocket ship. Ming the Merciless. I shuddered as I drew the outline of Ming's gaunt face, like a skeleton, with his narrow, up-slanting eyes. I saved Dale Arden for last. I drew her tied to the stake in her flimsy slip. Her breasts were bigger than my mother's. I concentrated on getting them just right and lost track of time, until my mother called up to me, "Time for bed, Patty. And shut off the light." I put Dale's drawing under all the others so Ma wouldn't see it. She was always poking around my bedroom looking for, I didn't know what. Then I got into bed in darkness and turned on my radio on the nightstand beside my pillow. For the next two hours, I listened to radio programs. *The Shadow*, *The Green Hornet*, *The Lone Ranger*. I closed my eyes and tried to picture in my mind what the Shadow looked like. A wisp of smoke with an odd name, Lamont Cranston. I decided the Green Hornet must look like a praying mantis, and the Lone Ranger, with his black mask, like a raccoon. His faithful Indian, Tonto, had a black, pulled-back-tight ponytail, bronzed skin, and a nose like a hawk. Tonto never painted his face with war paint like the Indians Roy Rogers shot. Tonto was a good Indian. He called the Lone Ranger "Kemosabe," his faithful friend. But that was the 1950s. Years later I would learn that Kemosabe was a Spanish word for "he who understands nothing," and Tonto was an Indian word for "idiot."

After the kids' programs went off, the adult programs came on. *Fibber McGee and Molly*, and my favorite, *The Bickersons*, a married couple named John and Blanche Bickerson. The program always began with them getting in bed at night. Before they even turned off the nightlight they began to argue, like my parents. I wondered if Mr. Bickerson was a gambler, too, like my father. Were they Italian, too? They must be, I thought, despite their last name. The parents of my white bread friends never raised their voices or argued. Only Italians argued. So, I decided, John and Blanche must be Italian, too. I concentrated on what the Bickersons said to each other to see if I could understand what caused adults to argue. But it was hard to figure that out. It always seemed like their arguments began over nothing. Blanche's feelings were hurt because John forgot to say good night. So John said, "Good night, Blanche." Blanche said, "You didn't mean it." He said, "I meant it, Blanche." She was silent, still hurt, then she said, "You don't love me." He said, "Of course, I do." She said, "Then why don't you say it?" He said, "Awright, Blanche. I love you."

Silence. Then she said, "You used to be so considerate. Since you got married to me, you haven't got any sympathy anymore."

"I have, too," John said. "I've got everybody's sympathy."

"Believe me, there's better fish in the ocean than the one I caught."

"There's better bait, too."

"I don't see how you can go to bed without kissing me good night."

"I can do it."

"You'd better say you're sorry for that, John."

"Ok, I'm sorry. I'm sorry, I'm sorry."

"You are not."

"I am, too. I'm the sorriest man that was ever born."

"You stopped loving me the day we were married."

"That wasn't the day at all."

Finally, Blanche tells him she wished her beloved "Grand daddy" was still alive because "he could have settled our problems."

John said, "How do you know?"

"Because when I get to heaven, I'll ask him."

"Suppose he isn't in heaven?"

"Then you can ask him."

And so it went, until finally, exhausted from arguing, they said, "Good night," and went to sleep. I did, too.

# CHAPTER TWENTY-FIVE

My brother taught me how to pitch. We went to the park two days a week after he'd established himself as a lawyer. He pulled up to my house in his Lincoln and rolled down the window. I was sitting on the front steps with my gloves and a ball. He called to me, "Time to work, brother." I ran to his car and got in.

That's what he called it now, in the late spring when I was nine, work. It was no longer my brother fulfilling his obligation to my father to raise me or amuse me or have a catch with me. I didn't go to the park "to throw" some baseballs with my brother now. I went to pitch. It was work, because by then my brother saw that I had a very real and exceptional talent as a pitcher.

We began my work with wind sprints. I ran from home plate to first base, walked back to home plate, ran again to first base, walked back, ran, over and over, with my brother standing at first base shouting at me, "Dig! Dig it out! Faster! You're quitting! You want to be a quitter? Then work!"

He said the purpose of those wind sprints was to make sure I didn't get out of shape. I believed him then. It wasn't until my late teens that I would kid him, "Remember those wind sprints, bro? How does a nine-year-old get out of shape?"

My brother would smile at me then, and say, "I had to exhaust you, brother. You were such a hyper kid. So full of energy. I was afraid if we went right to the mound you would be so jacked up you wouldn't be able to concentrate on what I taught you."

When I was finally exhausted, bent over, gasping for breath, my brother would say, "OK, brother. Time to hit the mound."

We stood on the big-league mound while my brother explained to me the intricacies of a pitcher's motion. He had been a pitcher himself at Prep, until he hurt his arm. He said, "It's many parts, Patty, all of which have to flow one into another smoothly." I nodded. He stood on the rubber and showed me what he meant. A tall, wiry man, 6'4", in a button-down collared shirt with his rep tie askew, his gray flannel slacks and wingtip cordovans. My brother was not a handsome man. He had bristly hair like Brillo and a horsey face, with small eyes and a receding chin. Like my father, my brother's look never changed before my eyes. He always looked the same to me. He looked like a man in his fifties when he was only thirty, and when he was fifty, he still looked fifty. Even at eighty-nine, he still looked fifty, his hair salt and pepper, while I, at seventy-eight, with my white hair and white beard, looked like the older brother.

In high school he looked like an old man, too, although I don't remember him then. But I do remember the nickname his high school friends gave him. They called him Moose, which was apt. Not only because he had a long moose-like face, but because he had the demeanor of that stolid, plodding, graceless creature. I was always the beautiful deer, swift, graceful, talented. My mother used to say, "Patty was the pretty one, George was the good one." She called him Saint George. When I was in my thirties and George was in his fifties, I used to kid him, on the sly, "You know, brother, I would have liked to have been the good son just once." He gave me a sad smile and said, "Yeah, brother, and I would have liked to have been the pretty one just once." Too late. Our mother had already defined us.

He put his right toe on the pitching rubber with his glove hand hanging down at his left side and his ball hand at his right side. He began his motion, slowly, explaining to me each step of the motion as he went through it. His hands at his sides, and then his hands swinging up past his face, his ball hand in his glove now as if he was praying, his two hands swinging up over his head as his upper body leaned back. Then his right foot turned sideways to the rubber and his body turned, too, so that he faced third base while, simultaneously, his left leg was rising now, until his thigh was level with his waist, and his right foot was planted in the dirt for balance. He held this position for a split second, balanced on his right leg. He called it the Crane position. Then his two hands over his head moved forward and down and separated in front of his face, the one with the ball reaching back behind his body, the one with the glove swinging toward home plate. Everything speeded up as his body lunged toward the batter, his left leg swinging out in a half circle toward the first base line, his upper body lunging downward toward the imaginary batter, his right arm with the ball, bent in an L-shape, swinging past his right ear toward the plate. He released the ball precisely when he could see it off to the right of his eyes as his right foot hit the ground and kicked up dirt.

The ball crossed the plate and rattled the home plate screen. He turned to me and said, "Now you try it, brother."

He took his catcher's mitt and went behind home plate into a crouch. "Now show me what you got, brother." I began to pitch, warming up slowly, remembering each part of my motion that he'd begun to teach me when I was five years old. Finally, my motion smoothed out, became all of a piece, and my arm was warmed up. I stood on the mound and said, "Fastball now, brother." I went into my motion, so effortless now, each of my body parts in rhythm, the ball in my hand as light as a feather, so that when I released it I felt no exertion, as if it was all a slow-motion dream. Then everything speeded up again, my head jerked down, and I lost sight of the ball until I heard it explode in George's glove.

I looked up as my brother leaped out of his crouch like an excited child. Not his usual demeanor. My brother was always a didactically serious man, not childishly exuberant like me. Except on those days when we worked on my pitching and our demeanors were reversed. The joy he took in my pitching freed something in him, a lightness he never had, or maybe just never revealed until now. While simultaneously my pitching imposed on me the seriousness of a discipline not then in my nature.

My brother's face was beaming as if he'd seen a vision. He said, "You got it, brother." He fired the ball back to me as hard as he could. "Again," he said. I snapped my glove at the thrown ball with disdain. I owned it now.

And so it began, my education in pitching. Day after day, pitch after pitch, year after year, with my brother correcting my flaws. "You didn't raise your left leg high enough." My left leg rose higher and higher as I got older, over those years when my fastball was electric and my pitching accomplishments seemed to have no bounds, defied gravity, seemed otherworldly to others, but not me.

At nine, I was the best pitcher on my Little League team. At ten, I was the best pitcher in our league. At eleven, I was the best Little League pitcher in New England. At twelve, I was the best Little League pitcher in the country. People traveled hundreds of miles to see me pitch a Little League game.

I remember every one of those days with my brother when I was a boy and we were as close as we would ever be. To understand how close we were it is only necessary to know this. When I was eleven, a big kid for my age, my brother became the basketball coach at Prep. When his team won an especially important game, my brother's name appeared in the *Bridgeport Post Telegram*, praising his coaching. I cut out that story and brought it to school to show my classmates. I said, "That's my brother." One boy scoffed, "No, it isn't. He has a different last name." I insisted, "But he *is!*" The kid laughed at me. I had tears in my eyes, could think of nothing to convince him. So I punched him in the nose and got suspended from school. When I told my parents why I got suspended, they looked at each other. Then my father explained why George and I had different last names. "But it doesn't matter," he said. "You're brothers, that's all that matters." Which was always the point.

I've always wondered why George and I made such a fetish over calling each other brother. Was it some psychic tic to artificially reinforce a tenuous relationship that we knew, or feared, was not natural? A lot of people in Fairfield didn't know that the successful lawyer and basketball coach and the young pitching phenom were brothers. We were not much alike. We had different last names. We were not full-blooded brothers. Our natures were diametrically opposed. We were separated by a fourteen-year age gap. We were closer in age to a father and son than brothers. Or was it just a psychological tic of our parents, so determined to impose on us a relationship *they* feared was tenuous? But to me, it was never tenuous. It was as real, as natural, and as deep as any brotherly relationship could be.

In my late twenties, my brother and I weren't so close anymore. It made Dad sick in the heart. Over the next forty years, we would be estranged periodically until we cautiously reconnected again later in our lives. We became close again in my seventies and his late eighties, closer than ever at just the right time. But not the right time for Dad. He was gone by then. Mom was gone, too, but she was always less invested in her two sons' brotherhood than Dad was. She was more invested in maintaining the primacy of her oldest son. It was Dad who was fixated on our brotherhood. And now it was too late for him to see his sons' relationship as he always wanted it to be. That made me sick in the heart now. Until I realized that maybe Dad, and Mom, had to be gone. They had burdened us both.

Without our parents, George and I were free to be the natural brothers we were. Now, while we waited out the dirt nap, we reminisced over the phone about those innocent days of my youth, the way old men do. "But you forgot what Casey Stengel said when you were twelve," he said.

I said, "I don't remember."

"At Yankee Stadium. Casey said, 'I guess your fielders don't need no gloves when you pitch, Sonny.'"

And then I would remember it, the year I was twelve. I pitched six six-inning games that year. Four were consecutive no-hitters, two were one-hitters, both hits bunt singles. I struck out every batter I faced in four games, and in the other two, I struck out every batter but one in each game. I approached the sun like Icarus, at twelve.

In one game, the best hitter in the league hit a soft line drive off the end of his bat into foul territory behind third base. The fans rose in their seats as one and gave him a standing ovation. The batter tipped his hat in appreciation. I heard my brother's voice from the stands, "Show him, Patty. Show him what you got." My face was red with fury. I faced the batter and threw a fastball that he swung at after it was in the catcher's glove. The third time I'd struck him out.

His shoulders sagged as he walked back to the dugout. I called out loudly to him, "Why don't ya tip your hat now?" The fans hissed and booed me. But I didn't care. I cared only that I heard my brother's voice, "Thatta boy, brother."

"They hated you," my brother said over the phone. "Don't you remember?"

But I didn't remember. I said, "I'm seventy-five years old, brother. I don't remember what I had for breakfast two hours ago."

He didn't laugh. "They tried to get you banned from the league," he said.

"Who?"

"The parents of the other players. When you were eleven. They said it wasn't fair. You ruined the game for the other players. You humiliated them at bat. You destroyed their confidence. They said your fastball could kill one of the batters someday. They got up a petition, but it didn't go anywhere. So they brought pots and pans to your games and beat them with big metal spoons to distract you."

I laughed. "You're kidding?"

"A fact."

"I never heard it."

"Of course you didn't, brother." Then he added, "Remember the Little League banquet that year?"

I did. The president of the league handed out trophies at a dinner with the players and their parents. He called out the name of the league's home run leader. I went up to get my trophy. Applause. Then he called the name of the player with the highest batting average. I went up to get my trophy. Polite applause. Then he called out the name of the best pitcher in the league. I went up to get my trophy. A faint smattering of applause. Then he called out the name of the league's Most Valuable Player. I went up to get my trophy. Silence.

George laughed. Then he said, "But by the time you were twelve, they gave up. Most of them, anyway. You know, you can't beat 'em, join 'em. They were your biggest fans now." That, I remembered, too.

Adults came early to my games to see me arrive at the park. I felt their eyes on me from the stands as I walked to the dugout. They pointed me out. After the game, girls came up to me. They were thirteen, fourteen years old, wearing eye makeup and lipstick. They told me how wonderful I was. Did I ever hang out at the ice cream parlor on the Post Road downtown? I said, why?

Ma and Dad went to all my games that year when I was twelve. They sat high up in the bleachers along the third base line. A couple. Respectable now. People deferred to them because of my talent. Those old Yankee Fairfield WASPs approached them with deference, as if they were royalty. They acknowledged my parents with a nod and respectful, "Hellos." They complimented them on their son. "Such a fine boy, Mr. and Mrs. Jordan. You should be proud." To those parents, with their pale, wispy sons with sandy hair, like Frank Skeffington's son in his yachting cap, my talent was a metaphor for my character that their own sons lacked, because they could not throw a baseball as fast as I could. It must have been all that WASP inbreeding.

Imagine! Wops from The Hollow! All those signs on storefronts from my parents' youth, "No Italians need apply." My mother's fear, put to rest now, that we would be discovered in Fairfield for what we were. Guineas with dark skin. Gamblers, con men, grifters. The Other.

But we weren't The Other now. We were white now. Whiter than white. Whiter than those pale-blooded WASPs.

My father watched me pitch in silence. My mother cheered my every pitch. Her shrill voice pierced the WASP silence, "Strike him out, Patty!" From the mound, I glanced at her and Dad. I winked, faced the batter, and struck him out to end the game.

As I walked off the mound toward my parents, I could see my mother smiling and clapping her hands, while my father hurried down those bleachers, and then half-walked, half-trotted toward the pay phone behind the left field fence.

Our fame spread beyond Fairfield. A researcher for Ripley's Believe It or Not! called our house. He wanted to verify certain facts about my pitching. Possibly my achievements in Little League would appear in one of their columns in a Sunday newspaper supplement. And they did, alongside a drawing of a Zulu warrior with a bone in his nose.

One night, a New York City *Daily News* sports columnist called our house. He interviewed my parents about my pitching over the phone. Then he interviewed me. I tried to be modest, but it didn't take. A few days later his column about the Connecticut Little League pitching phenom appeared in the *Daily News*. With a photo. A tall young boy all arms and legs in a baggy baseball uniform, the sleeves of his shirt rolled up to his shoulders, the bill of his cap low over his brow, casting a shadow over his eyes, glaring with enmity at someone unseen. He is in a pitcher's mid-motion, his glove hand and ball hand joined high over his head, his left leg raised almost to his chest, before he delivers his electric fastball.

Then the Yankees called. A voice invited my parents and me to Yankee Stadium to be guests on Mel Allen's pre-game TV show. We arrived at the stadium, my mother in a shirtwaist dress, my father and I in identical tan gabardine suits and rep ties. I carried a paper bag in my hand. We were greeted by a fawning low-level Yankees functionary in a silvery suit. "So this is our little pitcher," he said, grinning at me. "I'll bet he wants to be a Yankee when he grows up." I didn't think of myself even then as a little pitcher, nor did I think I needed to grow up before I could pitch for the Yankees.

He led us on a tour of the bowels of the stadium. The Yankees executives' exclusive dining room. Pinstripes everywhere, even the walls. Pictures of Ruth and Gehrig and DiMaggio. He looked at my parents to see if they were impressed. My father gave him a slight nod. My mother said, without expression, "Very nice." And then we were walking through a dark tunnel with a light far ahead, a muffled noise, the noise growing louder, until we stepped into the Yanks' dugout, the sun blinding, the sounds of bats against balls, coaches' palaver, players' laughing, fans applauding batting practice, a shout, "Mick! An autograph for the kid, Mick!"

When my eyes adjusted to the light, I was introduced to a hunched-over old man in a Yankee uniform, his wrinkled face like a furrowed field. He shook my hand and said in a gravelly voice, "I heard'a ya, Sonny. All them strikeouts. I guess your fielders don't need no gloves when you pitch."

We were seated in box seats along the third base line. I put my paper bag on the concrete between my feet. A man with a camera on a tripod aimed it at us. Mel Allen, my father, my mother, and me in the last seat, my paper bag at my feet. The cameraman nodded. Mel turned to his right, instantly smiling, and asked my parents questions. His lips peeled apart like an open wound. My father said something, then my mother. Self-conscious glances at the camera. I could barely hear them. It didn't matter. I sat there, waiting, my heart pounding in my chest, for that moment when Mel finally looked down at me, and said, "Pat, why don't you throw a few? Show the fans your stuff."

Then, I would take my glove out of the paper bag and step on the field, the camera zooming in close on me. A catcher would appear, and I'd begin throwing. Fastball after fastball exploding into his glove. How Vic Raschi would envy me, throwing in my suit and tie with more speed than he ever dreamed of having.

Fans would be looking down at me in amazement. The Yankees taking BP would stop and stare. Casey Stengel would walk over behind my catcher to better see my fastball. Finally, that old man would raise up one hand, "I seen enough, Sonny. How would you like to pitch for the New York Yankees?" He would withdraw a baseball contract from his back pocket, and I would sign it right there, against his hunched-over back.

My mother elbowed me out of my reverie and flashed her false smile. "Patty, Mr. Allen asked you a question." Mel leaned forward so he could see me down the aisle and asked the question again. I mumbled something. He returned to my parents. I fought back tears.

I looked out over the field. It was deserted now before game time. Only Vic Raschi was warming up behind home plate. I watched him throw, with his pathetic fastball.

# CHAPTER TWENTY-SIX

In the summer of 1953, after I became a Little League baseball star, I had no more time for kiddie movie matinees, or stamps, or drawing pictures, or silly radio programs at night. I had a serious interest now. I devoted every waking moment of my life to baseball that summer. I rode my bike to the baseball park every morning at eight o'clock. All the boys and girls in the neighborhood were there. The girls on the swings and tennis courts. The boys playing pickup baseball games all day. I returned home only when the sun was going down. But before I did, I stopped at the drugstore to read all the sports magazines from the magazine racks. I ordered a chocolate malted and sat at the soda fountain slurping my malt all over the magazines. The pharmacist, a skinny, red-faced man in a white doctor's smock, glared at me. Then he gulped down a bottle of Cheracol cough medicine to stop his hands from shaking.

Mostly I read stories about my family's favorite baseball team, the Yankees. My parents loved the great and elegant DiMaggio, the scrappy little Rizzuto, the hard-working Berra, and the sturdy pitcher, Vic Raschi. I liked them, too, but my idol was the Yankees' young, left-handed pitcher, with the pink, freckled skin and pale blue eyes, Whitey Ford. The sportswriters always referred to Whitey as a stylish southpaw, whatever that meant. I didn't tell my parents Whitey was my idol because I knew my mother thought of him as the hated Irisher. I didn't care. I just wished I could be a stylish southpaw like Whitey, too, so calm on the mound, nothing ever bothering him, not even the bases loaded, the fans screaming, his teammates yelling to him, the other team's players calling him names from the dugout, and Whitey, motionless on the mound, staring at the batter in Whitey's private world of silence, his eyes a cold, unreadable blue as he decided in his mind what pitch to throw, and where. And then he moved out of his stillness into his stylish southpaw delivery. But I could never be Whitey. I was a right-handed pitcher, and an Italian.

At night, in bed, I no longer listened to my child's programs on the radio. I listened only to the Yankee baseball games. And now it was Mel Allen's hypnotic voice, not the Bickersons' harsh quarreling, that lulled me to sleep.

In the fall after my Little League success, I told Dad I wanted to learn basketball, too. So he bought a plywood backboard, rim, and net to put up over the garage in the driveway. It took him all day. He grumbled and cursed as he hammered nails into the garage to hold up the backboard.

I was a natural as a pitcher from the first time I picked up a baseball. But I had no talent for basketball. I couldn't run fast, or jump high, or move quickly left or right. And I didn't have quick hands, like Dad did when he dealt cards from the bottom of the deck, so I couldn't dribble the ball with confidence. But I was big for my age and strong. So I spent hours practicing my jump shot in the driveway. I started close to the basket, and then week after week I moved farther and farther away until I was so far from the basket that I had to arc the ball over a tree limb that hung over the driveway. I couldn't go back any farther now, so I practiced shooting the ball quickly before my imaginary defender could block my shot. Then I began practicing my head fake so that my imaginary defender leaped in the air while my feet were still on the pavement. When he was at the height of his jump, I jumped, going up and passing him on his way down before I lofted, unobstructed, my beautiful, feathery-soft jump shot. Swish! I was a one trick pony, a phrase Dad used.

All the boys in my neighborhood, and even those farther away, met at Wittenberg's up the street from my house to play three-man basketball games. Mr. Wittenberg, the father of three teenaged daughters, ages fourteen, eighteen, and nineteen, had a long, wide driveway and a big three-car garage surrounded by spreading oak and maple trees and a vast lawn. He had put up an expensive metal backboard, rim, and net over the garage doors, which drew all the boys around. The younger boys like me, twelve, thirteen, and fourteen years old, pedaled our bikes up to Wittenberg's. The older boys, seniors in high school, drove their cars. His daughters and their girlfriends sat cross-legged on the lawn watching us play. I thought that strange. So I asked my father why Mr. Wittenberg had put up that backboard, since he had three daughters and no sons.

"Use your head," Dad said. "Why do you think?" I was thirteen now, and I figured it out.

Dad had known Sol Wittenberg since they were both boys playing on the same grammar school basketball team. I never knew Dad had played sports. So he showed me an old, yellowed newspaper clipping as dry as dust. It was only one paragraph. It said that Dad's team had won their game by a score of 7-4. The high scorer on Dad's team was "Patsy Giordano with four points, and the second highest scorer was his teammate Solomon Wittenberg with three points."

I said, "Dad, can I keep that article to show my friends?"

Dad said, "What's the point? It was in the past." It was the only thing from Dad's past he ever showed me. I never saw that newspaper clipping again.

The boys from the leafy, Waspy suburb of Fairfield, like me, thought of basketball as an autumn outdoor game for fun that was played on driveways like Mr. Wittenberg's. The paved driveway was lumpy, uneven, and littered with obstacles. A tree root pushing through the pavement for sunlight. A little girl's doll. Fallen leaves on the pavement which made driving to the basket treacherous. And even if we reached the hoop on a drive, we still had to avoid slamming into the garage doors or Mr. Wittenberg's black Cadillac parked in the garage. So we played a confined suburban game of mostly jump shots, and rebounds, and passes, but not much ball handling, or drives to the hoop. That kind of game was played in Bridgeport gymnasiums.

So I took long jump shots that barely cleared the low branches of a spreading maple tree. Swish! Our audience of girls, sitting cross-legged on the lawn, future cheerleaders, clapped their hands and called out, "Way to shoot, Patty." I blushed.

Very quickly, it all became too easy for me. My perfect jump shot was unstoppable, my opponents no match for it. I grew dissatisfied with those bucolic suburban games under the shade of trees with their falling red and gold leaves. So I began driving toward the basket, elbowing my opponents out of my way, slamming into the garage doors, missing the layup, leaping for the rebound on the backs of my opponents. I began to put off my white bread opponents, who, unlike myself, did not trace their ancestry back to the docks of Naples, Italy, or The Hollow, where Dad and Ma and my brother were born, and where I was born much later. The boys I played with in Fairfield could trace their ancestry back to England, Scotland, Germany, Sweden. They played a gentleman's game of "excuse me's" whenever they so much as breathed on an opponent. I was a mad man, slapping wrists, climbing backs, growing more wild-eyed and red-faced with each basket. I had to win. It was more than a game for me. Baseball, and now basketball, was everything for me. It proved I was better than everyone else. I was raised in a family that taught me that the pursuit of excellence was not enough. The achievement of excellence was everything.

Those games became so easy for me to excel in that I made it harder for myself to excel by picking the worst players for my team. Richie Greenberg in his crewneck sweater, pressed chino pants, and dusty buckskin shoes. Fat Lenny Blum. With a lousy supporting cast, I was always being guarded by two, even three opponents. Why not? Nobody else on my team could put the ball in the basket. Which gave me an added incentive to win. I had to work harder to shake the two players who guarded me at all times. I liked it when they held my arm on a shot, or pushed me off balance, and still I made the shot. Swish! And when I did miss it, I never cried foul. I wouldn't give them the satisfaction. I knew even then it was no fun winning when you were supposed to. So I stacked the deck against me, a term from Dad's sport, poker, although he always stacked the deck in his favor. Now when I won with an inferior team my satisfaction was sweeter, as it was for Richie Greenberg, who otherwise would never experience the delights of such triumphs over the more talented boys like Doug Holmquist and Davie Perkins.

Before long, the boys began avoiding me. When they saw me pedaling my bike towards Wittenberg's they disbanded their games, told me they'd been playing for hours, and went home. One day, a few hours later, I was riding in the car with Dad when we passed Wittenberg's and I saw that the boys had reconvened after I left.

I was fourteen in the fall of my freshman year at The Prep, a strict Jesuit high school in Fairfield that prided itself on taking in boys and turning them out as men. I was translating Latin sentences from Caesar's Gallic Wars for homework in my bedroom when, from the kitchen below me, I heard Ma and Dad talking about me.

"On Saturday, I'm taking him to the North End Boys' Club," Dad said.

"He's not ready," Ma said.

"It's time."

"They're too rough for him."

"That's the point," Dad said. "It'll make a man of him."

I already knew about the North End Boys' Club. It was in The Hollow, the Italian ghetto where I was born in 1941, in a hospital near Nanny Goat Park. But I remembered nothing of The Hollow since my parents had left it shortly after I was born.

The North End Boys' Club was where basketball players in the city met to play their three-man games that began when the club opened at 8 a.m. and finished only when the lights were turned off at 9 p.m. I'd heard about those games. The best players in grammar school, high school, college, and on barnstorming semipro teams played there. The Pork played there.

The Pork. Porky. Flo. Florindo Viera. A Portuguese immigrant, five feet, five inches tall, the greatest college basketball scorer in the country for four years in the early 1950s. He led the nation in scoring in his freshmen year, thirty-nine-plus points per game, for an unknown little Connecticut college called Quinnipiac. By the time he graduated, he had the highest four-year scoring average, over thirty-three points per game, of any college player. He once started a game by missing his first ten shots. He ended it with sixty-eight points.

Porky was too small for the NBA, so after college he played on semipro teams that barnstormed all over the East Coast. He played against Harry Bosley and Bobby Knight of the All-Black Milford

Chiefs. Bill Spivey and "Black Jack" Molinas, All-Americans, Spivey out of Kentucky, Molinas out of Columbia, who were banned from the NBA for fixing college games. Bosley, with his shaved head, and Molinas, with his scowl, roughed up The Pork whenever they could. He never complained. He just kept scoring his points, thirty, forty, fifty.

I saw The Pork with my father when I was fifteen, at the University of Bridgeport gym, in a three-night tournament against other former college stars. Porky scored sixty-five the first night. Seventy-two the next. Seventy-seven the night after that.

He outscored every famous NBA player he ever played against in exhibition games. He scored twenty-seven against Sihugo Green and the Knicks, twenty-eight in a half against Hot Rod Hundley and the Lakers, then fifty-five against Goose Tatum's All Stars.

He outscored Wilt head-to-head in the Catskills. Thirty-eight points to Wilt's thirty-three. Nobody stopped The Pork. Not Wilt. Not even Topsy. Topsy DelGobbo had a nice game. Smooth. Slick, really. He never sweated. A southpaw with black hair in a D.A. and a spit curl hanging over his forehead. He wore white sweat socks to his knees and an immaculate uniform. Still, he gave Porky fits in his wrinkled, sweat-stained uniform.

Topsy glued himself to Porky like a sandwich board, dogging him, with a smile, while Porky screamed at his teammates in his little girl's voice, "Gimme the ball! Gimme the fuckin' ball! Gimme the mutha-fuckin' ball!"

Once in a while, Topsy would have a good game dogging The Pork. A nice game, really, nice enough at the game's end for the crowd to give Topsy a standing ovation for holding The Pork under fifty.

During all the years of Porky's greatness, he always returned to the North End Boys' Club to play ferocious three-man games that meant nothing, except to him. He would drive to the Boys' Club after a Quinnipiac practice at 5 p.m., and play in those games into the night.

"Those three-man games were more important to me than the Quinnipiac games," he told me once. "I'd knock people down. Kick over lockers if I lost. Get in fights. Guys had to hold me back. People thought I was crazy. They'd say, 'Pork, you're leading the nation in scoring and you're killing yourself at the North End Boys' Club. You could get hurt.' But I didn't care. I wouldn't give up those three-man games for nothing. Shiiit! After college, I played in the College All-Star Game in Madison Square Garden. At practice I told those All-Americans, 'You guys ain't shit. I can go to the North End Boys' Club right now and round up five guys who will beat the shit outta all of ya.'"

Porky looked at me with a smile. "Wasn't that the truth, Pat?" he said. "The Boys' Club was where it was at. You should know. You were there."

# CHAPTER TWENTY-SEVEN

On that Saturday when I was fourteen, Dad drove me into The Hollow, past Frank's Market and Sorrento's Importing. When we reached Pacelli's Bakery, alongside the city jail, Dad stopped the car across the street from the jail alongside the North End Boys' Club. I waited for him to shut off the engine.

Finally, he said, "Go on now. You're on your own."

I grabbed my gym bag from the back seat and got out. Dad drove off. I stood there with my gym bag stuffed with my clean white T-shirt, white basketball shorts, white socks, and white, high-top Converse sneakers, and watched Dad's car disappear into The Hollow toward the Venice A.C.

The North End Boys' Club was a low brick building that looked like a warehouse. It sat on a scruffy grassless patch of weeds across the street from the high jail walls with razor wire and the little wood building that was Pacelli's. The jail was set much lower than the Boys' Club in its own hollow so that I could look from the Boys' Club over the jail walls and see the prisoners in khaki prison uniforms hoeing and watering rows of prison vegetables. To the left of the jail, I also saw a line of people waiting to get into Pacelli's. I could smell the hot baked ciabatta bread and grinders from across the street. Finally, I went inside the North End Boys' Club.

The boys my age who played basketball at the Boys' Club were nothing like my suburban friends in Fairfield. Nor were they much like me. They were city kids who played basketball in their black dress shirts, black gabardine pants and black, high-top Keds. They never showered after our games like I did, and then changed into my fresh clothes, khaki chinos and dusty bucks. They just played basketball in their street clothes until the club closed, then walked out in their sweaty clothes into the dark night of the city streets. They walked up the street to a candy store and hung out in front of it talking to olive-skinned girls with black hair and tight black Capri pants.

Although I played basketball with them for years, I never once went with them to that candy store at night. I just watched them go up the street, jostling each other, yelling at the jailbirds behind the wall, laughing, while I waited in front of the club for Dad to pick me up. I was a part of them, but not of them. They were wild and wise in ways I wasn't. They seemed so exotic to me then, as they still do now.

They were Black and white, Italians and Poles, Hunkies and Czechs, Irish and Jews. They ragged each other with ethnic slurs. Micks were drunks, Polacks dumb, Jews cheap, wops criminals. Yet, since they were all thrown together in an ethnic bouillabaisse at the North End Boys' Club, they had no prejudice. Blacks, who traced their ancestry to Angola slaves, dated Italian girls. Blond, blue-eyed whites, who traced their ancestry to Krakow, dated Black girls. They mixed and matched any way they wanted to, long before the rest of America did.

Although I lost track of them when I became a man, I heard rumors about them all. They had become doctors, lawyers, bank robbers, beauty pageant promoters, murderers, high school teachers, car mechanics, beauticians, heroin addicts, pimps, *finocchios*, professional drag racers. Richie Bells, a Jew, became a stand-up comic in New York City, and then an actor in L.A. Bells had a thin, pock-marked, hatchet face, with greasy, swept-back, black hair when I knew him. He wore thick-lensed eyeglasses with black rims, and was always cracking jokes during our games, which pissed us off. "Shut the fuck up, Bells!" But he never did. Richie Bells was a lot funnier then, and a lot cooler than he is today as Richard Belzer, the self-consciously hip TV actor with blow-dried hair and tinted shades.

What I thought was my rough game on the Wittenberg's driveway in the suburbs, I found out quickly, was a pussy's game at the North End Boys' Club. Of course you climbed an opponent's back for a rebound. Of course you pushed an opponent with your elbows when he drove to the hoop. Of course you lowered your shoulder and slammed it into an opponent when you set a pick. Of course you tugged on an opponent's shirt to slow him down, or planted your hand in his back and pushed him forward when he tried to back you into the hoop. Of course you hooked your elbow around your opponent's arm to keep him from jumping for a rebound, and then you jumped for the rebound with your elbows out to clip him in the jaw if he dared jump with you.

You did all these things and more at the North End Boys' Club, and anyone who called a foul was a pussy. There was only one rule at the North End Boys' Club: No blood, no foul.

And you cheated, too. Any way you could. You fought over every ball that went out of bounds. "I never touched it! It nicked your shirt! I saw it! I swear to God!" You hoped God was busy elsewhere. The game stopped. Curses were thrown back and forth. Players threatened to quit. "Good ahead, pussy, quit!" They called your bluff and stomped off to the locker room. You waited, got a drink of water from the fountain, shot around awhile until they returned and you knew you had them. The matter was settled with matching foul shots. Finally, the game resumed. Until the next argument and you lied again. "You kicked it out!" More curses. Insults. Matching foul shots. The game resumed. Anyone who didn't cheat was worse than a pussy. He was a *finocchio*.

I loved it all. The pushing, shoving, cursing, the fierceness of every moment of those games.

We held the court from 9 a.m. until 5 p.m. Our feet were so blistered, inflamed, that we could barely walk. We went outside and hobbled across the street like the ragged remnants of a defeated army. We bought powdered jelly donuts or hot grinders with butter and a quart of milk for dinner at Pacelli's. We ate and drank as we crossed the street in a hurry to get back in the gym even though for us, our games were over. The older guys in their twenties would take over the court now. College stars. Semipros. The Pork.

We stood with our backs against the tiled gym wall, one leg bent, our sneakered foot planted against the wall, and watched The Pork play.

Porky had the purest of games, despite his unorthodox shots. A high, arcing, two-hand set shot. A fade away jump shot he flung from behind his head on a high arc. A straight, hard drive to the basket which ended in a hook shot which Porky fired low off his right hip, with a little spin on the ball that hit high up off the right side of the backboard, and fell through the hoop.

We watched from the sidelines in amazement, but to no avail. Nobody could copy Porky's game. It was said at the North End Boys' Club that Porky Viera ruined the games of more young basketball players than any player who played the game. Even my father, who last played the game when the ball had laces, told me once, "Don't ever try to copy Florindo's shots. Just copy his intensity."

One night at the club, I was standing against the wall with the other boys my age, watching Porky play. His team was tied at fourteen-all in a fifteen-point game. One of his players went up for a rebound and landed awkwardly on his ankle. He limped off the court. Porky screamed at him, "Where the fuck you going? The game ain't over." The player waved his hand in disgust at Porky and hobbled on one leg toward the locker room. Porky screamed again, "You ain't done until we win this fuckin' game!"

Porky looked around, wild-eyed, saw me, grabbed me by the neck of my shirt, and pulled me onto the court. "You're takin' his place." I was terrified. Porky said to me, "We only need one basket, kid. You get the ball, you pass it to me. Understand." I nodded.

Play began. Players cut back and forth, jostled me, banged me around like a ten pin, until I was disoriented. I stood at the top of the keyhole, blinking stupidly. Someone took a shot. Players leaped for it. The ball bounced high in the air. I looked up at it. It started to come down, straight to me. I put my hands up to deflect it, but instead caught it, unguarded, alone at the key. Instinctively, I went up for one of my jump shots. I heard Porky's shrill scream, "No! You fuckin' asshole!" and saw him leaping at me, his hands outspread to block my shot. The ball left my hand with perfect spin just as Porky knocked me to the floor on my ass. I watched the ball drop softly into the net. I jumped up, smiling, and reached out my hand for Porky to slap it in congratulation. He knocked my hand away with the back of his hand.

"What the fuck's the matter with you?" he said.

"But, Pork, I made it. We won."

"Made it! Made it! Are you fuckin' crazy?" He poked his finger into my chest. "Nobody takes the last shot on Porky's team! Nobody but The Pork. Never! Do you fucking understand?"

I lowered my eyes and nodded. "I'm sorry, Pork."

After that night, whenever his team was down a man, Porky would always pull me onto the court with a smile on his face. "I like this kid," he'd say. "He's the only guy in this fuckin' club with the balls to take the last shot on The Pork's team."

On those nights when I played on Porky's team, I subordinated my game to Porky's game. I passed Porky the ball, set picks for him, fought those older players for the rebound, grabbed the ball, spun around, and fired the ball to The Pork.

When Porky's team, my team, too, was comfortably ahead, say, thirteen points to six, he would pass me the ball at the top of the key. "Go ahead, kid. Show 'em that jump shot." And I would. Swish.

"Fuckin' kid can shoot," Porky would say.

It was a good discipline for me, subordinating my game to Porky's game. It prepared me for that day in the not too distant future when I would no longer be a star. It was one of the many things I learned at the North End Boys' Club. The most important being that, in sports, as in life, no blood, no foul. Not even when there was blood.

By the time I was fifteen, a sophomore at Fairfield Prep, I was a budding basketball star with the junior varsity, averaging almost twenty points a game. Because The Prep was a private Jesuit school, we couldn't play in any of the city leagues. We had to barnstorm all over the state to get games. One night, we took a bus north to Naugatuck, a hick factory and farm town in the Naugatuck Valley. I had one of my best games, scoring over twenty points in a narrow, tiny gym. After I showered and dressed, instead of going into the stands to watch our varsity play, I went outside to replay the game in my head in the quiet of the night.

There was a young girl my age standing outside with her back against the gym building wall. She was smoking a cigarette a few yards from a streetlight. She was short, with blue eyes and sandy-colored hair pulled tight into a long ponytail. She wore dungarees rolled up into cuffs above her ankle and saddle shoes with white socks. A little Valley girl wearing an oversized sweatshirt with the words Quinnipiac Athletic Dept. printed across her chest. The Pork's college.

She smiled at me. I smiled at her, and said, "Why aren't you watching the game?"

She said, "Bored, I guess. I only went because my girlfriends insisted I get out for a change."

"Don't you like to go out?"

"Sometimes. When I can."

"What's your name?"

"Suzzane... With two zs and an e on the end." I laughed. She blushed. "My mother's French." I told her my name was Pat. She said, "I know. I watched you play. You were good." She lowered her eyes as if embarrassed by her compliment.

"Thanks," I said. She offered me a cigarette. "I don't smoke."

She said, "Because you're an athlete, right?"

I nodded. "And what about you? Are you an athlete?" I pointed at her baggy sweatshirt.

She laughed. "Me? No. It's my older brother's sweatshirt. A hand-me-down."

"Then you must be a cheerleader."

She looked embarrassed again. "Oh, no. I don't have time for stuff like that. I'm just a Valley girl. I help my father on the farm."

"Doing what?"

"Feed the pigs and milk the cows. Muck the horses' stalls."

"What does muck mean?"

She laughed again. "I forgot. You're a city boy down there in Fairfield."

"It isn't really a city," I said. "But I was a city boy because I spent a lot of time in Bridgeport."

"Anything south of the Valley is a big city to us." Then she said, "Muck means to clean out the horses' stalls and put in fresh hay."

"You mean, the horse shit?" She nodded. "Do you like doing that?"

"I don't mind. I like the animals."

We were silent for a moment, thinking of what else to say. Finally I said, "Want to go for a walk?"

"Sure." She dropped her cigarette and stubbed it out with her saddle shoe.

We walked on the sidewalk up a small hill. We didn't say anything for a while. When we got past the streetlights of the gymnasium we were in darkness. We came to a huge oak tree, its branches spreading low over the sidewalk. We stopped. She leaned her back against the tree, facing me. I moved closer to her. She put her arms around my neck. I pressed my body against hers and felt her soft breasts against my chest. Then I kissed her. I opened my mouth, and then she did too. We breathed in, sucking the air out of each other, and then our tongues touched. She pulled her head back from mine and looked down.

"I never kissed a boy like that before," she said.

"But you're French?" I asked.

She laughed. "Not all French girls my age French Kiss."

"I'm sorry. I just figured..."

"That's all right..." She looked up at me. "I liked it."

"Me, too." Then I heard from down below us the fans leaving the gym. I said, "I better get back, or I'll miss the team bus."

She said, "You wouldn't want to do that. Be stuck here in the Valley."

When we got back to the gym, the team bus was parked in front, its engine idling loudly, smoke billowing from its exhaust.

I said, "I'd better get on the bus."

She said, "Do you want to see me again?"

"Sure."

"Maybe I could come to Fairfield on the train sometime."

"The Big City," I said.

She smiled, "Yes. The Big City." She reached into the back pocket of her dungarees, pulled out a little pad and pencil, and wrote something on it. She ripped off a piece of paper and handed it to me. "Here," she said. "Call me."

I said, "Sure." Then she turned away. I watched her walk back up the hill until she was gone. I looked at the piece of paper. She had written on it her name, "Suzzane, two zzs and an e at the end," and her telephone number. Below that she wrote, "Don't forget."

A few weeks later I called her. When she answered the phone, I said, "This is Pat, the Prep basketball player. Remember me?"

"I didn't think you'd call," she said.

"Well, I did. Do you want to go to a Prep mixer with me?"

"Really?"

"What do you mean?"

"Nothing. Just kidding. Of course I do."

"It's no big dance. Just a sock hop in the cafeteria. We don't even have a gym. All the priests will be standing around watching us. You know. It sort of takes the fun out of it."

"I don't care. I like to dance. I'd like to dance with you."

On the night of the dance, my father dropped me off at the Fairfield railroad station at seven o'clock. It was deserted and cold. I was wearing Dad's old camel hair topcoat, which fit me perfectly. Dad was only five-feet-eight and I was already almost six feet tall. When the train from New Haven stopped, she was the only person to get off. A little girl wearing a worn, blue cloth coat so big for her that only her saddle shoes showed. She had a scarf looped around her neck, and a hand-crocheted hat that was halfway between a beret and a stocking cap, pulled down over her forehead. Probably an older sister's hand-me-down. Her hair was bunched under her cap so that only her blue eyes and mouth were visible in her oversized coat and cap. She wore bright red lipstick that made her lips look fat, and something blue around her eyes which made her look older, like Debbie Reynolds. Only she looked more real than Debbie Reynolds.

We walked up the hill alongside the road toward The Prep. I had to walk slowly so she could keep up with me. She stopped to light a cigarette. "I smoke when I'm nervous," she said.

"Why would you be nervous? It'll only be a record player with some rock and roll songs and a few ballads. There won't be anything to eat or drink, except cokes and potato chips. I should have told you. I hope you ate something."

"I was too excited to eat anything. Then the train made me nervous. I kept looking out the window at the signs at each station."

She laughed. "I was afraid I'd miss the Fairfield station and end up in New York City."

"Well, you made it."

"Yes, I did. All by myself." Then she blurted out, "I was afraid, too, you might not meet me at the train."

I looked at her. "Why would I do that?"

She shrugged. "Some boys do things like that. They think it's funny."

"What's funny about that?" She smiled at me.

When we got to the dance, I took off my coat and threw it over a chair. I got her a coke and some chips, and we sat at a small, round table. She was still wearing her coat, as if afraid to take it off. The cafeteria was brightly lighted and noisy from the music and the other boys and girls talking and laughing. The room was hot from the damp steam hissing out of the radiators along the walls. The Jesuits in their black dresses and white collars stood with their backs against the walls, eyeballing the boys and girls dancing to a fast rock and roll song, "Mr. John Law," by a local Bridgeport band called Dick Grass and the Hoppers. I told her the song hadn't been released to the public yet. She asked me how I knew that.

I said, "Because I know Dick Grass."

"Really?" she said. "That's cool."

"Well, he wasn't a cool rock and roll guy when I knew him. He was just Dickie Grassia, an Italian kid like me. He played third base on my American Legion team."

"What position did you play?"

"I was a pitcher. I still am, at The Prep."

"Are you good?"

"Pretty good."

"I'll bet you're just being modest."

I shrugged.

"You must be hot in that coat," I said. "Let me help you off with it." We stood up. She took off her hat, and then her coat. I laid them over an empty chair and turned toward her. Her long, sandy-colored ponytail I remembered was now long, wild, reddish-blond ringlets that framed her beautiful face. In the light now I saw her face was lightly freckled.

She was wearing a long, tight gray skirt buttoned down her front almost to her calves, a wide, black belt cinched at her small waist, and a pale blue sweater. The sweater was tight, too, buttoned down her back. Now I realized why she hesitated taking off her coat. She was embarrassed by her breasts. They were round and full and too big for such a small girl. Most of the girls I knew wore pointy, stiff bras that made their breasts look bigger than they were, like the bullet bumpers of Buicks. Her breasts looked natural, like Marilyn Monroe's breasts.

I tried not to stare at her breasts, but she saw me looking at them. She crossed her arms across her chest, which made her breasts rise up more noticeably.

"Want to dance?" I asked. It was a slow ballad now, "Earth Angel," by the Penguins.

She smiled at me, and exhaled a deep breath. "That's why I'm here, isn't? To dance with you." I led her by the hand on to the dance floor. Her skirt was so tight she had to take mincing, little girl-can't-help-it steps like Jayne Mansfield.

The moment I put my arm around her to dance, she pressed her body against mine and nestled her face against my chest. She put her arms around my waist and held me tight as if I could save her from something. I could feel her breasts against my chest, soft and firm at the same time. We danced like this for a few moments until a Jesuit appeared behind her. He glared over her at me and said, "Leave room for the Holy Ghost, Mr. Gi-Or-Dano." Suzzane and I separated. Her face was red. The Jesuit walked back to the wall.

She said, "Did we do something wrong?"

"No."

"I didn't get you in trouble, did I?"

"Fuck him," I said. She looked startled. I said, "Do you want to go to the second floor, see my classroom? We can be alone there." She nodded, like a child.

We went up the stairs to the second floor of classrooms. She said, "Why did that priest call you Mr. Giordano? I thought your name was Jordan."

"It is. My father changed his name a few weeks before I was born. He wanted me to have an American name. It didn't fool those mick priests though."

The hallway was lined on both sides with lockers. It smelled of teenaged boys' sweat. I showed her the door of my classroom, the top half glass, the bottom half old wood scarred by the knives of boys who carved their initials into it. PJ 1956. "My desk is in the last row," I said. "In the far, right hand corner."

She pressed her face close to the glass and peered into the dark room. "Why is your desk in the last row in a corner?" she said, still staring at it.

"It's where the Jesuits bury the guys who give them a hard time. They never call on us. They make believe we don't exist. Which is fine by me."

She turned around to face me, her back against the door. She looked pained, and said, "That's a terrible thing to do. What could you be doing that was so bad?"

"Not doing what they want. Asking the wrong questions. Defying them. When they tell the Irish boys they should pray to the Blessed Mother for a priestly vocation of celibacy, those mick boys bow their heads and say they do every night before bed."

Suzzane said, "What do the Italian boys like you say, when the priests tell you to pray for a vocation of priestly celibacy?"

"We laugh in their faces." I felt myself getting hot just thinking about those Jesuits.

She reached up and put her hand on my face. "Don't think about it. It doesn't matter now." She stood on her tip toes and kissed me on the cheek. It took me a moment to forget those Jesuits until she kissed me again, on the lips. I opened my mouth and she opened hers. Our tongues touched, and I forgot about the Jesuits, and thought only about what we were doing. I put my hands on her breasts and felt their soft firmness. She stiffened. She pulled her face back from mine, but she didn't take my hands off her breasts. She just looked up at me with a sad, sweet smile that haunts me still. She said, "Is this why you invited me to the dance?"

# CHAPTER TWENTY-EIGHT

In the summer of 1957, I pitched against men. Thirty-, forty-year-olds, a few pushing fifty. Bricklayers, carpenters, roofers, painters, plumbers, electricians, machinists at the Brass Factory. They had wives, children. Their kids were my age, sixteen, and older. They drove to our games at Seaside Park, across the street from Long Island Sound, in old cars, pickup trucks loaded with tools, vans with the names of their self-owned businesses painted on the panels: Gus Viera, Mason Contractor.

They parked under the shade of an oak tree. They rested a moment in their vehicles, dragged on a cigarette, exhausted. Then they began to take off their work belts with their tools and their construction boots and filthy jeans and painters' pants and ripped T-shirts. They threw them in the back of their vehicles. They sat there in their boxer shorts, stubbed out their cigarettes, then began to change into their baseball uniforms. It was cramped in their vehicles, but there was no clubhouse at Seaside Park. Only a men's facility frequented at night by *finocchios*. Finally, they emerged into the fading afternoon sunlight in their uniforms: The Lenox AA, The White Eagles, The Stratford Merchants, The Highlanders. They walked across the parking lot toward the diamond in that shoulder-shifting strut of athletes, rather than that plowman's plod of working men. The fans stared at them. Fathers whispered names to their young sons, pointed them out. They recounted for their sons the players' athletic exploits of years ago in high school, college, the pros, before they became working men with unshaven faces. Their caps were pulled low over their forehead as if to hide their weary eyes. Their hands and arms were marked with cuts, bruises, scabs, coated with white lime or mechanic's grease or paint. Their uniforms were kept in their gym bag all week, wrinkled, smelly, caked with dirt, patched in places by their wives. But no matter. Every time they wore those dirty uniforms, they were reminded of a time when they had been someone, looked up to, admired, set apart, with a future.

I can still remember their names. My brother had taken me to their games ever since I was in Little League. They were my idols. Ronnie "The Globe" DelBianco, shaped like a globe with sticks for arms and legs. He moved in little mincing steps, like Minnesota Fats around a pool table. He played third base with hands so quick the eye could barely see him snap up a hot ground ball. But in the minor leagues with the Dodgers' chain, he had been a catcher who caught Don Newcombe.

The Pork was there, too. A swarthy, little madman with a jaw like a cantaloupe. He chased down fly balls in centerfield like a banshee. Once, one of his cronies told him he was out of shape. The Pork screamed, "Outta fuckin' shape!" A bet was wagered. The Pork would run from Bridgeport to Danbury, thirty miles, in his black dress pants and hard-soled shoes. His cronies puttered alongside him in a car, exhorting him on. Traffic backed up behind them, horns blaring. When he reached the Danbury city limits, Porky stopped. The car pulled over to the side of the road. The Pork went over to the driver's window, not even breathing heavy, and said, "Double or nuthin', assholes. I'll run back." A chorus shouted at him, "Just get in the fuckin' car."

Porky's older brother, Gus, was as tall and placid of temperament as Porky was short and manic. Gus had the flat-featured face of a Mexican bandit. He had a look in his eyes as if he'd seen things he wished he hadn't. I learned years later that he had been an alcoholic whose only respite from his torment was the order he found on a pitcher's mound. He was a pitcher of meticulous mannerisms on the mound. I studied him like a student. The way he landscaped the mound's dirt with the toe of his spikes, fluffed out his shirt, rotated his shoulders, tugged on his cap with a raised pinky, before he delivered the ball with a pitcher's textbook motion.

Big Al Bike was a barrel-chested catcher in his forties, always scowling, pissed off. He blocked home plate with the ball in his glove, waited for the collision with the runner charging in from third base. Just before he lunged at the runner's face with the ball, Big Al smiled.

John "Whitey" McCall was a pale, delicate-looking man, always smooth shaven, with neatly parted blond hair, like a small-town banker. He was shy, soft spoken, the gentlest of men. His teammates never cursed in Whitey's presence. Even The Pork kept his "muthafucking cocksuckers" to himself around Whitey. He was a southpaw first baseman who fielded his position with a dancer's grace. He was also one of the few players in the SCL whose uniform was always spotless. It was laundered each week, and pressed with an iron, by the housekeeper in the rectory of St. Augustine's Cathedral, where Whitey was known as Father John McCall.

Fred "Fritzy" Luciano was a slight, dark man, with the long, sad face of a Mafia hit man, dour and prissy at the same time. Fritzy had pitched in the minor leagues for over ten years and never rose above a Class C league, with his tiny slider. His career was interrupted for a few years when he became a gunner's mate on a bomber in World War II. He returned home in the 1950s to drive a hearse and, on weekends, pitch for The Highlanders, mostly guineas from The Hollow.

Rufus Baker was as Black as a plum, as stoic as a cigar store Indian. He was a slick fielding infielder who ran like the wind, until he lost a step in his forties. He had played for the New York Black Yankees in the 1940s and early 1950s, before he returned to Bridgeport and the SCL. He rarely spoke, just nodded.

Tommy Casagrande, aka Tommy Big House, was a southpaw pitcher as big as Paul Bunyan. He had freckled, pink skin and arms like hams dusted with blond hairs. Tommy had a southpaw's stylish motion like the Yankees' Whitey Ford, only Tommy had had better stuff. He'd been given a $40,000 bonus by the Phillies, with whom he sipped an espresso in the majors, until he hurt his arm and retired. Now, like all of my idols, he was just keeping his hand in the game he loved in Bridgeport, Connecticut's famous Senior City League.

The fans were mostly fathers with their sons, Puerto Rican families spending a day at the beach across the street, and the wives and girlfriends of the players. The wives absentmindedly rocked their babies in carriages, glanced around for their older sons and daughters, then fixed their eyes back on their husbands in the field. They worried about their husbands, not for them to do well, but for them not to get hurt, be laid up for weeks, unable to work. After the half inning, their husbands would jog off the field, past the dugout bench to their wives, who had a lighted cigarette for them. Their husbands took a few drags, exhaled smoke, then lifted their babies out of the carriage and kissed them. A teammate called to them. They handed their cigarette to their wife, kissed her and went back to the bench. They picked out a bat, took a few practice swings, and went up to hit.

A clutch of old men stood under the shade of a tree. Old men of even more distant repute than the players. They clustered together, aged crones clucking their tongues like the witches from *Macbeth*, double, double, toil and trouble. They were trouble, full of mean-ness and spite. They rooted against the players on the field, dispar-aged their talents, both now and from years ago when those players were young. Those players had never been good enough, not Fritzy Luciano or Tommy Big House, and certainly not Rufus Baker, not even in their prime.

And then there was me. Those old men disparaged me before I pitched an inning in the SCL. The gall to think I could pitch in this league. Against men. Who did I think I was? A pink-faced sophomore in high school. With a crew cut and a new Herb Score model glove, kangaroo skin spikes and a spotless uniform. But with no girlfriend, like Suzzane, two zzs and an e at the end. I never talked to her again after that Prep dance. I was too ashamed to call her. So now, I had just my mother and father and brother in tow. They sat in the stands, watching me pitch, not for amusement, like parents of other boys my age in the American Legion League. My family watched me with an appraising eye, jewelers examining an uncut diamond through a loupe. By then it was clear that baseball was no longer just a game for me. It would be my destiny. I would sign a huge bonus contract when I graduated from high school. I would pay off my parents' mortgage, buy my brother a car. Then go off to my career. After a few years in the minors, for a little seasoning, I would be called up to the majors to begin my Hall of Fame career.

No major league scouts ever went to those SCL games. What was there to see? Men with a past and no future. Young prospects my age were playing against boys their age in the Babe Ruth League or with an American Legion team. So the scouts went to those games, looking for me. The scouts had already heard of me. My nineteen strikeouts out of twenty-one batters, a state record, in my first high school game when I was fifteen. That night, a Cincinnati Reds scout called our house and offered me a $20,000 bonus. He was shocked to discover I was only fifteen. "A boy," he said. "By the time you graduate high school, you'll be out of my league. But remember I was here first."

It took the scouts only a week at those Babe Ruth and Legion games to discover where I was. So the following Sunday, they appeared at Seaside Park for my first SCL game. My team was the Lenox AA, mostly Hunkies and college graduates, like The Pork, some ex-minor leaguers, and a few older guys like Rufus and Whitey McCall. My opponents were the White Eagles, the SCL Polack version of the New York Yankees. They paid their players fifty dollars a game. Most of them were older players like Red Grunik, or ex-minor leaguers like Vinnie Corda, and, of course, Tommy Big House. He was fresh from the majors, so they paid him one hundred dollars a game. He still had good stuff, a nice fastball that had lost a few precious mph, and a pretty curve not so sharp as it once was. But he still looked like a pitcher who didn't belong in some working man's semipro league in Bridgeport, Conn. Tommy, my idol, would be my pitching opponent in my first SCL game.

I did not strike out fifteen, sixteen, seventeen, eighteen batters as I had in Little League and high school in my first ever nine-inning game in the SCL. I struck out nine batters, walked two, gave up five hits, a few hard-hit outs, and an earned run.

I started the game feeling my way around on the mound. The new kid, just trying to throw strikes, not embarrass himself in front of his idols, trying to look like a pitcher with an idea. I paced myself through the first three innings, retiring all nine batters I faced. Two strikeouts, a few easy groundballs, one hot shot to Rufus at second base that he back-handed, and a few lazy fly balls to the outfield. It was easy pitching to these men. I didn't have to throw so many pitches. They didn't swing and miss as many of my pitches as high school batters did. They attacked my first pitch fastball and popped it up to first base. Or pounded my overhand curveball into the dirt for a routine groundball out. Six pitches, side retired.

They started to make better contact in the fourth and fifth inning. A line drive to Whitey who snapped it out of the air like swatting a fly. A long fly ball over Porky's head in center. He ran it down and caught it over his shoulder, just a long out. In the seventh I gave up a run on a walk and a double between center and right that Porky cut off before it rolled across the street for a ground rule home run. Runner on second, one out, the score 2-1, my favor. I fidgeted on the mound, walked the next batter on four pitches. Whitey came over to the mound and said, "Take a breath, Pat. Remember who you are." I said, "Yes, Fath...Whitey."

Ronnie "The Globe" DelBianco was up. He glared at me with red eyes, a fat dragon spewing fire. The kid had struck him out previously on a fastball in on his hands. He shouted to me, "Throw that shit next time, you little prick, see what happens." Now he was grinding the bat in his hands, just waiting, the kid on the ropes, not knowing what to do except what he always did with overmatched kids, rear back and throw heat. I threw The Globe a first pitch overhand curveball, the ball floating toward the plate waist high, and then collapsing to the dirt just as The Globe lunged at it, too soon, the bat slipping out of one hand, the ball bouncing back to me on one hop. I caught it, whirled and fired it to Rufus at second. He tagged the bag, pivoted, leaped to avoid the sliding runner with his spikes high, and fired it to Whitey stretching toward him at first base. I saw out of the corner of my eye, The Globe's mincing little feet churning under the weight of his massive body, Whitey stretching low to the ground, swiping the ball out of the dirt with a disdainful backhand before The Globe's little feet hit the bag.

As I walked off the mound Rufus jogged past me, his eyes downcast. I almost didn't hear what he said, "You the man, boy." Then The Pork ran past me and said, "Fucking balls, kid." Whitey came over to me as I crossed the first base line toward our dugout. He put his hand on my shoulder as if to give me a blessing. Then he did. He smiled, the faintest of smiles, and nodded, once. I smiled back at him, "Thanks, Whitey." I felt a lightness in my chest as if I could levitate. It surpassed any feeling I ever had when overpowering teenagers my age.

I struck out four of the last six batters in the eighth and ninth inning to end the game. I beat Tommy Big House 2-1 that afternoon.

After the game, players from both teams went to the White Eagle Hall for beer and sandwiches. The Pork said, "You comin', kid?" I said, "I dunno, Pork. I have to ask my parents." Porky stared at me with his black, glistening eyes, and said, "You don't have to ask your parents shit no more, kid."

My parents dropped me off at the White Eagle Hall and told me they'd pick me up in an hour. I went inside. The players were still in their sweaty, dirty uniforms, drinking beer, laughing, taking a bite out of their kielbasa sandwiches. I didn't know what to do. What to say to these men. I stood off to the side by myself. Then through the crowd of players I saw Big Tommy Casagrande parting the crowd as he came toward me with two beer bottles in one hand, and a cigarette dangling from his lips. He handed a beer to me, "Here, kid, you deserve it." I said, "Thanks, Tommy." I took a sip, the first beer I'd ever tasted. It was bitter, con gassata. I belched. Tommy laughed and dropped his big arm on my shoulders like a falling tree limb. Then Tommy pulled a pack of Camels out of his back pocket, shuffled one out of the pack, and reached it toward me. I shook my head. "I don't smoke, Tommy," I said.

He smiled and said, "Sure, you don't. I forgot you're still a kid."

Tommy Big House put his pack of cigarettes in his back pocket. He looked at me seriously now. He said, "But you don't pitch like a kid. You're gonna be a big leaguer someday soon."

When my parents picked me up, I told them what Tommy had said. Dad said, "Tommy should know." But he didn't.

# CHAPTER TWENTY-NINE

After I graduated from high school, I signed a $50,000 bonus contract with the Milwaukee Braves. I paid off the mortgage on my parents' house. I tried to buy my brother a car, but he wouldn't let me. "It's your money, brother," he said. "You earned it."

I left home to begin my adult life in the minor leagues. After four years of diminishing success and then outright failure in the minor leagues, I returned home in the spring. I lived with my parents for a few months. I had my old room back. My Little League trophies had collected dust on the windowsill, illuminated in a haze by the morning sunlight. I saw the scuffed baseballs on which were written the hieroglyphics of my past successes. Numbers and letters, 18 ks, 0 hits, 0 bb, 0 er. I slept late, rarely left the house. I went back up to my room in the afternoon and lay on my bed staring at the trophies and baseballs. I wanted to put them in a box in the attic, but I didn't have the will to do it. Downstairs I heard my mother say, "Is he ever going to do something?" My father said, "Give him time."

One Sunday afternoon I ventured out like a frightened caveman into the dangerous world of the Senior City League at Seaside Park. I arrived after the game had begun so I wouldn't be noticed. I stood behind the old crones standing under the shade of a tree. I felt like that boy in the Sherwood Anderson story, "Sophistication," flattened against a dark doorway, fearful he'd be discovered, revealed as nothing more than a leaf blown by the wind.

"Jordan's back, I hear."

"Not surprised."

"I never thought he had the stuff."

"He didn't have the guts."

I fled in tears.

My future was now my past. The first twenty-one years of my life had been about my future. Now I had none. It was so sudden. I thought you lost your future gradually so that you could see its bright light dimming through the years like a dying star. In your forties, the light was extinguished, and you saw only darkness where the light had been. You accepted the fact now that your future was gone. It was the natural order of lives. Now, you had only the present which would remain the same until you died.

In your forties, you were what you would always be, only increasingly older. But that was OK. You'd had your future for over forty years. But not me. I was confronted with a lifetime of the present at twenty-one, which present for me now, was nothing. I didn't know what to do. So I got a job.

I became a working man. I was a laborer on a construction crew that built expensive homes in Fairfield County. The foreman dropped me off at a deserted site in the early morning. The trees were all chopped down, the tree stumps cleared out to reveal an open space, a square patch of dirt, outlined by string, with a high mound of dirt in the middle. He gave me a shovel and told me to spread the mound of dirt evenly over the square space marked off by the string. Then he left me alone. After I had spread the dirt evenly, I compacted it with a handheld steam roller, like a lawn mower, but with a metal cylinder instead of the blades of a lawn mower. I supplied the steam. I rolled it over the loose dirt until it was compacted firmly. The foreman returned in the afternoon. He pulled up in a cement dump truck. He backed it up to the square space and pulled down a long chute so that its open end was in the middle of the square. Then he emptied wet concrete mixed with small stones into the square space until it, too, was a high mound. He gave me a rake this time and told me to rake the concrete and stones evenly over the dirt before the mason came later. Then he left me alone again.

All day in a hot sun I shoveled, rolled, and raked. It was a back-breaking and solitary task for a young man who had always performed with grace before an audience. There was nothing to do in the solitude except work and sweat and think. I wondered what had happened to my future, why it was gone, but I had no answer. I thought of what I would do next in my life. What I would be. But I could think of nothing. I felt betrayed. By whom? My mother, father, brother? Fate? God? Myself?

And then I thought of Dad. Born into nothing. No mother, father, siblings, future. His curse, and yet his blessing, too. He made a life out of that nothing. So, one morning I had got out of bed and got a job as a working man. And then I got another job, and another, and another, and another over the years until, pushing thirty, I had a future again.

# CHAPTER THIRTY

**M**y brother had a nervous breakdown on a commuter plane returning to Connecticut from Boston where he'd seen *The Exorcist* ten times in one weekend. He was pushing fifty at the time, a prosperous lawyer fourteen years older than me. I was naked on a bed in a No-Tell motel room in Orlando, Florida, with a woman who was not my wife, when my first wife called from Fairfield to tell me the news.

"It's your brother," my wife said.

"He killed himself," I said. The naked woman on the bed beside me sat up, her eyes opened wide.

My wife was silent on the other end, then said, "No, it was a nervous breakdown."

"Thank God." The woman on the bed closed her eyes and exhaled.

"He thought he was God," my wife said.

"Of course."

My wife said nothing in that reproachful way of hers. It was how we'd communicated these past years. I'd say something she disapproved of and she'd fall silent. She'd give me enough time to reproach myself, then she'd speak again. Now she said, "He walked up and down the aisle raving that all the passengers were damned if they didn't repent."

"That's a flight they'll never forget."

I could see my brother raging up and down that aisle. A towering man with a horsey face and beady eyes that did not blink from the sun glinting off the silvery wings of that plane. A crazed Ahab in a gray, worsted suit off the racks of J. Press Clothiers in New Haven. He shouted and waved his arms. A stiff, unbending man capable only of breaking.

I had seen him only a few days before on the sidewalk in downtown Fairfield. He was staring up into a blinding sun, without blinking, as if defying God to strike him blind.

I said, "What the hell you doing, brother?"

Still staring at the sun, he smiled and said, "It's a good discipline, brother."

I got him to follow me to my office on the third floor of a Victorian house next to the Post Office. I had worked in an attic room in my house for years. It was a dark and silent refuge from five young children and a failing marriage. When my two oldest daughters became teenagers, I turned my attic office into a double bedroom for them. Then I took this office downtown, hoping it might inspire me to work harder, so I could save money for my daughters' college education. It didn't. All it did was become another refuge from a failed marriage, a place where I often slept after a night of drinking, and where I brought women, whose names I seldom knew. I picked them up, two or three a day, at my weightlifting gym in the morning, the beach in the afternoon, the Nautilus bar off the beach at twilight, dinner at Mario's Restaurant in Westport, Bunyan's singles' bar down the street from Mario's late at night. I had sex with them on my office floor, with a pillow for their heads and, if necessary, another pillow for their asses. Sometimes I had sex with those women as in an old Playboy cartoon. The businessman sitting in a chair at his desk, talking on his phone, his pants bunched around his ankles, glancing down at his secretary kneeling between his legs, her head bobbing up and down, her hair long or short, blonde or brunette, faceless.

I wondered what their names were, their ages, where they worked, were they married or divorced or single? Did they have children? I never asked. It didn't matter.

The following day, when I passed them on the sidewalk in Fairfield, they gave me a knowing smile. I smiled back, but I didn't know them.

I sat at my desk looking down over the street. George sat in a director's chair and stared at the yellow arrow I had painted horizontally around the wall that ended at a big, orange question mark.

"So how's it going, brother?" he asked.

"Not so hot. Money's tight."

"How's the wife holding up?" He'd known her for twenty years, but I still didn't think he knew her first name. He'd call our house. She'd answer the phone. He'd say, "Is this Patty's wife?" It never bothered her.

"The same," I said. "She's silent a lot." He nodded. I said, "I'm thinking of leaving for a while." I smiled at him. "A little sabbatical."

He shook his head. "Brother, you can't run away from life's responsibilities."

I stared out the window at the traffic below.

When I was nineteen and about to marry my wife, George summoned me to his office for what he called "a little talk, brother, about the responsibilities of marriage." He told me that sex was only for procreation, never pleasure, because then it would give women power over men. After ten years of a Jesuit education, George had learned his lessons well. "Men have to rule their families," he told me. "With that comes responsibilities. You have to make as much money as possible so your family is secure. This frees your children to find their happiness." I interrupted him. I told him I thought it was a man's job to work at something that made him happy. His happiness would permeate his family. My brother shook his head at me as if I was a child. "That's being selfish, brother," he said. "It's not a man's place in this life to be happy. It's to be responsible."

I got married when I left baseball, or rather baseball left me. Then I had children, became a high school English teacher, a newspaper reporter, and finally, my dream, I became a successful freelance writer at thirty. During those years of my twenties and early thirties, I began to formulate my own ideas of what it meant to be a man. Often, those ideas conflicted with my brother's beliefs. Now when we met for our little lunches in a diner downtown in Fairfield, I no longer just sat there, absorbing my brother's monologues. I spoke up, disagreed with him, expressed my own views. When he dismissed those views as childish, I got hot, my fatal flaw, stood up, my face flushed, "You're fucking crazy," and stormed out. He'd call me as soon as I got back home. "You can't fight me, brother," he'd say. But I did fight him, and hung up.

The last straw came in 1970, after I published my first story in *Sports Illustrated*. I was so excited that I brought the magazine to one of our little lunches to show my brother. He looked at my name, my photo in the editor's notes, the story, and then at me with a pained smile. He said, "Why do you always have to be better than me, brother?"

I was momentarily stunned. It was as if he'd revealed to me a facet of our relationship that had always burdened him, but of which I was unaware. Then I remembered one time when my brother and I were at the table in his kitchen. Mil was cooking at the stove. George and I were talking about failed dreams. My baseball career. I said, "It was a blessing in disguise, brother. I never would have become a writer if I didn't fail in baseball. It made me a better man. I woulda been a real shit if I became a baseball star." In a moment of weakness, my brother said, "My great frustration in life was I never had a talent."

Over the years, I began to realize that my brother's interest in my life had only to do with things in my life he controlled, like my baseball. It was his way of fulfilling his role that Dad had prescribed for him. The older, wiser brother making a man of the younger, immature brother, precisely up to that point, but never beyond it, at which I would become independent of him.

It was all so confusing to me. They all preached to me that I should achieve excellence. I took them at face value. But what they really meant was, "...as long as that excellence was through George." My brother coached me in baseball and I excelled. When I went off to the minor leagues on my own, I failed. Proof I could never achieve excellence without my brother's steady hand on my shoulder. Now when I'd become a successful writer without my brother's guidance, I thought they'd all be proud of me, making my own way in the world finally. But they saw my writing success as my attempt to diminish my brother. This was my mother's greatest fear when I was born.

My parents constantly referred to my brother to me as poor George, as if, like Job, his life was doomed to constant suffering.

Poor George became my brother's persona, his cross and his salvation. Suffering became George's currency. So he cultivated it. During a routine doctor's checkup X-rays revealed a growth inside his head near his ear. It was of only mild concern to his doctor. Still, George summoned all his children around him and told them he had brain cancer. They wailed in an orgy of grief. Then he vanished. Mil called me in a panic and told me what happened. "Find him, Patty!" she cried. "Please!" So I tracked my brother's disappearance to a town in Minnesota, Rochester, the home of the Mayo Clinic for cancer patients. I called the hospital, but they had no record of him as a patient. The receptionist said, "Maybe he's an outpatient staying at one of the motels near the clinic." I called every hotel near the clinic until I found him in his room. He said, "Brother, how did you find me?" I said, "I'm a fucking reporter, brother. It's my job to find people." A few days later he told me that the growth was benign and harmless.

When I was trying to be a writer in my late twenties, I affected what I thought was a writer's look. I had unkempt, long hair and I dressed in blue work shirts and jeans and cowboy boots. Ma would say, "You trying to be Hopalong *Casa Dice*, Patty?" Dad would say, "You look like a bum. Look at the way your brother dresses." I'd say, "He's a fucking lawyer, Dad." Dad would say, again, "You coulda been a lawyer in his firm if you had a brain. A partner eventually." I'd say, "Yeah, a junior partner all my life."

It was a crushing blow for Dad to see his two sons drifting apart. "After all your brother's done for you," Dad said. "He changed your diapers, for chrissakes. He tried to make a man of you."

Dad was right. My brother did try to make a man of me. But he made manhood so elusive for me. It shifted with his whims that I was never privy to. Which was the point. I would never be a man, in his eyes, and mine, as long as he kept shifting its definition.

When I was the star player on his Prep basketball team, I twisted my ankle in an important game. The refs called timeout and I limped off the court. George snapped at me, "Can't you play with a little pain? Be a man." So I returned to the court and scored twenty-three points. The next day my swollen ankle was in a cast. The doctor told George I couldn't play in the next three games. George said to me,

"See how selfish you are. You didn't think of the team. You played on a bad ankle just to score your points."

When I got fat in my early twenties, my brother told me that was a sign of moral weakness. "No discipline, brother," he said. "You can't control your appetites." George and Mil, and even their kids began calling me Uncle Pot. Then I lost the weight in my late twenties and began lifting weights. My body got lean, hard and muscular. George just shook his head in despair, "Brother, your obsession with your body is a woman's vanity."

Dad tried to shame me into a rapprochement with my brother. When he found out about my women in the 1970s, he said, "A real womanizer, eh?"

I said, "You told me to pick one, Dad. Broads, booze, or gambling. I made my choice."

"Don't be such a smartass. What if your brother found out?"

I looked at him and said, "More to the point. What if it had been George? Would you call him a womanizer?"

Dad looked truly pained, not acting now. "I could never do that to your brother," he said. "It would hurt him."

I could hear my wife's voice from a great distance in my motel room in Orlando, Florida. It got closer and closer until I could make out what she was saying. "He's in a sanitarium in Fairfield County. Where the Kennedys go to dry out."

The naked woman got off the bed and began putting on her clothes with her back to me. She bent over at the waist in a pose that reminded me of a famous statue of a naked woman, or was it a drawing? I couldn't remember who the artist was.

My wife was waiting for a response from me. When she didn't get it, she said, "Are you coming home?"

I said nothing.

She went on as if nothing had passed between us. "They're all going crazy without your brother. Your father said he's going to break him out of the sanitarium. He said you're the one who should be in a nut house."

"Naturally."

She was silent for a moment, then said, "Your mother blames his wife for everything. She said if she had a gun, she would kill her."

"Oh, Christ!"

My brother's wife, Mildred, was a sweet, uncomplicated woman. More an Old World Italian than a New. My mother felt that George married beneath himself. But then, she would have felt that no matter what woman took her son from her. I always thought George married precisely the woman he wanted to. Beautiful, compliant, domestic. The ideal wife for a padrone.

When George was nineteen, he gave Mil an engagement ring, without telling his mother. When Ma found out, she demanded he take it back. He did. That moment of thoughtless betrayal by George affected all our lives. That sealed Mil's contentious relationship with my mother until the day my mother died. Of course, it was Ma who told me this story as a lesson to me. I should learn from George how to be so devoted to my mother. But yet, in my ears, I'd always heard Dad's admonition to me, "Love is more important than blood."

The woman in my motel room was dressed, seated in a chair by the window, waiting. I heard my wife's voice again, "Mildred is hysterical. If she doesn't commit your brother, the sanitarium will have to let him out in ten days. He's still raving. He said the psychiatrist is Satan. Mildred doesn't know what to do. She calls here every day, asking, 'When's Patty coming home?'"

"What do you tell her?"

"The truth. I told her, 'I don't know, Mil. You know him better than I do.'"

"What does she expect me to do? Make it all go away?"

"She wants you to sign the papers to commit him. If she signs them your parents will claim it's her plot to get his money. Mildred said, 'Patty's the only one. They're afraid of him.'"

After I hung up the phone I got dressed, then sat and talked with the woman. When it got dark, she stood up and said, "I have to get home, make dinner for my husband."

"Of course," I said. "Thank you." She kissed me on the cheek and left.

That night I sat at a round metal table under an umbrella outside my motel room by the pool. On the table I had a bottle of bourbon, a paper cup, and a yellow legal pad and a pen. I poured myself a drink. It was a soft, warm Florida night with a full moon and a gentle breeze rustling the big fronds of the palm trees.

I wondered what the woman had cooked for her husband. She was a terrific cook, and a dutiful wife. One night after she left me, she got home before her husband returned from work. He was a nationally-known gourmet chef at a Michelin-starred restaurant. When he finally arrived home late that night, she told me the next day, "He looked exhausted, stressed. I felt so sorry for him. I made him relax in his easy chair. I brought him a stiff drink. Then I got down on my knees and took off his shoes. I massaged his feet. Then I gave him a blow job."

We had been meeting in Florida for years, two or three days at a time, maybe twice each year. We rarely left the motel room except to eat. Mostly, we just had sex, and then we talked for hours, naked on a bed. Then we had more sex.

She had a big-featured, expressive face, with a wide, lascivious mouth, wild chestnut-colored hair and a zaftig body. The first time we had sex in a motel, she lay on the bed while I took her clothes off until she was naked. She had pendulous breasts and wide hips and pregnancy stretch marks, jagged red scars across her stomach as if she had been slashed with a knife. The first time we had sex I avoided looking at those stretch marks. But only that first time. After so much sex over the years, and so much talking, I never noticed them again.

She told me once, after sex, "I hope you don't take this the wrong way. I mean, I love the sex and all. But it's the talking I'm here for." I laughed, and said, "Me, too."

When I tried to talk to my wife, she'd say to me, "Why do you have to talk and ruin everything?" This woman told me that the only thing she ever talked to her husband about at dinner "was cuts of meat." For each of us, at that time in our lives, we were the first person to whom we revealed our most intimate thoughts, and fears. She told me, without emotion, the story of her infant son. She had rushed him to a hospital when he started bleeding from his mouth. The hospital administrator wouldn't admit her son until she gave him all her health insurance information. While the woman answered questions about deductibles, coverage, etc., her son died in her arms.

When she finished that story, she was looking into my eyes. She said, "You don't have to say anything." But I felt such a fool, burdening her with my self-inflicted melodrama of family slights, innuendo, deceits in the face of her tragedy. She knew what I was thinking. She said, "Everybody suffers, Patty. It's not up to us to judge the depth of another's suffering." Then she smiled. She looked beautiful. She said, "His name is Peter."

Sitting by the pool, I began to write by the light of the moon. I wrote nonstop, eight pages, and then, exhausted, I put the pen down. I poured myself another drink.

The next morning, the woman picked me up at the motel and drove me to the airport. Before I got out of her car, she put her hand on my arm and said, "Don't worry. You'll do the right thing." I nodded. Then I handed her the eight yellow legal pages with a fax number and a name at the top. "Could you fax these for me?" I said.

She took them and said, "Of course."

I said, "I'd like them to be there before I arrive."

She smiled at me, "I'll take care of it."

# CHAPTER THIRTY-ONE

When I got back to Fairfield, I drove to my brother's colonial estate on a hill. Mildred was waiting for me outside, in front of the stable where they kept their horses. Her oldest daughter, Beth, was an equestrian. She performed at Madison Square Garden.

I waited in the car as Mildred walked toward me. She was still a beautiful woman, would always be until the day she died. Jet-black hair, vivid blue eyes, a straight Greek nose. She looked like my father's mother, Rose, might have looked. Mil had a photograph in her bedroom I had seen only once. I pointed to it and said, "Mil, why the hell do you have a photo of Ava Gardner in a silk peignoir in your bedroom?" She laughed and said, "That's me, Patty, before you knew me."

When George married Mil I was only a child, but I loved her from the first moment I met her. She was the only softness in my family. She cooked special meals for me, like pastina with butter and grated Parmesan. She did things with me. She taught me how to draw and write in script with a pen, and how to add and subtract from flash cards. She'd hold up a card, 4 + 3 =?, and say, "What's the answer, Patty?" I'd think, then blurt out, "Seven." She'd say, "Are you sure?" I'd nod. She'd say again, "You sure, Patty?" I'd say, "Yes! Yes!" She'd turn the card over to reveal a big number 7. I'd clap my hands and Mil would smile, "Good boy, Patty."

Every year, Mil made me help her decorate our Christmas tree. The lights first, then the ornaments. "Spread the ornaments out, Patty," she'd say, "and alternate the colors." Then we'd tear off pieces of cotton and put them on the branches so they looked like snow. She finished the tree off by wrapping a gauzy film of spun fiberglass around the tree, like a spider's web, so that it looked haunted and decaying, like a tree in Miss Havisham's Satis House. When the tree was finished she brought in a stepladder and steadied it while I climbed to the top step. She handed up to me an angel, with spread white wings and a golden halo, and I put it on top of the tree.

My mother and Mildred fought a war of attrition for my brother's affections, or maybe just for his attention, until the day my mother died. Their conflict was exacerbated by my brother's refusal ever to take his wife's side in an argument with his mother, no matter how egregiously unfair Ma was. Sometimes I wandered into their line of fire. Mil and Ma lobbed shells down on each other. George was the prize. I was collateral damage. It confused me when I was a child. I thought both women loved me. When I got older, I understood.

As we drove to the sanitarium, Mildred cried softly beside me. In between sobs, she said, "It's my fault, Patty. I fought him so much over your mother. He began to resent me. But he never let on. He was always just this loving husband who was never really there. The pressure must have made him snap." She turned to me, "You know how he keeps everything in, Patty! Like a stone wall around him!" I nodded. Mildred went silent.

We turned into a long, winding driveway that led to the sanitarium. Maple and oak trees shaded the drive. We passed a pond with lily pads and white swans floating by. Then past an expanse of perfectly manicured green lawn. The sanitarium was set on a small hill. It was a white colonial mansion, like my brother's house, only bigger and more recently built. My brother's house had a plaque on the front door which read, "Josiah Perry, 1688." His dark and musty dining room was paneled in scarred old mahogany. It had a six-foot, stone walk-in fireplace where Perry's women cooked their meals. Looking down on George's family eating at a circular table were two huge posters coated in resin to give them the thick texture of oil paint. They were in elaborate gilt frames. George Washington and Abe Lincoln. I used to kid my brother about those posters, and the plaque alongside his door. "The family tree, eh, bro," I would say. "Poor old Josiah, turning over in his grave, his ancestral manse now owned by a wop from The Hollow." George would give me his pained smile, "Give me a break, brother." But I wouldn't. I said, "Assuming, of course, old Josiah even knew what a wop was 300 years ago."

I parked in the sanitarium's gravel drive and told Mildred to wait in the car. She clutched my arm with a strength that stunned me.

"Patty, please! Do it for me."

"Don't worry. I'll take care of it."

She let go of my arm and said, "I'm sorry, Patty. For all those years. It wasn't you."

"I know, Mil. You didn't mean it."

"You were the only one who defended me against your mother."

I remembered a late afternoon in my twenties. We were sitting around the kitchen table at George's house, Ma, Dad, George, me. Mil stood at the stove cooking. Ma snapped at Mil for some reason, I couldn't remember what, only that it was so inconsequential. I snapped at Ma, "Give Mil a fucking break, Ma!"

George said, "Don't talk to your mother like that, brother."

I caught a glimpse of Mil, bracing herself against the stove with her two hands as if she was trying to push it away. Her eyes were closed.

"Why do you have to be like that?" Dad said to me. "We were having a good time."

"Fuck you all," I said, and stormed out. Which was the point now. My uncontrollable temper.

"Why shouldn't I defend you?" I said to Mil in the car. "You're my sister." We had an unspoken bond all those years, like twins, who were both on the periphery of a tightly knit family.

As a child and young boy I drew pictures to please Mil. I practiced writing in script like she had taught me. When I showed her in private what I had done, she would kiss my cheek and say, "You're a good boy, Patty." But when I showed her what I had done in front of my mother, Mil would laugh at me and say, "That's what girls do, Patty, practice their penmanship." This infuriated my mother, for whom manliness was paramount in her sons. My mother always thought I was the less manly son. My obvious love for Mildred was, for my mother, a sign of my weakness. I did feminine things with Mil, drawing pictures and decorating a Christmas tree. Worse, even, my affection for Mil was a kind of betrayal of my mother. Ma felt that, like George, I had to choose between her and Mil, and that, unlike my brother, I had made the wrong choice.

"You understood then?" Mil said to me in the car. I nodded. She shuddered, then began to cry, her beautiful face ugly now. I waited until she stopped. Then I got out of the car.

I went inside to see my brother. The psychiatrist was sitting in his office behind his desk. He was a spectrally thin man with taut skin over a skeletal face. He had a Mephistophelean beard. My brother was never that far off in his perceptions.

"You're the half-brother," he said.

"I'm his brother."

He held up the eight yellow legal sheets I had written. "You wrote this?" I nodded. "Then why didn't you tell all this to your brother, and your parents?"

"I tried. They'd say, 'Why are you jealous of your brother? You're the crazy one.'" I shrugged. "I was the younger brother. Much younger. I came late in their lives. They were already settled by then."

He nodded. "I understand. It's a shame. You could have saved them all heartache."

In those eight pages, I had written to the shrink how my parents had spent their lives praising George for his brilliance, his talent, his saintliness, his manliness. They did this because they knew my brother was a limited man and they wanted to give him confidence. He was smart enough to know what they were doing and why. This put a terrible burden on him. To fulfill their false expectations of him, while knowing, in his heart of hearts, it was all a lie. He knew himself. He had wanted to be a fishmonger.

Since my brother couldn't be the man of his parents' expectations, he could at least present to them the façade of that man – the loving son, dutiful brother, caring father, faithful husband, brilliant lawyer, and compassionate and moral man. His false life finally overwhelmed him on that airplane, and he broke.

The shrink put on his reading glasses and scanned my yellow sheets as if looking for something. Finally, he looked up at me, took off his glasses, and said, "Why didn't you mention his women in this?"

I said, "What women?"

"You didn't know?"

"Know what?"

"Your brother had mistresses for years."

"How do you know that?"

"When your brother was in the hospital, he was raving. He told your parents, his children, and his wife, that he'd had affairs for years." The shrink shook his head in his attempt to express sadness. "He must have been obsessed with guilt. His defenses were gone. So to expiate his guilt he told everyone what he'd been hiding for years."

He put the yellow legal sheets down, cleared his throat, and assumed his authoritative voice now. He picked up some official looking pages with a Connecticut State seal on top of the first page. "Your brother's wife told me you would sign these papers." He handed them to me. I scanned them quickly.

"We can only keep him ten days against his will," he said, "unless a family member signs him in. No one in your family will sign these papers. We can hold him for three months. It's my recommendation that he needs extensive therapy. He can't be let loose in society. He's a danger to himself, and maybe others, too." I said nothing. He said, "Do you understand?"

"Yes. But I'd like to see my brother before I sign anything." He looked at me with the annoyance of a professional when crossed by a layman.

"If you insist. But be prepared for a shock. He's not the brother you knew."

He led me down a narrow hallway through a house in need of repair. It had that weathered look of WASP great houses whose descendants had fallen on hard times. He ushered me into a room with original, eighteen-inch-wide wood floorboards partially covered over with curling up, cheap linoleum. He stayed at the door, and said, "It's better if he doesn't see me." He closed the door behind me. The room was completely bare. No plants, no pictures on the walls, no lamps, no chairs, nothing a patient could use to hurt himself, or others.

The psychiatrist was wrong. When my brother entered the room I did know him. That long, tragic face, the Gant button-down shirt, gray slacks, and wingtip cordovans. George was holding up his pants with one hand because he had no belt, or shoelaces. He moved slowly toward me as if in a dream, or as if sedated. His eyes were glazed over and his face diffused with an ethereal smile. He held out his arms wide as if to embrace me, or be crucified. His pants began to slide off his hips. He grabbed them with one hand, then hugged me with his free arm.

"Brother," he said. I smelled his stale smell I remembered from my childhood when I slept with him in his bed.

I began to cry into the crook of his neck. He gripped my shoulder with a superhuman strength and held me at arm's length. "Why are you crying, brother?" he said. "There's nothing wrong."

I forced myself to stop crying. "I love you, brother," I said.

He smiled his ethereal smile, and said, "Yes, that's always been the problem, hasn't it, brother?"

We didn't say anything for a few minutes. Finally, George spoke. "Why have you come here, brother? Mil told me you flew up from Florida especially to see me. You didn't have to do that. You can see me anytime."

"I know. I just thought maybe you'd want to see me..."

"I always want to see my brother." Then he wasn't smiling anymore. He said, "What did Mil tell you?" I didn't say anything. "That I wasn't myself?" I nodded. "But brother, now I am finally myself, don't you see?"

"Yes."

"So, brother...have you made up your mind?" I looked at him as if confused. He said, "Are you going to sign the papers, brother? Keep your brother locked up in this place for months?"

Before I could answer, two men in white coats came for my brother. They stood on either side of him, each of them holding him by his elbow, and led him out of the bare room into the sanitarium. I walked back down the narrow hallway to the psychiatrist's office. He was waiting for me behind his desk. He looked up and said, "I told you." He pushed the papers for me to sign across his desk.

I looked at the papers. I saw in my mind's eye, my brother, my father, myself, in our delicate house of cards I could blow over with the faintest of breaths. "Your relationship was sick," I had told my father. But now I understood it all, their common bond. Both men rejected by their fathers. My father was determined that George would never feel the emptiness he had felt, alone, unwanted, diminished. So what if their relationship was at my expense? I was supposed to understand this. A man would. These two men loved me. Despite everything. What I had felt all those years was nothing but the self-pity of a self-absorbed, pampered child who had never realized how blessed he was to have, not one, but two fathers.

I heard the shrink's voice again. "He's not the brother you knew." He held up the papers for me to sign.

"Yes, he is," I said. And then I left.

# CHAPTER THIRTY-TWO

After his breakdown, my brother was never the same again. When he returned to his home from the sanitarium he retreated into the bosom of his family. He rebuilt a wall around himself, and his wife, children, grandchildren, Ma, Dad. If he could no longer control the outside world, at least he could control all the people in his immediate world. So, he reaffirmed his marriage vows to his wife in a private Catholic ceremony performed by a priest. Only he and his wife and his kids and Ma and Dad were invited.

Now, my brother sat for hours at his circular kitchen table while his family waited on him. The potentate of a diminished kingdom. After a long journey, and many glorious battles. "It little profits that an idle king, / By this still hearth, among these barren crags, / Match'd with an aged wife." But my brother, unlike Ulysses, no longer lusted after his days of glorious battles. He was content now by that still hearth with his aged wife. His family hovered over him. They acquiesced to his whims out of fear. If they crossed him, they could be responsible for pushing him over the edge of sanity again. It was painful to watch, at least for me. The self-assured, strong-willed brother I knew, my rock, the dispenser of unassailable truths that were never unassailable, was now reduced to being a hectoring dictator over the minuscule.

"Mil, not too much garlic in the sauce," he'd say. Mil, stirring the sauce at the stove, would say, "Yes, George." Then he would say, "The last time you put in too much garlic, Mil." Mil would say, "Yes, George." George would reply, "You know I don't like too much garlic in the sauce." Mil closed her eyes.

When his four daughters fluttered over him like guinea hens, he smothered them with effusive compliments. How beautiful this one or that one was. He'd turn to me and say, "Isn't she gorgeous, brother?" I'd smile at one of my attractive nieces, and say, "Of course, she is." Even I was complicit.

Which was why I didn't visit my brother as much as I used to when I was a boy and on into my early thirties. In those days his house was always filled with life. His kids, his assistant coaches and the Jesuit teachers at The Prep, where he coached basketball, and later his coaches and Jesuits at Fairfield University, where he'd become the basketball coach.

The dining room table would be crowded with all those people. They talked about basketball, Catholic theology, philosophy, books, movies, plays, Marilyn Monroe, Sophia Loren, Saul Bellow, Hemingway, Mailer, *Catcher in the Rye*, Studs Lonigan, Saroyan, and the weakness of the Catholic social activism of the Berrigan Brothers. All the while Mil hustled back and forth from the kitchen to the dining room, serving ten and twelve people an eight-course gourmet Italian dinner.

George sat at the head of the table, listening, the padrone, while everyone ate and talked. One of the Jesuits directed a question to him, "What do you think, coach?" Faces looked up, turned toward George. George spoke. The table went silent. George finished, "Which is why ultimately Hemingway is an amoral writer." The Jesuits nodded in rispetto. And why not? It was a small price to pay for those mick priests, as fat and pink as pigs, to have such a sumptuous Italian meal. Delicate foods and expensive wines they never knew existed back in the Old Sod of Guinness Stout and boiled potatoes and soda bread as hard and tasteless as a plank of wood. In front of their greedy eyes was now a feast of *bruschetta, prosciutto e melone, pasta e fagioli, bistecca* Florentine, Asiago and *pesca,* Baba rum and tiramisu. Limoncello. So they stuffed their fat faces and condescended to the homely wop at the head of the table who fancied himself an Old World padrone. The Pope of his personal realm.

So why did I go in those days? I went because I hated those mick priests who used my brother and Mil. My anger was a kind of fuel. I waited for those mick priests to direct a question toward me, the younger brother dressed like a 1960s radical, a wop Weatherman who wanted to blow it all up. And in a way, they were right. I did. They just didn't know that the it was them. The least they could do for their host was to draw his sullen kid brother into a discussion. "And what about you, Pat? You're some kind of writer, aren't you?" My brother would see a look in my eyes. He'd shake his head, no. "Who's your favorite author?" one obviously gay priest said. "... Mickey Spillane?" I smiled, an idiot's grin, "Yeah, he is Father, actually. You ever seen one of his books? The sexy blondes on the covers are all versions of his wife." I looked at him. "She's really hot. If that's your taste...Father."

"More wine?" George asked.

After his breakdown, my brother's house turned silent. All were banished except his family. Which didn't always include me. The coaches and priests were gone. The sumptuous meals. The discussions of Catholic theology and philosophy. God, too. Banished because He had betrayed my brother, and so my brother betrayed Him right back. "There is no God, brother," he told me. "There's only man."

George went from being a dogmatic Roman Catholic moralist to a relativist Humanist. Mankind was his God now. The poor, the oppressed, the downtrodden. He picked up filthy vagabonds hitchhiking along the side of the road and brought them back to his house. He had Mil feed them. Then he gave them money.

Every certitude he'd ever preached to me was turned on its head. The achievement of excellence was now the greatest sin because it came at the expense of the downtrodden. Money was the root of all evil. So give it away. Well, yes, but in sawbucks, not G-notes. "That's all this country is about," my brother told me now, driving in his new Mercedes-Benz. "The pursuit of money. I *hate* this country." It was the temper tantrum of a child the first time he had been denied.

One year his daughters arranged a surprise wedding anniversary party for George and Mil. They didn't send me an invitation. When I found out about it, after the fact, I called Beth, furious. "How could you forget me?" I snapped.

Beth said, "It was only for the immediate family, Uncle Pat." She had a point.

The only enthusiasm George showed now was when he was talking about his grandson, Tony, Beth's son. Tony was a handsome boy, like a male model, and a high school baseball player of some talent. He was a light-hitting infielder for average, but with long ball power. He would eventually earn a baseball scholarship to Stanford, and then sign with the Dodgers, where he played for 10 years in their minor league system, and after that, two years in an independent league. Tony never had money worries since his father, Harley, was a multimillionaire businessman. "The Window King of Omaha," Dad told me. Harley had his own Learjet so he and Beth could fly to wherever Tony was playing in the minors during the summer.

One afternoon, at the kitchen table, George was regaling me with his grandson's baseball successes in high school. I said, "Why don't I work with him a little, brother? Pitch him some batting practice. I might be able to help him identify different pitches as they leave a pitcher's hand." George said, "That's not necessary, brother. I'm coaching him."

One day I took George and Tony to a Yankee game in the Bronx. At that time, the Yankees were managed by my old minor league catcher, Joe Torre. Before the game I brought Tony and George to the railing behind home plate to introduce them to Torre. Joe shook their hands. Then he said to Tony, "Your uncle here could throw bullets, you know."

As my brother's life shriveled, after his breakdown, mine blossomed a bit. I acquired a small renown as a writer. In the early 1970s I wrote a well-received memoir about my baseball failure. I gave it to George to read since he told me he'd never understood what had happened to me as a pitcher once I left home. "You'll find out in the book, bro," I said. When he finished reading it, he showed me where he had underlined passages in red ink. "Places where you got it wrong," he said.

One day, George called to ask me to help him carry a wingchair up a stairway to the second-floor guest bedroom. It was a big chair and a narrow doorway. We struggled with it, turning it this way and that, but it wouldn't fit through the doorway. Finally, I got a ruler and measured the doorway, thirty-three inches wide, and the chair's width, thirty-six inches. I said, "No way, brother," and went home. A few hours later, George called, "I got it up the stairway, brother. You quit too soon."

"Impossible! How'd you do it?"

"I cut the legs off."

I remember one afternoon when I visited my brother, shortly before I moved to Florida. I knew I might not see him much anymore, so I increased my visits to him before I left his life. When I walked through the kitchen door, the house was in an uproar. Mil was sweating at the kitchen stove over a variety of pots while her four daughters were chopping and dicing behind her. George would stick his head into the kitchen to check on their progress and then go back to the dining room where he was setting the table with their best china, Waterford crystal, and silverware. I went into the dining room to help him.

"I told you never to fuss over me, brother," I said. He didn't smile. "Who's the guest of honor, Tony?" He ignored me.

"I don't have time, brother," he said. "He'll be here in a little while."

"Who?"

"My father."

"What? Is it Dad's birthday?"

Finally, he looked up at me. "George Senior is coming."

His natural father had ignored my brother all his life, except for this one day when he condescended to visit his son along with his young wife and George's two half-sisters. My brother was determined to show them all how successful he was, like his father, a wealthy man, with a loving family, and the old manse on a hill.

When Dad found out from George about that visit of a man he detested all his adult life, he told me a few days later that he said nothing to George. But I saw the look on Dad's face. The only time I remember that his son ever hurt Dad's feelings.

George Senior arrived with his family amid much fanfare, as if The Pope had come to give the peasants a blessing. The women went inside while George walked his father around his property. He showed his father his barns, the horses, his BMW 7 Series and

Mil's Mercedes-Benz convertible with the "Milly II" license plate, his abandoned granary, tennis courts, a small lake, and then back to the manse. His father and wife and his half-sisters ate a quick meal and then left, never to return.

My brother's father and my mother were married in Stamford, Connecticut, in 1927, and divorced in 1932. My mother was twenty-six, and George Senior was thirty. He then abandoned my mother and his three-year-old son and fled to Eastover, Massachusetts, in the Berkshires to make his new life. According to a book written about George Senior (*George Bisacca, His Life, His Way*, by Steve Crowe), he found his inspiration for that new life when he visited a resort called Ted Hilton's. He had gone to Hilton's resort at the urging of a friend who wanted a respite from his wife and nine children. His friend told his wife that he and George were going fishing. "I played ball with him" in deceiving his friend's wife, said George Senior. However, George Senior's understanding, young second wife, Ruth, "gave me a three-day reprieve" to party at that resort. (I can't imagine my fierce mother would have been so understanding.) George Senior spent that reprieve at Ted Hilton's dancing the nights away "with the prettiest Southern girls," according to that book. He told his friend, "This is the business I want to get into!" So he opened a dude ranch with the money he'd received from his sale of a number of gas stations he'd owned in the Stamford area before his divorce from my mother. (When his biographer asked him about that divorce, George Senior said only, "We were young.")

George Senior called his new venture Eastover. He said he didn't court "the moneyed crowd from New York, Boston, and Philadelphia," but rather young, working-class men and women he referred to as "a young swinging group." At first, however, there were always more young women than men at Eastover. So he handed out free passes to single men who would entertain the secretaries and school teachers and hair dressers and shop girls yearning for romance, or, at least, sex. His advertising brochures from those days showed a photo of a beautiful young woman in a bathing suit staring up into the eyes of a handsome young man in a skimpy bathing suit, his bare chest rippling with muscles. Eastover's brochures promised, "Around-the-Clock Fun. Frolic. Gaiety. Recreation. Romance." A *Saturday Evening Post* article extolling Eastover was titled "Working Girls on a Frolic." George Sr. admitted that he, too, was not "immune to flirtation," and that it was a temptation for him not to "get infatuated - especially when you're married - with too many girls."

It was understandable why so many girls would become infatuated with George Sr. He had the easy smile of a man confident in his charm. And unlike his son, George Sr. was a handsome man, with thick, wavy, black hair, and a tanned, fit body, more Cary Grant than Walter Matthau.

It was never explained to me (one of the many things my family never explained to me about their past) why George Sr. decided to visit his son that one time, with his family. It was just a thing that happened. There was no point that made sense to me. It was not the first of many such meetings so that his father could forge a relationship with his son. It was the first, and last of such meetings. Maybe George Sr. and his family were just passing through on their way to New York City. My brother's old colonial house served as a convenient way station, one of those Revolutionary War colonial inns that serviced stagecoach passengers and Pony Express riders on their long journeys. A warm fire, a pipe, some grog, and a bit of rest. Then refreshed, a few glasses of Madeira, or rum, and a slab of beef delivered to their table by a saucy serving wench. Then they were off again with a running leap onto their ponies and the thunder of hooves on their way to protest the Stamp Act in New York City in 1765.

Or maybe they were just going to see *My Fair Lady* on Broadway, and didn't want to pay for lunch in New York City.

I once asked Dad why he never legally adopted George and changed his last name to Jordan. He said, "I have nothing to leave George. His father's a millionaire many times over." Dad thought that before George Sr. died, he would be forced to acknowledge his namesake in his will, and leave his son an inheritance, no matter how little, to give my brother some peace of mind. But his father didn't.

# CHAPTER THIRTY-THREE

In the early summer of 1979, I went to Fairfield beach one afternoon, as I often did. I walked through the hot sand, past a woman
in an orange two-piece bathing suit, lying on her stomach on a
beach towel. She was reading a book. When I got to the rocky
jetty that led out into the water, I hopped from rock to rock until
I reached the last rock a few hundred yards from the beach. I put
my towel on the flat rock and sat down, facing the beach. The sand
was crowded with sunbathers, but I was able to pick out the woman
in the orange suit because she was lying apart from the others. She
was still lying in the sand a few hours later when I left the jetty and
walked past her on my way to the Nautilus bar.

She was there on the beach, reading, every afternoon for the
next four days. I glanced at her as I walked past her. One day, I noticed she had long, black hair. The next day, I noticed she had the
three-dimensional blue eyes of a startled child. On the third day, I
noticed she had the furrowed black brows of someone contemplating insoluble problems in her life. On the fourth day, I noticed that
her old bathing suit was too big for her. Her breasts were shriveled
in her bra, and the skin on her arms and legs was slack as if she had
lost a great deal of weight too quickly. I continued past her onto the
rocks, and sat on the last rock from the beach. Every so often she
would look up from her book and catch me staring at her. She stared
back at me for a few minutes, then went back to her book.

On the fourth day, leaving the beach, I stopped in front of her.
She looked up at me and shaded her eyes from the sun behind me
with the flat of her hand. She had the lined face of a once beautiful
woman, now just attractive for her age, past fifty. But she wasn't past
fifty. I could tell. She was barely forty, worn out.

"Do you read every day?" I asked.

She said, "Yes. I like to read. It's a comforting escape. Don't you like to read?"

"No. I have other escapes. What are you reading?" She held up the cover of her paperback book, *The Complete Plays of Tennessee Williams.* I said, "Are you an actress?"

"I used to be." She seemed embarrassed to admit this. "But I'm a teacher now, at a boarding school. Theater arts." She paused, as if she'd caught herself in a lie. "Actually, I'm still a casting director in New York. But I'll be a teacher in September." She waited for me to say something. When I didn't, she said, "What do you do?"

"I used to be a baseball player."

"That must be like acting. Performing in front of an audience."

"Not really. I never had a script. The outcome was always in doubt."

"Well, plays are like that. Every night is a different performance. You find a new nuance every night."

"I missed a lot of nuances in my career."

"What did you do after baseball?"

I shrugged. "I was a teacher for five years. An All-Girls Catholic high school. Teeny boppers and nuns."

"That must have been challenging after baseball."

"In a way. I was only twenty-three when I started. The girls were, seventeen, eighteen. Lots of temptations."

"Did you succumb...to the temptations?"

"No. I never did. I thought it was unfair. They were only kids."

She smiled at me. "Well, good for you."

"I made up for it." She looked embarrassed. I wasn't sure if it was for herself, or for me.

She changed the subject. "What do you do now?"

"I'm a writer. Magazines. Some books."

"And you don't read?"

"When you're not on stage, are you still acting?"

She smiled. "I see what you mean. Might I have read any of your books?"

I laughed. "You mightn't have. Nobody much buys my books." I was getting bored talking about myself. "Listen, why don't you meet me on the rocks tomorrow?" I smiled. "A different escape for a change."

She looked at me with her startled blue eyes. "Oh, I don't think so. I have my reading. But thank you anyway."

"No problem." I walked off toward the Nautilus. Just before I left the beach, I looked back. She was reading again.

The next afternoon, she wasn't lying on the sand. I walked out to the end of the jetty and sat down. A few minutes later, I saw her walk onto the sand. She looked around like a mother searching for a lost child. When she saw me far out on the rocks she hurried across the sand, stepped onto the rocks and walked quickly toward me. She had long legs and a slim-hipped body. Then she began to walk faster, hopping from rock to rock. She jogged over the last few rocks until she stood before me, smiling, a little breathless. She looked younger, prettier, with makeup.

"I was afraid you might not be here," she said.

"When I didn't see you today, I thought I'd scared you off the beach."

"Maybe a little. I was going to read at home. But then, I just found myself rushing over here."

"Why did you change your mind?"

She looked at me, and said, "I didn't have a reason not to."

"Most people change their minds only when they have a good reason to."

"I know. I tried to think of a good reason, but I couldn't."

I smiled at her. "Good for you."

She smiled at me. "Did I make a mistake?"

"Maybe. Maybe not."

She sat down beside me, this young-old woman. We began to talk. We talked for hours, until the sun began to set, and the tide began to come in, washing over the rocks, splashing us in cold sea water. We didn't even notice the water rats scampering past us toward shore, single file, like a routed army, until we stood up to leave in the cold twilight. She shivered and hugged herself. I wrapped my towel around her shoulders and rubbed her back dry. Then we walked off the rocks toward the deserted beach.

We met the next day on the rocks, and the next, and for days after that, for the rest of the summer. We never brought a picnic basket with sandwiches, fruit, cheese, wine, or a portable radio to listen to music, or a book to read, or anything that would interfere with our talking. When it got cold and dark, we left the beach and went to the Nautilus Bar. We warmed ourselves with bourbon neat for me and vodka rocks for her. We talked for another two hours until she had to go back to her father's house, where she was living for the summer.

"He expects me for dinner," she said that first night.

"Of course," I said. I watched her leave the bar and walk up the street to her father's house. When she passed under a streetlight, I saw she had a small, high ass in her baggy bathing suit. Then she was gone. I drove to Mario's for dinner, and then to Bunyan's Bar, which was always crowded with women. I had a drink, then left.

What did we talk about all those hours, days, weeks, for two months? Everything. Books, plays, movies, actors, writers, at first, and then finally our lost dreams. Her acting career, my baseball career, our unhappy marriages, ungrateful children, her four, my five, her cold, Germanic father, my parents and my brother, her beloved mother, so fragile. "My divorce killed her," she said. "She got cancer. It was my fault."

"Then you shoulda stayed married," I said.

She looked at me, her face red. "I couldn't. It would have killed me."

"You can escape your husband or your wife," I said. "Your siblings, too. Even your kids. But never your parents." She nodded, fighting back tears.

Finally, she told me that her marriage was loveless, her husband aloof, distant, uninterested in sex with her. "Except that first time before we were married," she said. "I got pregnant the first time I ever had sex. He felt obligated to marry me. We were married for seventeen years. He never talked."

"You don't talk, you die."

"Yes. Sam Shepard was right."

"People think they want someone to love them. Not true. They want someone to know them." She nodded. I said, "Except for your ex-husband and my wife. They should have got married. A silent marriage made in Heaven, or wherever."

"But I don't know your wife."

"Neither do I."

When she left her husband, fled was the word she used, she left her four children with him. For the first few years after her divorce, she lived with theater friends in big, old, dilapidated colonial houses in small towns north of Fairfield. "Like communes," she said, "until I got a job as a casting director in New York City. I thought I'd make enough money in a few years to get my children back." She was paid $6000 a year, not even enough to survive in the many sublets she moved to from year to year. So she made a few TV commercials, French's Mustard, Hills Brothers coffee, that helped sustain her in the city. She flashed me her 8x10 glossy smile, and said, "The face that launched a thousand coffee cups."

I faked a shudder. "Brrr! I hope you never smile at me like that."

"It paid the rent," she said.

She met men in New York, a doctor, a businessman, an actor, a famous TV critic on CBS. The doctor offered to give her a face lift, if she slept with him. The businessman took her to his company's volleyball picnic on the beach where he knocked her, face down, into the sand in the heat of the action. The actor was gay. The TV critic was a handsome, distinguished-looking man with silver hair. She got two free passes from a TV commercial director one night for a performance of *The Taming of the Shrew* in Shakespeare in the Park in Central Park. She invited the TV critic. When she led him up the bleachers toward the top row, far from the stage, he stopped in a panic, and said, "I can't be seen up here! I have a reputation!" He fled, leaving her standing in the aisle.

"So what did you do?" I asked.

"Watched the play." She smiled at me. "I've never really had much luck with men...less even with sex."

"Your luck could change."

"I'm not sure I want it to, now." Then she said, "What about you?"

I knew what she meant. So I told her about the women I didn't know, except sexually, so many of them.

"What were you looking for?" she asked.

"Sex, I guess."

"Come on! Really?"

"OK. Escape then."

"Did they help you escape?"

"For a few minutes. Maybe I should have taken up reading."

"Didn't you find even one woman you wanted to know?" I told her about the woman in Florida whose baby died in her arms. "I knew her," I said.

She said, "Then why didn't you pursue a relationship with her?"

"We were separated by too much distance," I said. "I never gave it a chance. I don't think I wanted to. So I defined it as just sex. I preferred guilt rather than happiness."

"I know," she said. "It can be very comforting, guilt."

A few nights a week we went to the movies, or to dinner at Mario's. One August night we were at the movies when an actor on screen said a word she didn't know. She blurted out, "What does it mean, twat?" People around us stared at her. She wasn't even blushing. I told her what twat meant. She looked at me and said, "No! Really?"

"Would I lie to you?"

"OK. Then what's its etymology? I mean, can I find twat in the Oxford Dictionary?"

I laughed out loud, while on screen someone was being murdered. "I don't know," I said. "That's one place where I never looked for twat." Then I looked at her, and said, "Ya know, you're a funny broad." People sitting around us were staring at us.

"But I'm not trying to be funny."

"I know. That's what's so funny."

Then she said, "No man ever called me a broad before."

"You don't like it?"

"It's not that. It's just that I never thought of myself as a broad. I never had the hips. Or the big fanny."

I laughed again. "Fanny? You're kidding?"

"I'm glad I make you laugh," she said, "even if I'm not sure why." Then she smiled. "But I think it might be fun to be a broad, just once.

Like a femme fatale in a film noir." She tried to give me a sultry look, but it didn't work.

"Maybe you need a cigarette dangling from your lips."

"Yes, that would work. A prop always helped me get in character on stage." She gave me another sultry look that did work, and said, "Maybe you should start calling me Baby. Isn't that what the men in film noirs call their femme fatales?"

"Yeah, Baby." We both laughed so loud that now people around us hissed at us. So we got up and left the theater. We went to Mario's for dinner, where we could talk until the waiters started eyeballing us. "I think they need the table, Baby," I said. We went outside into the night. We felt the whoosh of hot air as the last commuter train roared past us. When it was gone, I said, "Want to stop for a drink? I know this place."

"Of course." So I took her to Bunyan's. She looked around at all the predatory women and said, "I've never been to such a place. So many...broads. Is it easy to pick up a broad here?"

"For me, it is."

We sat at the bar and I ordered our drinks. Finally she said, "Why did you take me here?"

"I wanted you to see it."

She nodded. "No secrets."

"No secrets."

Late that night I drove her back to her car in the parking lot below my third-floor office downtown. I parked alongside her beat-up, old Pinto and we talked a few minutes, the engine idling. I waited for her to get out of my car. But she didn't. She put her hand on my forearm and said, "It's about time, don't you think?"

"You sure?"

"Oh, I'm positive."

We went up to my office and had sex. But it was different. I knew her name, her face, her.

She came with a gasp and a wide-eyed look of wonder on her face. Then she laughed like a girl. "Oh, that was fun!" When she stopped laughing, she said, "It's been a long time...you could probably tell...I'm not very experienced."

"Experience is overrated. Enthusiasm is better."

She sat up. "Oh, my God! Was I too enthusiastic?"

"No such thing."

She was quiet for a moment. Then she said, "It's been two months... Why did you wait so long?"

"I didn't want to ruin it."

"Do you think we ruined it?"

"What do you think?"

"You didn't ruin it for me." Then she looked embarrassed. She said, "I'm just afraid I'm not sexual enough for you."

"You really don't know yourself, do you?"

"Well, maybe you could teach me."

"I could teach you things, if you want."

"I'd like that... Maybe I could teach you some things, too." And she did.

# PART THREE

# CHAPTER THIRTY-FOUR

I married my second wife, Susan Ryan, in a bar in Ft. Lauderdale, Florida, on December 24, 1984. Our wedding was officiated by a drunken Justice of the Peace, a rangy, red-faced, female Florida cracker. She was an older version of those tattooed, redneck girls sitting on an ice chest in front of a 7-11, swinging their dirty, bare feet. One of the waiters was my best man. Susan's bridesmaid was the barmaid. We had no friends that first year in Florida, after we'd fled our past lives. We lived in a tiny, two-room apartment on a canal off the Intracoastal Waterway. No one from our past lives knew about our marriage, except Barbara.

Barbara was the naked woman on the bed in that Florida No-Tell Motel when my now ex-wife had called to tell me that my brother had had a nervous breakdown. That was the last time I had seen Barbara, although we'd kept in touch over the years with long-distance telephone calls. Susan knew all about Barbara. I told Susan that Barbara had finally divorced her chef husband and remarried a younger man who scammed her out of her divorce settlement, then left her. I had told Barbara about my relationship with Susan, contentious as it was at times. "It's hard for her," I said, "being the mistress of a married man with five kids, no money, and guilt." Finally, I told Barbara I had moved to Ft. Lauderdale with Susan after my divorce.

"I'm happy for you both," Barbara said.

Eight years after the last time I'd seen Barbara, Susan and I got married in Ft. Lauderdale. I called Barbara and told her the news. She was on a business trip in Miami. "I'd love to see you again," Barbara said. "Would Susan mind if I came for a visit?"

"Mind?" I asked. "She's heard so much about you, she'd love to meet you."

The next day Barbara parked her big Cadillac in front of our small complex and came to our front door with a wedding present. She looked the same, with her beautiful face and zaftig body. I looked older, with my salt-and-pepper beard and graying hair.

Barbara came into our apartment with her gift wrapped in gold paper with a big red bow. When she gave it to Susan, Susan hugged her. She kissed Barbara on the cheek and said, "I've always wanted to meet you."

"But, why?" Barbara said.

"To thank you," Susan said. Barbara looked confused. Susan smiled at her, and said, "For taking care of Patty before I knew him. He was so unhappy in those years, except for those times he was with you."

Barbara said, "It went both ways, Susan."

There was a card taped to the present. Before Susan opened the present, she read the card. It was just a long, thin book marker with a cartoonish painting of flowers with smiling human faces. On it, Barbara had written, "Do that which makes you happy. It's a wonderful life. To Susan and Pat. From: Barbara."

It wasn't until a few years after our marriage that I told my mother that her youngest son had married an Irisher in Florida. My mother had met Susan only that one time when we had gone to my parents' apartment in Bridgeport.

"I remember her," my mother said. Then nothing.

The next morning, I picked up the ringing phone. My mother's voice said, "Patty, Dad and I are coming to Florida to visit you...and your Irish wife."

"But, Ma, I have to..."

"Pick us up at the airport tomorrow morning." Click, buzz...

I told Susan. Her face went white. "Did she sound angry we didn't tell her?"

"You kidding? She always sounds angry."

"But we only have one bed!"

"I'll get them a hotel room."

"No. That's not right. We'll give them our bed. We'll sleep on the chaise lounges on the deck."

"With the possums, raccoons, and water rats?"

"Yes!"

So, the next morning, Susan, forty-six, and I, forty-four, drove to the airport to pick up my mother, eighty, and my father, seventy-six, for their five-day Inquisition.

Susan said, "Your poor mother. She must be wracked with guilt." I looked across at her. "I mean, where did she go wrong? Her youngest son marries an Irish girl. What *umilliazione!*" Susan and I had spent the last four summers in Florence, where she became almost fluent in a cultured Florentine accent. As an actress, one of her talents was for languages.

"Not to scare you," I said, "but it must be serious. Ma hates to fly. Especially to a godforsaken place like Florida. She thinks it's a foreign country of Yentas, white trash, spics, and no Italians."

Susie recognized my mother as soon as she got through the tunnel to the gate. "I told you," she said. My mother was wearing her mink coat that Dad had bought her for Christmas.

"It's 84 degrees," I said. "How did you know?"

"A woman can always find an excuse to wear her mink."

They came toward us. An old couple I hadn't seen in four years. They looked timid to me, now, and small. Hesitant. No longer the fierce Italian parents who raised me.

My father wore his fedora and navy blazer with brass buttons. My mother held his arm tightly. Her other hand held a big paper bag filled with long rounds of Genoa salami and Italian bread that stuck out of the bag like baseball bats. I knew what she had in the bottom of that bag. Parmesan and Pecorino cheese, roasted sweet red peppers in olive oil, and God knew what else.

Dad came up to me and kissed me on the cheek like he and my brother and I have always kissed each other. "My Patty," he said. He smelled musty, like an old man. Then he smiled at Susan and said, "How's my beautiful daughter-in-law?" Before she could answer, he kissed her on the cheek. My mother looked up and glared at Dad. Then she gave Susan her thin smile.

Susan smiled at her and said, "It's wonderful to see you again, Mother."

"Yes."

"Can I help you with your bags, Mother?"

"No. I can manage."

As we walked toward the exit, I heard Susie gushing over Ma's mink coat. Ma pulled it tight to her and said, "It was so cold on the plane." Susie glanced at me.

Ma and Dad settled into the back seat of our small, old Alfa Romeo sedan. Dad said, "It's cramped. Why don't you get a Lincoln like your brother?"

"I'm not a rich lawyer, Dad." I remembered the day I told Dad I wanted to be a writer. I was twenty-three, just graduated from college. He said, "Writer? That's not a man's job."

"You could have been a lawyer," Dad said from the backseat. "I told you to go to law school like your brother. You would have been a partner in his firm by now." I never told Dad what George had told me about the law. "It's just pushing papers, brother. The money's the only satisfaction. Be a writer if it's your dream." I asked my brother what his dream had been. He said, "I can't remember." I said, "Then why did you become a lawyer?" He shrugged, gave me a weak smile, "Dad."

I glanced at Dad through the rearview mirror, and said, "I would always have been the junior partner, Dad." He shook his head.

"You could have been a *professore*, too, at an Ivy League college, like Darthmuth."

"Your alma mater?"

Susan put her hand on my arm. She said, "Are you comfortable back there, Mother?"

Ma said, "I'm fine."

"It's an Italian car, you know, Mother." I looked across at Susan.

Ma said, "It's a pretty red."

"It has rust on it," Dad said. "I thought you said your writing was going good. Is this all you can afford?"

"We're doing OK," I said. "It's not expensive to live here. Not like Connecticut."

"Connecticut is exclusive," Dad said.

"Too exclusive for us, pop," I said.

"Patty has a story in *Playboy* this month, Dad," Susan said.

"Naked women?" Dad asked. "Who will even read it with all those pictures?"

Before I could answer, we were caught in bumper-to-bumper traffic. Tourists heading to the beach. Construction all around us, the sounds of jackhammers. I turned on the air conditioning. Ma made a production of shivering. "Oh, no, Patty. It's too cold." I shut it off and opened my window. A gust of hot air blew in. Dust swirled in the heat. I inched the car along and stopped at a red light. One of the hookers who worked Federal Highway came up to my window. She leaned over, flashing her tits in a tube top, and smiled.

"Wanna party, hon?" she asked.

I gave her a head fake toward the backseat. "You got a group rate, sweetheart?"

She stuck her head through the window and looked back at my small parents, then at Susan. "Oh, I'm sorry, hon." She moved up to the next car.

"Who was that, Patty?" my mother asked.

"Nobody, Ma. Just a hooker."

"A what?"

"*Puttana*, Flo!" Dad said.

Ma nodded. She looked up at the girl working another car in the hot sun. "Poor thing," Ma said. "It's too hot to work the street today."

Susan put her hand over her mouth to stifle a laugh just as we heard the screech of tires and first one crash, then another behind us, until finally we felt the impact. Everyone was jolted forward in the car, but no one was hurt. I got out to inspect the damage. My rear bumper was dented and hanging loose.

The guy who had hit my car was standing in the street screaming at his wife who was in the car. She was screaming back. They were in their sixties, fat, slovenly. I went over to him. He had swollen ankles and his shoes had no laces. I said, "Relax, it's no big deal. Your insurance will cover it."

"What insurance?"

"Aw, great." I went back to my car and got in.

Ma was poking Susan in the back. "Go ahead, tell him, Susan. Tell him."

"Tell me what?"

Susan looked at me. "I think I hurt my neck."

"Whiplash!" Ma said. "You can sue him."

Before I could ask Susan if she was hurt, she turned toward the backseat and said, "It's not that bad, Mother. I'm all right really." Ma glared at her. My Irish wife had betrayed her already. I interceded.

"Besides, Ma. The guy's got no insurance."

"No insurance! What kind of place is this?"

When we finally got to our little apartment, Ma feigned enthusiasm. "It's so...Florida." She looked at the glass and chrome coffee table, the Art Deco prints of 1920s flappers. "Pink walls," she said.

"Coral, Ma," I said. "A Florida color."

I went back to the car to bring in their bags. Susie showed them their bedroom and our deck on the canal where we would sleep. A white motor yacht was docked by our bedroom window. "Very nice people live on it," Susie said.

"Someone lives on it?" my mother asked. I was putting their suitcases in the bedroom and the paper bags of food in the galley kitchen. "They can see through these windows," Ma said.

"We'll draw the shades for you," Susie said.

"I hope Dad doesn't get any ideas."

I said, "Dad still gets ideas?"

Susie cleared her throat and said, "Let me show you the kitchen, Mother."

Ma went into the kitchen and took the food out of the bags and put it in the refrigerator. "I'll cook a nice Italian dinner tonight," she said to Susan. She turned to face her. "But first I have to get some things." She put her hands on her hips. "I don't suppose you know of an Italian importing store around here."

Susie smiled at her. "I have just the store."

Dad and I stayed at the apartment while Ma and Susie went shopping. I poured us both stiff drinks, scotch for him, bourbon for me. We sat in the living room in silence for a moment. Dad was getting his bearings. Finally I said, "What do you think, pop? How long should I give them before I call the cops?"

Dad waved a hand at me. "Aw, don't worry. Ma's mellowed."

Susie followed Ma up and down the narrow aisles of Fernando's Italian Importing Store on Federal Highway. Ma carried a wicker basket in her hand, like a bent, aged, steely-haired Little Bo Peep. She was trailed by a tall, thin, tanned woman with short, spiked-blonde hair. Ma wore her mink. Susie wore her white T-shirt, blue satin shorts, and white running shoes. Women stared at them. A South Florida stripper and her guinea mother-in-law.

Ma stopped at the delicatessen counter and looked at stuffed peppers behind the glass. "I always make my own," Ma said. "I never buy breadcrumbs. I toast my own bread and grate it."

Susie nodded, "I see, Mother."

My mother explained how to mix the ingredients to stuff the peppers. "The raisins are the secret," she said. "They cut the fishy taste of the *alicia*."

Susie nodded. The deli man came over behind the counter and smiled at Susan. He greeted her in Florentine Italian and Susan answered him in Florentine Italian. Then the man greeted my mother in Florentine Italian. My mother was speechless. She stared at the young man with his pink cheeks and swept-back, black hair. Susan said to him, "*Pietro, mia suocera, Firenze, e una Napolitana.*"

The young man nodded, "*Ah, si. Signora e Napolitana.*" Then he said something to Ma in a Neapolitan dialect. Still, she didn't speak. She looked frozen. Susan rescued her.

"Peter says he has some nicely salted *baccalà* for the *signora*," Susan said. "Do you want some *baccalà*, Mother?" Ma shook her head, no. Finally she spoke, "Just *alicia*."

When they got back to the apartment, they were silent. They put the bags of groceries in the kitchen. Dad and I looked at each other. The kitchen was silent except for the rustle of paper. We could see them from the living room. We drained our drinks. Finally, we heard Susie speak.

"There are a lot of Italians in Florida, Mother. The weather and the sea reminds them of Italy."

Ma flung the back of her hand at Susan. "It wasn't that," she said. She caught herself. "I'm sorry, Susan. It wasn't your fault. I was embarrassed." My mother sounded weak, not herself. "Your Italian, Susan. You speak it beautifully. How did you learn?" Susie told her about our trips to Florence. Ma said, "Of course. I forgot. Patty told me." She was silent for a moment, then said, "I have always been ashamed of my Italian, Susan. My Neapolitan accent, it's for peasants. Not even real Italian in the States. Just bastardized with American words. Dad and I don't speak much Italian anymore. You forget over the years."

"Of course," Susie said, "It's only natural... I've forgotten all my Gaelic."

Ma shrieked with laughter. "Gaelic! Mother of God! What have I done to deserve this? A daughter-in-law who speaks Gaelic." They were both laughing now.

Then my mother began to tell Susan stories, about her girlhood in The Hollow, her mother's store, the Irish cop Grandma had to bribe. "They made fun of us," Ma said. "The Irish. Our broken English. They called us wops, guineas, greaseballs, those lace curtain Irish bastards who lived in pigsties." Ma stopped herself. She said, "I'm sorry, dear. Things happened. You get prejudiced."

"But that was long ago, Mother," Susan said. "Things change."

"I know. I know. But I'm an old woman. I'll always be prejudiced against the Irish. I told Patty, never bring home the hated Irisher girl. But he never listened to me like George."

"I understand, Mother."

Ma said, "I don't suppose you have any Italian blood, do you?"

"No. Just English, Irish, and some German."

"All the same. White bread."

"There is a tiny bit of Spanish way back," Susan said. "In the 1500s, the Spanish boats docked off the Irish coast. The sailors came ashore and mingled with the Irish girls. The result was the black Irish, black-haired babies with blue eyes."

"Oh, don't tell me!" Ma said. "The Spanish! God forbid! They cut each other up with knives." They both laughed, again. When Ma caught her breath, she said, "You know why Italian mothers don't want their sons to marry an Irish girl?" Susan said, no. Ma said, "Because when an Italian husband strikes his Irish wife, she calls the *polizia*. And who comes to the door? An Irish cop. He sees this poor Irish girl with a face like a potato and her red cheek! Who's he going to hit with his nightstick?"

Susan laughed, then said, "And what does a good Italian wife do when her husband strikes her?"

"She never calls the *polizia*." Ma paused for effect. "She just waits until her Italian husband goes to sleep, then she sticks a knife in his heart. Just like the Spanish."

They were both laughing when they came out of the kitchen into the living room, where Dad and I stared at them.

That night, Susie and I slept on chaise lounges on the deck with our eyes closed tightly. The rhythmic lapping of the water and the patter of tiny animal feet lulled us to sleep. I woke with a start to an ancient ghost bending over me in 6 a.m. darkness. Ma held a dish of prunes cooked in lemon juice. She reached one out on a spoon for me.

"Come on, Patty. They'll help you go to the bathroom," she said.

"Ma, I'm not awake. Later."

"Now." So I ate a prune. It was good, sweet and tart at the same time. I told her to give me another one. She said, "No. Only one." Then she cupped her hand under my mouth. "Spit out the pit."

She went over to Susan, still asleep. I got up quickly and went inside. Susan came in a few minutes later, half asleep. I said, "How'd you like your prune?"

While Susie made breakfast for Ma and Dad, I went out to the parking lot with a wire coat hanger. I twisted the hanger around the sagging rear bumper of our Alfa and fastened it to the car's undercarriage.

That evening, we invited some of our friends from our apartment complex over for drinks and to meet my parents. Phil, from Detroit, the owner of the Booby Trap, Home of Stylish Nude Entertainment, came with his girlfriend, Brenda, from Two Dot, Montana, who danced naked at the Trap. Sol was our next-door neighbor, a Jew from Brooklyn, now a pot smuggler in Florida. Fred was a Jew from Manhattan, who had been a district attorney. Now, in Florida, Fred was a degenerate gambler, but only on the ponies. They were all younger than us, Fred and Sol, late thirties, Phil, twenty-nine,

Brenda, twenty-three. We sat around our small apartment drinking and talking.

Fred, the gambler, sat on the living room floor cross-legged like a coed, listening to Dad's hustling stories, A.R., The Canuck with the knife, The Palm Beach Heiress, as if Dad really was *Il Professore* of Con. Ma was sitting on the sofa alongside Brenda in her black T-shirt with "Beyond Bitch" scripted in gold on her tits, and her tight short-shorts that barely covered her ass. Phil, Sol, Susan, and I were sitting on the deck drinking and talking. Susan pointed through the open sliding glass doors to Ma and Brenda. She whispered, "Isn't that cute?"

We heard my mother say to Brenda, "And what do you do, dear?"

"I'm an entertainer."

"Oh, an actress like my daughter-in-law?"

"Kinda. You could call it acting."

"Is that how you entertain people?"

Brenda was starting to blush. "Actually, I'm a dancer."

"Of course you are. You have beautiful, long legs." Brenda smiled at the compliment. Ma added, "And how do you dance? With your clothes on, or off?" Sol choked on his drink. Phil and I laughed. Susie's mouth opened.

Brenda, her face red, said, "Off, mostly."

Ma said, "I'll bet you look gorgeous naked."

On their third night with us, we went to Pompano Beach to Laura DiNapoli's condo for dinner. Ma and Laura went way back to their teenaged years in The Hollow. Now, Laura was a widow living out her years overlooking the ocean from the window of her twenty-first floor condo she seldom left.

We all stood behind Ma at Laura's front door while Ma pressed the buzzer. "Laura, it's Firenze DiMenna!" The door opened and a smiling, tiny, black-haired woman appeared. Ma turned, grabbed Susan by the arm and pulled her toward Laura.

"Laura, this is my daughter-in-law Susan, Patty's wife." Laura nodded, still smiling, and shook Susan's hand. Ma's voice said firmly, "Susan's Spanish, you know."

# CHAPTER THIRTY-FIVE

By my parents' fourth day with us, Susan and Ma were going out every morning and not coming back until late in the afternoon. Susan took Ma to the beach, thrift stores, shopping at the Galleria Mall, and then a ladies' lunch in the mall before an afternoon trip back to Fernando's, where Ma talked to Peter in Italian now. She told him about the *"povera puttana"* who had solicited them in the car outside the airport. Peter blushed.

I was stuck with Dad in our tiny apartment, running out of things to do with him. He was getting grouchy, bored. I offered to take him to Hialeah for the ponies, but he wasn't interested. "I don't suppose you know where there's a crap game?" he asked. I shook my head. He just grumbled, moped around the apartment, or went for little walks by himself. When he left for his walk, he said, "Call your brother." Each time he came back, he said, "Did you call your brother?"

"I was busy." I tried to call my brother as infrequently as possible in those days.

"Call your brother."

So I called George when Dad was out on one of his walks. "How's it going with Ma and Dad, brother?" he asked.

I said, "Ma and Susie are bosom buddies. Susie's teaching Ma Gaelic." He didn't laugh. He was concentrating on what he really wanted to say.

"What about Dad?"

"He's a pain in the ass. He won't do anything. He wants to shoot craps."

"So find him a game."

"Brother, I'm a fucking writer. You're a fucking lawyer. You know criminals. You find him a game."

"You know criminals there."

"Yeah, but they're smugglers. They don't gamble. They're businessmen."

"Then take him to the track."

"He won't go to the track. You know how he is about the ponies."

"Well, find him a pool game, for chrissakes!" George said. "Even better, you take him out to shoot pool. You can bond with the old man. Remember your fishing trip with Dad? How you bonded with him in the Maine woods?" Now my brother laughed.

"Yeah, I fished for golf balls while he booked bets at the 19th Hole."

"This will be different. You'll be doing something together. You're a good shooter. You'll give him a good game. It'll keep him occupied. You used to love to shoot pool with the old man when you were younger. But don't play him for money."

"He only plays for money. You think he's gonna play just to keep score, like in Little League, you're out of your mind."

"Don't say I didn't warn you."

"About what?"

"He'll own you."

I drove Dad to a bar-pool hall out on Dixie Highway, west from the beaches. A redneck place next to body shops and biker clubs and the Dixie Gun Range alongside the railroad tracks. Every other pickup truck had a Confederate flag on its rear window. Dad stared out the window as we passed all the motorcycles lined up in front of the Pagans' clubhouse.

"Where the hell are you taking me?" he asked.

"The real Florida, pop. The beaches are for Yankee transplants and tourists. Nobody but Florida crackers goes out here much."

I parked in a gravel parking lot next to a '69 Chevelle Super Sport painted lime green with a brush. We could hear country and western music coming from inside the low, dilapidated building with boarded-up windows and a sign, "Mis-Cue Lounge."

It was dark inside and smelled of stale beer, cigarette smoke, and baby powder. There was a circular bar near the front door, and beyond it, a dozen pool tables. There were a few derelicts, slumped over, staring into their shot glasses at the bar. I went over to the barmaid washing glasses in a sink. She didn't look up. I waited, Dad behind me, fingering his fedora like a frightened old man. His con. I knew what he was thinking. Humor the kid for a few games, then find a real Mark.

The barmaid looked up; I asked for a rack of balls. She gestured with her head toward Dad beside me now. "For you and pops, huh?" She had stiff, teased, black hair like thin sticks, and a scar running from her cheek to her ear.

"Yeah," I smiled. "The old man shoots a pretty good game."

"I'll bet." She handed me a rack of balls. "Take your pick of tables."

All the Brunswick tables were deserted. Dad walked around them, running the flat of his hand over the green felt, shaking his head, until finally, he said, "This one." We got pool cues from the rack. Dad rolled his cue stick over the green felt as if he was rolling out dough for ciabatta bread. The cue stick wobbled. He got another, and another, until finally he got one that didn't wobble. I racked the balls.

"A game of straight, Dad. One hundred and twenty-five points. A buck a point."

He gave me one of his disgusted looks. "You want to play me for money? I'm your father, for chrissakes. I give you money; I don't take it from you."

He let me break. I played a safety, the cue ball kissing the rack so lightly only one ball popped out and settled against the rail. The cue ball rolled slowly back toward me until it rested against the rail. A long, straight-in shot, rail to rail. Tough, but it could be made. If you had the eyes. Dad went over to the barmaid and got some Johnson's baby powder. He splashed it on his hands and brought it back for me.

Dad bent over the table, sighted his shot, his pudgy fingers firm around the stick, his stroke still smooth, not jerky. He hit the cue ball and it rolled towards the object ball, clipped it and both bounced off the rail and nudged the rack, separating a ball. I bent over the table and slammed the object ball into the corner pocket. My cue ball ricocheted back into the rack spreading the balls over the table.

I looked at the spread out balls, then methodically began pocketing each one. Dad stood by the table, holding his cue stick like a long rifle, as if at attention.

I ran out the rack while Dad watched. He never said a word. When there was only one ball left on the table, Dad racked all the other balls. I sighted the loose ball down my cue stick, powered the cue ball into it. The object ball slammed into a side pocket, the cue ball ricocheting into the rack again. Only a few balls jumped out this time. My cue ball was wedged behind another ball against the rail. I had no shot except to play safe. I remembered what Dad had told me years ago during one of our games.

"You play an old man," he had said, "always leave him long. The eyes go before the stroke." He tapped his head with one finger. "This never goes."

Playing him now, Dad pushing eighty, he still had that firm bridge and smooth southpaw's stroke that I always tried to emulate, but never could. Twenty years ago, I was a pretty fair shooter. I used to hustle working men on their lunch hour at a pool hall in Fairfield. I wore dirty work boots and jeans and T-shirt, too, just like them. They should have checked my hands. Not a callus or a cut.

In those days, Dad and I used to play for hours. But I could never beat him. I'd get sweaty and hot tempered. The hotter I got, the colder he got. I just stood there, watching him pocket ball after ball, so effortlessly with his maddeningly methodical stroke and those blue-gray eyes as cold as ice, unblinking as they sighted the object ball that looked as big as a balloon. To him! Not to me.

During those games, other players around us stopped their game to watch Dad shoot. I was proud of his talent, but I wanted to beat him, too, more than anything. Not to embarrass him. But just to show him how good I was at my father's game.

It was always my fantasy that I had been born before George, and it was I, not George, who went with Dad on his hustling trips. It was Dad's firm I wanted to be a partner in, not my brother's. I fantasized that Dad and I would go into some shady pool hall in Maine, separately, ignoring each other. Then I, the green kid, would get in a nine-ball game with some rednecked farmers so eager to rake the kid over the coals. They beat up the kid like a rented mule for a few racks. The kid gets pissed off. He flings his crumpled bills on the table after blowing a nine-ball shot. And then this old man approaches the table, bowing and scraping, his eyes averted. "Got room for another stick?" he'd say. The farmers couldn't believe their good fortune. Two mules to beat now. The problem for the farmers was, the old man and the kid were so pitiful that when they missed a shot, they stupidly set up each other for a shot on the nine. And even then they had to get lucky on the nine ball, taking some crazy bank shot even they didn't expect to make. "Holy shit!" the kid said. "Do you believe that shot!"

The old man was even more embarrassed when he lucked out on the nine. "Oh, jeez! I'm sorry, fellows. One in a million." He gave them a weak smile, "You get old, you get lucky, I guess."

But I was born too late. All I was left with over the years was my old man beating me game after game. Looking back, I think that was his way of teaching me a lesson. I could never follow in his footsteps. So I'd better get a legitimate job, *L'avocat*.

Dad always played me hard and ruthless. He never let up on me, like fathers do. Give the kid a break. Miss a shot. Let him play, too. Make a few balls. Feel good about himself before you drop the hammer and run the rack. Forget about letting me ever *win* a game! Even I didn't expect that. It would have made me sick to see Dad deliberately miss shots so his sonny boy could win a game, like a child. I never beat my father in pool once in over twenty years. Not even close. I just stood by the table, leaning on my cue stick like a statue, watching him make ball after ball with his fucking maddeningly methodical stroke. I wanted to strangle him! Imagine? My own father.

Until now, in the Mis-Cue Lounge. I rolled the cue ball the length of the table, as far from the object ball as possible, for a safety. A long, straight-in shot for an old man with fading eyesight. He missed it. I ran out the second rack, too. Dad stood by the table leaning on his cue stick like I had for years. How does he like it now! Our roles reversed. His son playing him hard and ruthless *now*. Him feeling helpless.

After an hour of play I was up on him, one hundred balls to seventy. I stepped back from the table to survey the spread out balls for my next shot. My heart was beating in my chest. I looked at my father standing across the table from me. An old man with a friar's tuft of gray hair, a little bent over, motionless, staring at the hazy balls on the table. Behind him I saw the barmaid who had been watching us play all this time. She was smiling. I shook my head to clear it. Then I leaned over the table, sighted a straight-in shot, and slammed the cue ball into the object ball with such force that the object ball hit the back rim of the pocket and bounced out.

"What the hell's a matter with you?" Dad asked. "You got a touch like a blacksmith." He bent over the table now, and ran out the rack. I racked the balls. He said, "That's what happens when you get careless 'cause you're up."

I lost the game by three balls, 125 to 122. I threw my arm over my old man's shoulders and said, "I had you on the ropes this time, pop. When you're ninety, I'm gonna beat your ass."

"You shoulda beat me this time. You got careless." He looked up at me. "As usual."

I returned the rack of balls to the barmaid and paid the bill. "The old man took you to the cleaners, huh?" she said.

I shook my head. "I can never beat the old man. He's the best."

She gave me a sly smile and said, "I'll bet."

That night, my parents and my wife and I had dinner on the outside deck overlooking the water. It was a warm, soft Florida night with a faint breeze that rustled the big fronds of the palm trees. The sky was a dark purple felt cloth littered with diamonds. The boats along the dock swayed gently while we ate. I raised a glass of wine and said, "To Ma and Dad. A toast." We all clinked glasses over the table heaped with food, our faces illuminated by the flickering lights of candles. Ma. Dad. Susie. And me.

My mother said, "Who won, Patty?" I looked at her. "In pool," she said. "Did you beat Dad?"

"Are you kidding, Ma? You know I can never beat the old man."

Dad stopped eating. "He had me beat, Flo. Then he got careless. Just once or twice, but enough."

"Oh!" Ma said. "You mean, Patty let you win?"

Dad looked at her, then at me. "You sunuvabitch! Did you let me win?"

I looked him right in the eye and said, "You think I get you on the ropes, old man, I'm gonna go in the tank? After all these fucking years you never let me win." I shook my head in disgust.

The old man kept staring at me, looking for a tell. His face got red. "You sunuvabitch. You let me win."

"You think I'm that good? Great. I hope it keeps you up all night."

But he didn't hear me. He just looked at me with an anger I'd never seen on his face before in my life. Coldness, yes, I'd seen him look at me coldly when he thought I did something stupid. Or weak. Or rash. Or without thinking. Or in anger. Or in innocence. Like a Mark. But this was different. I had taken away from him the one thing that defined his life. Not because I'd let him win a game of pool. But because I'd done it so effortlessly, deviously, that he'd never caught on. I'd made him the Mark. I had conned *Il Professore* of Con.

Dad never again in his lifetime looked at me in the same way he always had. I had gained something I always wanted, and at the same time, lost something I never wanted to lose.

Dad was up all that night. I heard him prowling through the small apartment, going out the front door to sit by the pool, stare at the moon, thinking, then coming in hours later while I feigned sleep on the back deck. I knew what he was doing. He was looking for a tell. He was going through in his mind everything I had ever said to him, done for him, promised him, swore to him was true, and then all the things I never told him, all the things I told him that were never true, all the thoughts I had I never revealed to him, all the things I'd done he never knew, all the things I was I never let him see. He was trying to find that point in time when it had begun, and he'd missed it. But he couldn't find that tell, because he didn't go back far enough to that cold winter day when I was four and a half years old and he took me to the Waldorf Cafeteria, and then back home to my mother, who asked me, "Patty, did you have fun with your father?"

# CHAPTER THIRTY-SIX

At fourteen, I pitched for our town's American Legion team. My teammates were seventeen and eighteen. We played our games on the big-league diamond next to the Little League diamond where I'd had almost unqualified success the year before. But I wasn't untouchable now. No perfect games in which I struck out every batter. I was merely the best pitcher on my legion team now. Ten strikeouts, five hits, three-two wins. Games like that.

The park was a quarter of a mile from a few stores, a market, barber shop, drugstore, and in the other direction, a quarter of a mile from Woodfield, Home for Unwed Mothers. It was a big, old mansion on a hill that once belonged to an eccentric WASP spinster who bequeathed the mansion to the town on the condition that it be used for unwed mothers. The townspeople weren't enthused about that, but accepted that condition as the only way they could get their hands on that valuable property.

I would be on the mound, a runner on third base, concentrating on my next pitch, when I would be distracted by a young girl, maybe fifteen, walking on the sidewalk toward the drugstore. They were plain-faced girls with no makeup, lank hair, and they all had the same glazed, distant stare of someone contemplating a problem beyond their years. They held their big bellies in both hands as if afraid if they let go, their baby would drop out to the sidewalk.

After one game, driving home with Mom and Dad in the front seat, I said from the backseat, "Ma, are those Woodfield girls bad girls?"

My mother turned on me and said sternly, "Don't ever say that, Patty. They're good girls."

"Then why are they having babies so young?"

"Because only good girls get caught. Bad girls know how to protect themselves." Then she said, "You'll be dating girls soon. When you do, remember one thing. Don't buy them a hamburger and squeeze it out of them afterwards."

"What does that mean, Ma?"

"You'll know when it's time." But I didn't. I forgot her admonition when I put my hands on the breasts of that little Naugatuck Valley girl, Suzzane, two zzs and an e at the end, in the darkened hallway outside my Prep classroom. But when Suzzane looked up at me with her faint, sad smile, I never forget Ma's admonition again.

Dad piped up, "Yeah, son, and remember what the strongest thing in the world is."

I said, "What, Dad?"

"One hair from between a woman's legs."

I was fourteen, but I didn't blush. I said, "But why, Dad?"

He said, "Because it will make a man do things that nothing else in this world will."

My parents never spoke to me as if I was a child. They were raising me to be an adult. I drank wine, laced with water, for dinner like the adults did when I was five. I was taught to stand up to bullies no matter how much older and bigger they were than me. At five, I saw my mother's naked breasts when I burst into their bedroom early one morning. She made no attempt to cover herself. At other times, I heard my parents having sex in their bedroom down the hall from mine. Grunts and moans and the squeak of bedsprings and then a high-pitched gasp of surrender. I knew what they were doing. Well, not exactly, but I had an idea.

I remember once when I was ten, lying on the floor with my glove and baseball, tossing the ball toward the ceiling and catching it, while behind me on the sofa, my parents watched the Bob Hope Comedy Hour. One night, Bob Hope leered at the audience and said, "Did you hear the one about the little girl who swallowed a safety pin when she was seven?" Pause. Lascivious grin. "She didn't feel a prick until she was seventeen."

Behind me, my parents laughed. I turned around and looked up at them. My mother flapped her hand at me and said, "Soon, Patty. Soon you'll get it."

By the time I was sixteen, dating girls regularly, I had got it. My mother knew I had. So, one night, when I was leaving the house on a date, she stopped me at the front door. She handed me the keys to their car, and said, "You know now, Patty, that a woman is like a fine steak... Fillet...but for eat, too."

During the twenty-seven years Susan and I lived in Florida, I didn't see Mom and Dad, or my brother much anymore. I went back to Fairfield maybe ten times over those years. George visited us once, in our small apartment. He walked through the door, ran a finger over our glass bookshelves, and looked at his finger. "You keep a clean house, Susan," he said, "for an Irish girl." Mom and Dad visited us that one time, and Dad visited us after Ma died, when he was ninety-five. It didn't bother me much, not seeing them. We had set up a nice life for ourselves in Florida. We had our writing, our friends, our parrot, Francis, our six Shiba Inu dogs, Hoshi, Kiri, Stella, Nero, and his sons with Stella, Blue and Bubba. And of course Matthew, our retriever-spaniel rescue dog we called a Retraniel, our designer dog.

We had a house our last twenty years in Florida. A 1926 wood frame Key West bungalow in an old Ft. Lauderdale neighborhood a mile from the beach. We pedaled our bikes to the beach for years, until we got old. Susie lay in the sand while I sat on the low beach wall, reading the newspapers and watching the girls in g-strings roll-erblade past me.

Our house had a metal roof and Dade County pine walls and floors impervious to insects. We had foxtail and lady palms in our front yard and a mango tree. In our backyard, fenced in for the dogs, we had a grapefruit tree, a key lime and an avocado tree, and some date palms for shade.

It was a small house, but I had my own office now, and Susie had one, too. We both wrote until noon. Then we went to the beach, and at night to Phil's Booby Trap. I watched the naked girls dance, while Susie talked to Phil's girlfriend, Brenda, sitting beside her, topless.

Mostly, I kept in touch with my parents and my brother by phone. I called my parents twice a week and Dad called me at least once a week. I tried not to call my brother any more than I had to, maybe once a month. When I did, we invariably got into arguments. I got hot, lost my temper, and hung up.

"He's fucking impossible," I'd tell Susan. "He still treats me like a child."

"You're acting like a child," she'd say. "Call him back. He loves you."

But I didn't call him back. Instead I'd get in an argument with Susan. I ended up sleeping on the couch in the Florida room that night.

One morning in the mid-1990s, Dad called. At the time, I was fifty-four, he was eighty-five, Mom was eighty-eight.

"How's it going, pop?" I asked.

"Not so bad. I got a little hustle going."

"Great. Still keeping your hand in?"

"Yeah. These two *melanzanas* at the pool hall been hustling me for nickels and dimes the last two weeks. Arrogant bastards. They call me the old man."

"You are an old man."

"Not to them I'm not. They show me no respect. I'll teach 'em how old I am."

"Jeez, pop. Don't get in a trap. They could hurt you."

"They'll never know what hit 'em until I'm gone with the lettuce." He must have heard my disgusted sigh, because he got pissed off.

"You think I'm stupid now," he said. "Just because you beat me in pool."

"Jesus, Dad, that was years ago. Besides, I didn't beat you. Remember? You beat me, as usual."

"Don't play cute with me. I know what you did."

"What'd I do, Dad?"

"I don't want to talk about it." We were both silent for a moment. Then he changed the subject. "How are the dogs?" Dad loved hearing about our dogs, especially Matthew. They were both "illegitimate," Dad said. "Fellow bastards."

"Stella is pregnant. She's gonna have two puppies."

"How'd that happen?"

"How do you think? Nero nailed her outside behind the barbecue grill. I shoulda known something was up when he came in the house smoking a cigarette."

Dad laughed. I heard Ma giggling like a schoolgirl close to the phone. I said, "What the hell's Ma doing?"

Dad said, sheepishly, "Mom's sitting on my lap."

"I hope you're not getting a hard-on."

Ma called out, "Don't you worry, Patty. Dad can still get it up."

Dad said, "We have sex every so often."

He just dropped it matter-of-factly, an afterthought, like he was telling me he won a C-note shooting craps. A little tidbit of news from the home front Dad thought his sonny boy might like to hear. His eighty-year-old parents were still screwing.

"Well...I'm glad to hear that, Dad... And how are things otherwise?"

"Fine. And you and Susan?"

What'd he want me to say? "Oh, we're still fucking like rabbits." But if I did, I had this insane fear he'd ask me, "How often? Any interesting new positions?" And I'd say, "She likes it best when I bend her over the dishwasher, you know, the vibrations get her off."

I had to stop. I was losing it. I blurted out, "Susie got our house historically designated."

"Really?"

Was he disappointed? I could still cheer him up. I could tell him, "Of course, she had to give the guy at the historical society a blow job first."

Jesus, I had to get off the phone. "Well, Dad, great talking to you. I have to feed the dogs now."

"Tell Susan we said hello."

When I hung up, Susie asked how my parents were. I said, "Well, they're still fucking in their eighties."

"What?"

"That's what Dad said. Ma, too." I shook my head.

Susie laughed and said, "I wish I was raised by parents like yours." Her parents were devout, lace-curtain Irish Catholics. All she ever heard from them was, "What will people think?" Sex was something they never discussed because it was something dirty and a sin. Then she married me in her forties. A guinea con man's son whose parents hated the Irish, had never been in a Catholic Church except for their two sons' weddings, adhered to their own personal and idiosyncratic morality, were still fucking in their eighties, and bragging about it to their sonny boy.

"That's a conversation I never heard at my parents' dinner table," Susie said. "I wish I had."

"Yeah, well, there are other things that went with it maybe you wouldn't be so keen on."

"It didn't seem to affect you so badly." Then she quoted Ma to me. "'For eat, too.'" She gave me a lascivious grin. "Thank God you took that to heart."

"It's what I was taught. It was as natural to me as your silent dinners were to you."

She looked at me, not grinning now. She said sharply, "They were never natural to me. It was sick. I hated it. You should consider yourself lucky."

# CHAPTER THIRTY-SEVEN

When I was seven years old, all my friends had piggy banks. Their fathers had bought them so their sons could learn the value of money. When my friends did chores around the house, threw out the garbage, dried the dishes, mowed the lawn, their fathers would give them a few coins, nickels, dimes, quarters, rarely a dollar bill. When their piggy banks were stuffed my friends turned them over. They unscrewed the rubber plug on the pig's stomach and shook out all the coins. Then they all went downtown to Bridgeport to go to the Saturday matinee at the Globe Theater to watch cartoons, Bugs Bunny, the Roadrunner, and Flash Gordon serials. On those rare occasions when I went with them, I had to first ask my father for money. He never said, how much? He just reached into his pants pocket, produced some crumpled bills, three, five, seven dollars, whatever he had, and gave them all to me. "Pay for your friends' tickets," he said. "And buy them popcorn."

But those crumpled bills weren't the same as those shiny coins my friends had lovingly hoarded. Those coins were sacred, cherished, saved. My friends had earned them by doing chores for their mother. Those coins taught them about work and saving and delayed gratification. But I threw out the garbage, too! I just never got paid for it. I was never taught that important lesson about money and the barter system. You did something for someone, and they repaid you with money. In my house, it was assumed that I did things for my mother out of love, not because I expected to be paid. Money was an immediate gift from the one who had it to the one who needed it. Its very purpose was to forestall the anguish of delayed gratification. Dad knew a lot about delayed gratification. How it ate at him in the orphanage, wanting things he thought he would never have. Respect, family, love. And then, to his amazement, he'd got the real thing he ached for. A family, wife, two sons, love. He was so grateful for this gift that he became determined his sons would never feel the aching want he had for years. So money, with no strings attached, no quid pro quo, was his spontaneous gift of love.

One day, I got up the nerve to ask Dad for a piggy bank. He asked why? I said, "So I can save my own money." A pained look crossed his face. He left the room.

It wasn't until years later that I realized what I had done. I had told my father that I was taking away from him the only way he knew how to show me that he loved me.

When Dad was eighty-four, and I was fifty-three, a magazine offered to pay me to go gambling with Dad at the Foxwoods Casino on the Mashantucket Pequot Indian reservation near Ledyard, Connecticut. We drove two hours in a driving snowstorm, Dad hunched over the wheel of his old Beetle, while I stared out the window at cars abandoned in mounds of snow.

"The magazine gave me three C-notes for us to gamble with," I said.

"That's enough. We'll go down the line like Maggie Klein."

"Now what the hell does that mean?"

He looked across at me with a grin, "It's a Prohibition expression. It means we'll shoot it all until we're busted, or flush."

Jeez, the old man never changes.

I asked him what the thrill was in gambling. He said, "The possibility of loss. Hell for a gambler is a game he can never lose." He glanced at me. "Gamblers love to lose. The more they lose, the more of a man they think they are."

"It's a form of S&M."

"In a way."

"But without the sex."

"In place of sex."

Twenty miles from the casino, state police were directing traffic and tow trucks were pulling cars out of drifts. Dad didn't notice. He was still talking. "I always hated casinos, 'cause you can't beat the iron." I knew what that meant. The iron was the house winning percentage. "But Foxwoods is my style. It's not like Vegas or Atlantic City where people expect a steak, a show, girls, booze. There's no mob connection. The mob only comes in before the casino starts up, not after. Foxwoods is for hard-core, degenerate gamblers who can't help themselves."

His only complaint about Foxwoods was that the dealers and croupiers were not professional enough. "The games are too slow," he said. "The casino only manages about thirty decisions an hour instead of sixty like Vegas. Volume counts."

The parking lot was mounds of snow with humps of snow-covered cars that looked as if they had been there through the night.

Dad gave our coats and his fedora to the girl in the little hat check booth and gave me a tour of the casino. He showed me the slots, lined up in endless, brilliantly-colored rows of flashing lights and clanging bells. "Here's the profit," he said. "The casinos can regulate the payoffs by manipulating the machines, unlike with craps, roulette, and cards."

I went close to an unoccupied slot to check it out. A fat woman seated at the nearest slot put her meaty arm across the machine I was looking at, like a school crossing guard holding back a kid from a green light. "That's for my husband," she said. "He's been playing it all morning. He just went to the john."

"Oh, I'm sorry," I said, and backed away.

Dad said, "Machine gamblers are the lowest. No imagination, no brains, no guts for cards and craps. They crave instant gratification, so they pull a lever and hope three cherries come up."

We walked through the casino past a waterfall and the gaming tables, blackjack, craps, baccarat, roulette. Waitresses with drink trays wove in between us. They wore skimpy outfits with orthopedic-looking stockings and fat-heeled pumps too big for their feet. I saw they stuffed wads of cotton in the backs of their heels.

Dad caught me looking. "They don't look like much, do they?"

"Not in daylight," I said. "Maybe at 2 a.m. after a losing streak, they look better."

We stopped at a baccarat table with a beautiful, fresh-faced, young Chinese girl sitting at the table. She had short, lustrous, black hair and big, round eyeglasses. She could be a Wellesley student studying for exams, except for the cigarette dangling from her lips and the $500 chips she was betting. During the afternoon, I would come back to this table and the girl would still be there.

Dad tossed a head fake at the girl. "Asians are the best," he said. "They don't quit unless they go bust, or break the bank." He raised his eyebrows and grinned at me. "Tomorrow, you can come up here by yourself. She'll still be here."

I changed the subject and asked Dad if he wanted to shoot craps now. He looked down as if embarrassed. "I don't have to," he said.

"That's why we're here, pop. To go down the line like Maggie Klein."

"If you insist, son. If it'll help your story." I gave him $200 of our $300, and he went over to a craps table and bought some chips.

There was a lot of noise and action around the table as if it was a performance and the people there were the actors, extras, bit players, second bananas, the femme fatale and the darkly handsome, dangerous leading man. He was the guy with the bones in his hand, a good-looking guy with a beard. He rattled the bones, "Come on, baby," and flung them across the green felt. The femme fatale was behind him, massaging his shoulders. He didn't seem to notice. Some of the men around the table looked as if they had been there all night, disheveled, unshaven. They leaned against the table for support. The air was thick with cigarette smoke.

Dad said, "You know, you could put six police dogs in a room filled with smoke and they'd be dead in six hours. But crap shooters," he shook his head, "they could stay alive for days."

The stick man at the table was replaced by another man. The departing stick man raised his hands toward the ceiling in surrender before he left. Dad pointed to the glass ceiling and said, "He's showing the guy upstairs he's not taking any chips."

"You're a good reporter, pop." He smiled at me.

Nobody noticed Dad. He was just an old man down on his luck, a few sawbucks in his pocket, waiting his turn, then hoping to hit a few passes before he quit with rent money. Finally, the dice came to Dad. He stood at the head of the table, his head bowed, embarrassed, his con. I moved away from his line of vision. A wise guy called out, "Come on, old man, show us what you got." Dad flung the dice with a disdainful backhand toss without looking at them. He won. Then he won again. His eyes were quick and alert as he calculated the odds on each throw.

The wise guy shouted, "You got the luck, old man."

Dad flung the dice again and won.

The table came alive. "All right! All right!" People slapped down their chips.

Dad's chips began to pile up in front of him. Someone shouted out, "You're on a roll, old man."

Someone else shouted out, "He ain't an old man now. He's a winner."

Then Dad lost a few throws and my heart sank. I couldn't stand it, watching him play. I wanted him to win so badly. I didn't have the stomach for it. So I drifted away and went to a blackjack table. I took a seat and started playing blackjack. I looked across the room and saw the tufts of Dad's hair and heard the shouts around the table.

I played for an hour, was up $375, when a voice behind me said, "Can I get you a drink, sir?" I looked at the smiling waitress, annoyed at her interruption. I shook my head, no, and went back to my cards. I began to lose. I cursed the waitress who had broken my luck. I began to sweat. I heard another voice behind me.

"I hope you bust out."

I turned around to Dad and said, "I was just ready to quit, pop." He asked me how I did. I said, "I won a C-note, but I was up almost four hundred."

"Too bad. You should have lost it all."

I laughed. "You think a few C-notes are gonna make me want to become a gambler? Not to worry. I don't have the stomach for it."

He made a sweeping gesture with his arm. "They're gonna ruin the whole damned state with gambling."

"Except for the Indians."

"Indians? You see any goddamned Indians here?"

"How'd you do?"

"I won three hundred."

We cashed in our chips and headed for our coats. I threw my arm over his shoulder. He looked up at me and said, "Did I help you, son?"

"You're the best, Dad. You make a great reporter." He looked up at me with a child's smile, not a con's.

"I had a wonderful day, son."

Then I remembered something. I said, "You know, Dad, watching you shoot craps, I realized how it must have been for you watching me pitch all those years."

He turned on me. "What, are you crazy? You watched nothing! I watched a thunderbolt. I watched a talent."

# CHAPTER THIRTY-EIGHT

Before we left the casino, we stopped to pick up our coats and Dad's fedora from the girl in the booth. Dad handed her a folded bill. She thanked him without interest and we walked away. The girl unfolded the bill behind us.

She called out in disbelief, "Thank you, sir! Thanks a lot!"

Without looking back, Dad raised his fedora slightly and tipped it. I said, "How much did you leave her, Dad?"

"A C-note."

"A C-note! Jesus Christ, Dad, couldn't you just leave her a sawbuck?"

He glared at me. "For chrissakes, the poor girl's stuck in that stuffy hole all day. Whatsa matter with you?" Then he gave me the rest of his C-notes.

All my life, whenever I saw my father, he gave me money, whatever he had in his pocket. But that lesson about money never did take with me.

In many ways, I am my father's son. In some ways, not. I never had his purity of understanding of the true purpose of money. I never had his need to be loved. I had a father, a mother, a brother, a dog, a home, love. All my life I have been burdened, conflicted, cursed by my father's disdainful attitude toward money. I had a fearful need to hoard money to forestall that looming disaster always around the bend, the house foreclosed. The Hollow and Nanny Goat Park.

When I'm flush, I always pay for dinner with my friends. I whisper to the hostess as she leads us to a table. "Make sure I get the bill." I slip her a fin. I pay when I'm not flush, too. But that gnaws at me. Shamed by my weakness, I leave a too large tip to punish myself. It's a constant battle. I buy a twenty-dollar Cuban cigar to smoke on my birthday. All day I contemplate smoking that cigar after dinner.

A friend stops by to wish me a happy birthday. We have drinks. I light up one of my cheap cigars and ask him if he wants to try one of my Cubans, as if I have a box of them. He says, "Why not?" I light it for him. He savors it, exhales smoke, says, "There's nothing like a Cuban." I curse myself for my generosity because I know it's not in my nature.

When friends come to dinner, Susie suggests a rib roast. I tell her we can't afford it. Then, ashamed of myself, I hear my father's admonition in my ear, "What's the matter with you?" I tell Susie, "Fuck it, get the rib roast." I am like Pavlov's dog trapped in a programmed behavior I cannot overcome. My father's gift to me was my curse. I always fear the wolf at the door. He never did.

Throughout the 1970s, I was a contract writer for *Sports Illustrated*. When each story was published, I gave Dad a copy of that magazine. He said, "You don't have to do that, son." My feelings were hurt. Didn't he want to read my story? Then one day, I saw him downtown in Bridgeport. He was parked near the Waldorf Cafeteria, the trunk of his car opened. He was standing there with one of his cronies. He reached into the trunk and handed his crony a copy of *Sports Illustrated* with my latest story. I saw in the trunk dozens of that magazine. When I saw Dad later I told him he didn't have to buy all those magazines, I can get them for him for nothing. He said sheepishly, "Aw, son, I thought you got a percentage of every magazine that was sold."

Years later, Ma told me a story. Dad was on a flight to Puerto Rico to gamble. The stewardess had been reading a magazine in her seat during take-off. After the flight was in the air, she checked the names on the passenger list. Then she came over to my father in his seat and showed him the story she was reading in *S.I.* "Are you that Pat Jordan?" she said, pointing to my name. He blushed and nodded. She went back to the front of the plane and announced over the loudspeaker that they had a famous author on the plane. She asked my father to stand up. He did, to the applause of all the passengers.

Two years after I began writing for *S.I.*, my editor offered me a staff writer's position. It would pay me three times what I was making as a contract writer. I would also get an unlimited expense account, stock options, health insurance, and a pension fund. When I retired in twenty-five years I would be a rich man. There was only one drawback. Two, actually. One real, one psychological. *S.I.* would own all my stories. Which led to my second problem. I would be owned by an institution. My life, my work, no longer in my hands. When I told Dad about that offer, he said, "Didn't I teach you anything?" So I turned it down.

From my earliest youth, to manhood, and on into old age, I was always an obstreperously independent character. As a pitcher, and in life, I always wanted the ball in my hand, to win or lose. Was it because of Dad's admonitions to me? Or my own nature? Or both? Does it matter?

When I got my first newspaper job at the age of twenty-three, it was for a Jewish, liberal, left-wing paper called the *Connecticut Sunday Herald*. All these smelly old lefties, men and women, socialists at best, maybe even a darker shade of pink at worst. They sat around me furiously tapping out their columns and news stories that extolled the virtues of a paternalistic world order. I was a conservative Roman Catholic Republican even then. My political guru was Father Francis Fenton, the Catholic priest who was a member of the John Birch Society hierarchy. I had met him when he came to say Mass at the All-Girls Catholic High School where I had taught. He took a liking to me. He tried to convince me to join the JBS. "We could use young blood like you in the movement," he said. But I demurred. "I join nothing," I said.

One day, the staff of the *Herald* showed up at work to discover that the previous evening the paper had been sold to William Loeb, the fire-breathing, right-wing millionaire who owned the *New Hampshire Union Leader*. That day those old lefties circulated a petition among the writers to unionize the staff writers, which they hoped would protect their jobs. The editors were management so they couldn't unionize. That petition had to be unanimous for the staff to become unionized. I was the only member who refused to sign that petition. So the paper's editor fired me. The petition succeeded and the writers were unionized. I had the dubious distinction of being a worker who lost his job because of a union. That thirty-five dollar a week losst the time was a significant hit for me and my wife and two children. But then a week later I got a call at home from Bill Loeb. He'd heard about my refusal to go along with the unionization, and the subsequent loss of my job. "I appreciate your principles," he said. He told me that he couldn't rehire me as a writer, since the writers were now unionized, but that the editors weren't. So, he rehired me over the phone with an increase in salary to seventy-five dollars a week, gave me my own personal opinion column, and a new title, Assistant Managing Editor. Then he fired the Assistant Managing Editor who had fired me. A few weeks later our paper became a right-wing journal. The columns and news stories turned 180 degrees right, without a blink or a whimper from those old lefties.

Ten years later, after my first book was published, I got a letter from PEN offering me membership in that prestigious writer's organization. I never replied. PEN sent me another letter after my second book was published. I never replied. Then a third offer after my third book. When my fourth book was published, PEN sent me a letter beginning, "Your refusal to join PEN is incomprehensible to our committee members." So I wrote back, "I join nothing." And signed my name. No more letters from PEN on into my sixteenth book.

Then, over the years, reality intervened.

In my early forties, I was going through a divorce. I gave my wife everything. The house, car, alimony, child support, health insurance. It almost bankrupted me. So I fled to Ft. Lauderdale, where I could live more cheaply. I rented a tiny apartment for $500 a month. I had only my books, clothes, typewriter, and a rusted-out ten-year-old Alfa Romeo as possessions. But still I had over-extended myself, compounded by the fact that I was so depressed I had trouble writing. Soon, I was in debt. I used my credit cards to pay my bills. When I fell behind on my credit card bills, I stopped paying them altogether.

Bill collectors began calling my apartment demanding payment. They were understanding at first. It must be an oversight. I was such a valued customer. I explained I was sending all my money to my ex-wife. They said, "But you have an obligation to American Express." I said, "My obligation to my ex-wife comes first." No longer polite now, they said, "You divorced the bitch, Mack. Fuck her." I said, "Fuck you," and hung up. They called right back. The calls came every hour after hour all day and all night. They threatened to sue me. I said, "Get in line." We screamed obscenities at each other. Deadbeat. Cocksucker. Prick. Asshole. The companies were all different, Amex, Visa, Mastercard, but the voices all sounded the same. I had this insane idea that all the calls were from the same guy, in a cubicle, eating a Big Mac while he screamed at me, and then some other poor bastards. Finally, I just stopped answering my phone altogether. What the hell, nobody called me anyway but my credit card buddies.

Process servers knocked on my door day after day. I refused to answer. They left pages of legal documents on my step. I waited until they left, then I opened the door and peeked out. I saw the papers, took them to the communal dumpster in the parking lot, and tossed them inside.

I tapped out my credit cards to the tune of forty large. When I told the old man the whole sordid story, he said, "Good boy. Fuck 'em." Dad told George. My brother called me, "What's the problem?" I told him how I couldn't work. He said, "Then get a real job. Become a teacher, or something." I hung up on him. Then my problems got worse.

I got a letter from the IRS. They ordered me to report to their Ft. Lauderdale office with my tax records. The agent behind a desk said, "I'm your case worker."

I said, "I have a case?"

"This is just an interview."

"For what? A job?" He smiled at me. "Am I being audited?"

"That's a little premature. We'd just like to talk to you."

"You think I'm lonely? I need someone to talk to? Is this like therapy?"

"In a way. Fiscal therapy. We'd like to know why you didn't pay any income tax last year."

"I didn't make any money."

He looked at some papers on his desk. "Actually, you made $17,000 last year. But you spent $40,000. We'd like to know where that extra money you didn't declare came from."

"I'm a writer. I didn't sell many stories last year."

"Stephen King's a writer."

"I'm the other kind."

He looked me up and down. My tattered Hawaiian shirt, OP shorts, flip flops from Publix. I could see him thinking, another small-time smuggler in Paradise. Finally, he said, "We know where guys dressed like you get their money they don't declare."

"Wait here, I'll be right back."

I went back to my apartment, threw dozens of my magazine stories in a suitcase along with my five books, and went back to his office. I dumped the contents on his desk. "See!" I said. "A writer."

He nodded. "Yes, but that still doesn't explain the forty thousand."

I told him about the alimony, the debt, the credit cards. "Technically they're loans I have to pay back."

"I see. Prove it."

A few weeks after I had sent him my divorce decree and my credit card bills, he summoned me to his office for another fiscal therapy session. He told me he had closed my case file.

I said, "You mean, I'm cured?"

"In a manner of speaking." He handed me my suitcase with all my stories and books in them. I hefted the suitcase.

"It feels a little light," I said.

He reached into one of his desk drawers and pulled out two of my hard cover books. "I'd like to keep these two to read," he said. "Do you mind? I'll send them back to you." He grinned. "I know where you live."

"Knock yourself out." But he never did send those books back to me. Even the IRS agents are bent in Paradise.

He stood up and shook my hand. "It's been a pleasure. I'd never met a writer before." Pause. "Not even an unsuccessful one."

"Thanks. Something to tell your kids."

Then he shook his head and said, "Man, you really screwed up."

In his mind, maybe. Not mine. I was a con man's son. I had met my nut, my obligations to my ex-wife. So what if I had to screw Amex, Visa, and MC to do it.

When I married Susan, we struggled for a few years until I began to make enough money with my writing to support my ex-wife and my new wife. We lived frugally in our little apartment with a parrot and a dog. Then we accumulated a little money, enough for a down payment on a new car. The salesman said he wanted to check my credit first. I told him not to bother. He did anyway. "Man, this is ugly," he said. I told him I'd put down three Gs for the $24,000 car. He shook his head, no. I said, "Five Gs." He shook his head, no. I said, "Eight Gs." He smiled, "Congratulations. Sign here."

After seven years in our tiny apartment, Susan and I now had five dogs and a parrot. We began to look for a house in Ft. Lauderdale. We found one for $90,000. After the banker checked my credit for a mortgage, I said, "I know. I know. But I can put down fifteen Gs for the house." He shook his head, no. I said, "Twenty?" No. I said, "Thirty Gs?" He smiled and shook my hand. I had just learned a valuable lesson about bad credit ratings. No matter how bad your credit is, you can buy anything if you put 30 percent down. The only problem was I didn't have the thirty Gs. I only had $15,000 in our savings account.

A few days later, Dad called to ask me how the house hunting was going. I told him about the house and the banker. Dad said, "You like it. Buy the house." Three days later I received a FedEx envelope from Dad with $30,000 cash in it. I was afraid to ask him where he got it. He had told me once, "You send shady cash, never send it through the U.S. Postal Service. That's a federal rap." Finally, I did call him.

"I got the FedEx," I said. "You shouldn't have sent it. You and Ma need it in your old age."

"We can get by. We don't need anything. What am I gonna do? Wait until I die to leave you an inheritance? Deprive you for years. You'll put it to good use now. Make Susan happy."

"Thanks, Dad. You spoil me."

"You're my son, for chrissakes. Who else am I gonna spoil?"

"You got two sons, Dad."

"I know that. Who do you think insisted I send it to you? Your brother doesn't need it. You give to the one who needs it."

"The Prodigal son, eh?"

"He blew it on broads and booze and gambling. Then he went back to his old man for more. I wouldn't have given it to him then. I'm not a sucker. But you, you always work. You spend it for the right things. I got no worries how you use it."

Finally, I got up the nerve to ask him where he got it from.

"I borrowed it from your mother."

I blurted out, "Where does Ma get that kind of cash?"

"She saved the money you paid us for the house twenty years ago. That and the money I give her, she invests in CDs mostly. Twenty-fucking-percent in the 1970s. Worse than shylocks. She never listens to me." Ma was her mother's daughter after all.

"Yeah, but you always steal it back from her."

"Not all of it. She got wise to me. She hides some of it. It adds up."

"Do you have to pay her back?"

"Of course. I'll find a way. I don't have much of a nut anymore."

They were living in a rent-controlled apartment now. Dad was able to meet his nut on his fixed income. Any money he made with his scams was gravy. Dad always kept his nut to a minimum. I didn't have that luxury. Two wives, five children, two houses, six dogs, a parrot, insurance and taxes, and an exorbitant health insurance. Susan had had breast cancer in her late thirties, three months after we met on Fairfield beach. She had one breast for a year, and then another mastectomy, and then two implants, and then so many operations after that to get the implants right that the operations became a normal part of our life in Florida. Finally, after seven years, she had a perfect pair of tits like the ones you'd see on sixteen-year-old girls.

There were so many living things that depended on me for survival that often I would wake at 3 a.m., staring at the ceiling with the dreads. I should never have turned down that offer from *S.I.* What if I had joined PEN? Would that have helped my books become more successful? I cursed Dad's cavalier advice. No institutions, no paychecks, no investments, only cash, be your own man, give it all away. Easy for him to say with his minimal nut.

Like Dad, I rattled the bones and tossed them across the green felt table. But I knew they were not shaved. And if they were, I knew they were not shaved in my favor. Dad never rattled the bones unless he had an edge. I gambled always to make my life bigger, a house, more pets, a nicer life for Susan. Dad deliberately kept his life small, that rented apartment, that battered Volkswagen, his threadbare uniform. Dad never feared the wolf at the door. Why would he? There was nothing for the wolf at Dad's door. I always feared that wolf who could snatch the life I had created from my hands. Which is why I wonder now which of us was really the purest gambler.

# CHAPTER THIRTY-NINE

In my late fifties I flew up from Florida to visit my brother for a family reunion. George and Mil, my parents, and George's granddaughter whom I'd never met. I hadn't seen my family much after George's nervous breakdown, twenty years before.

I flew into New York City and spent the day making the rounds of magazine editors trying to drum up assignments. Late in the afternoon, exhausted from walking the city streets, I caught a train to Fairfield at Grand Central Station. I drifted off to sleep in my seat as the train pulled out. I woke at each stop, then forced myself back to sleep. When the train stopped at Greenwich, I heard voices.

"Oh, I just love bridal showers!" said a boy's breathless voice.

"You're going?" asked a girl's flat Midwestern voice.

"Of course!" said the boy.

"Timothy will be the only man there," said a girl's boarding school voice.

"I can dream, can't I?" said the boy. The girls giggled. The boy's voice said, "Are you going?"

"I'd love to," said the Midwestern girl. "But I have to read a book for my film study course." She sighed. "Besides, my grandfather expects me at dinner tonight. His younger brother's coming."

"Your uncle," said the boarding-school girl.

"I guess. I've never met him."

"You've never met your uncle?" asked the boy.

"He lives in Florida. He's a writer."

"How exciting," said the boy. "A writer."

"I dunno. Nobody talks about him. It's all very secretive. Something about a book he wrote. My grandfather was in it."

"A family memoir," said the boy. "How juicy!"

I opened my eyes and looked over at them, sitting across the aisle from me. The boarding-school girl was Chinese, sitting by the window. The boy was sitting across from her. The Midwestern girl was sitting on the aisle seat close to me. She was a beautiful girl, like Audrey Hepburn, only ethnic. A guinea or a Cubano. No, not Cubano. I wasn't in Miami now. She was a guinea, like her mother.

The Midwestern girl caught me staring at her. I smiled. She looked startled and turned away. She began telling her friends about her film course. She spoke quickly, nervously, every so often glancing at me. I was going to say something to her, but she didn't stop talking. So I closed my eyes and feigned sleep.

When the conductor announced the Fairfield stop, I got up with my bag and went to the door. They stayed in their seats. The train slowed to a stop. I still had time to grab a drink at the bar behind the station. Then I could walk back to the station and call my brother after the next train arrived.

I stepped off the train into a blinding late afternoon sunlight. I put on my sunglasses and looked for the bar.

"Brother!" a voice called from the parking lot. George was standing beside his new BMW. He looked the same, tall, with short, wiry gray hair like Ma's, and a Bloodhound's face.

"Brother!" I smiled. "I was gonna call you."

"I figured you'd be on this train," he said. We hugged each other. He looked over my shoulder and said, "Lois! Did you meet your uncle on the train?"

I turned and saw the Midwestern girl walking toward us. She was carrying a big canvas bag. George said, "Say hello to your uncle."

Lois tried to smile at me. I said, "We almost met on the train, brother. I tried to pick her up but she wasn't interested in an old man with a white beard." She tried to smile again. "Let me take your bag," I said.

George said, "I told her to look for you on the train. Didn't I describe him to a T, Lois?"

"How was that, bro?"

"I told her to look for a guy with a white beard wearing a black leather jacket, jeans, and cowboy boots."

I looked at Lois. She said, "I thought you'd be...older."

"Fifty-eight's not 'older'?" George asked.

"I was sitting across from you the entire ride," I said.

"I guess I just didn't notice you," she said.

"I have that trouble a lot," I said.

"I told her, 'Look for your uncle, you'll have an interesting conversation for an hour,'" George said.

"Maybe she didn't want an interesting conversation, brother."

She looked at me and said, "I was busy with my friends."

Lois got in the back seat of the BMW. I sat beside George. As we pulled out of the parking lot, he said, "Isn't she beautiful, brother?" I said, yes, she was. He said, "Beautiful." Lois said nothing, as if she was used to such compliments, either expected them, or just took them in stride from her grandfather.

I said, "So that's why you were at the station, bro. To meet Lois."

"You, too," he said.

George parked in front of his big red barn where he used to keep Beth's jumping horses when she was a teenager, competing at Madison Square Garden before Lois was born. I remember seeing pictures of Beth in her riding outfit. Black, hard-shell cap, fitted red coat, tight black jodhpurs, long, black, patent leather riding boots, and a riding crop in her hand. I told George once, "That's a little S&M, isn't it, brother?" He gave me a disgusted look and said, "It's your niece, for chrissakes."

As we walked toward the kitchen, the screen door swung open and George's big black Lab, Beau, came running out to us. Beau leaped on George first. George rough-housed with him, "My big guy." Then Beau sniffed my cowboy boots.

"He smells my dogs," I said. I scratched Beau behind his ears. He rolled over on his back. I scratched his belly.

"He likes you, brother," George said.

"Dogs can sense dog people," I said.

Beau went to Lois and put his paw on her white pants. "No, Beau! No! Down!" she said. Beau sat and looked at her, his tail wagging. She brushed his paw print off her pants.

"Bad dog!" George snapped. "Bad dog." He pointed toward the house. Beau slunk off, his tail between his legs.

"He was just excited to see us, bro," I said.

"He's got to learn, I'm the boss."

The screen door opened. Beau went into the kitchen and Mildred stepped outside into the late afternoon sun. She looked the same, too, with her dyed black hair, blue eyes and straight Grecian nose. She shaded her eyes from the sun with the flat of her hand, like an Indian scout scanning the horizon for the war party of a hostile tribe.

"Hello, Mildred," I said.

She smiled at me. "I thought it was your voice, Patty. The bad penny."

We all went into the small kitchen and sat at a round table while Mil checked the spaghetti sauce simmering on the stove.

George said, "Not too much garlic in the sauce, Mil."

"Yes, George," she said.

"I suppose you'll want a drink, brother," George said. "The bourbon's in the pantry."

I poured myself a Jim Beam Black, neat, and sat down at the table. "You remembered, brother," I said.

"Anything for my brother," he said. I lighted a cigar and took a puff. Lois, sitting across from me, wrinkled up her nose, and flapped a hand in front of her face.

"The smoke bother you, Lois?" I asked.

"It's smelly."

"I thought your father smoked cigars."

"He does."

"Does he put them out when you tell him, too?"

"I make him go outside."

"Amazing. Maybe you should just get used to it."

"It's a disgusting habit."

"I didn't mean the cigars."

George said, "Put it out, brother. You smoke too many of those damned things. They're not good for you."

"A man has to have his vices, brother."

"You've got enough vices, brother, don't you think?" Then he looked at his granddaughter and smiled. "She's beautiful, isn't she, brother?" Lois ignored another compliment and took a book out of her purse. She began reading it at the kitchen table.

"Are we that boring, Lois?" I asked. She ignored me.

George said, "She has to study for an exam. You're lucky she found time to come to dinner tonight. Just to meet her uncle."

"I feel honored."

Mil stirred the sauce. George stared at his beautiful granddaughter. I sipped my drink.

"So, brother," I said, "what time are Ma and Dad coming?"

"Seven," George said. His tone became serious now. "Don't be surprised when you see them. They got old. Dad doesn't look good."

"He sounds good over the phone."

"You aren't here to see him."

At dinner, we all sat around the circular table in the dining room, my parents, my brother, Lois, me. Mil was busy in the kitchen. The faux paintings of a stern George Washington and Abraham Lincoln were staring down at us. The old stone walk-in fireplace hadn't been lighted in forty years. The floorboards creaked as Mil moved around the table passing out bowels of spaghetti with puttanesca sauce. George uncorked a bottle of wine and filled everyone's glasses, except Lois's.

"Give the kid some, too, bro. It might loosen her up."

Lois glared at me. "I don't need loosening up," she said.

"You sure, honey?" George asked. She shook her head, no. George raised his glass and said, "Here's to Mom and Dad's sixty-fifth anniversary." Everyone, except Lois, clicked glasses over the table and said, "Happy anniversary!" George said, "Don't they look great, brother?"

I looked at my parents. They looked the same, as they always did to me since I was a child. My mother, small, dark, now with a puff of thinning white hair and a big nose. My father, bald, with his blue-gray eyes, and now a brush mustache. I said, "Not bad for pushing ninety."

George said, "Not bad! They look twenty years younger than their age. Ma's still a beauty."

"Come on, bro," I said. "Even Ma will admit she was never a beauty, right, Ma?"

Ma's face reddened. Lois gasped out loud. "That's terrible!" Lois said.

"Ma knows I'm only kidding," I said. "Don't they have irony out there in Omaha?"

"People in Omaha are a lot nicer than here," Lois said.

"Maybe they're not smart enough not to be nice," I said. Lois stared at me, but said nothing.

George said, "Omaha is beautiful, brother. You should see Lois's house, it's a mansion."

Mil cleared the pasta dishes and began handing out plates of lobster. Ma smiled and said, "Isn't my daughter-in-law wonderful? I have two wonderful daughters-in-law. I never had a cross word with either of them."

Mil glanced at me. I shrugged. George said, "What's that new Irish wife of yours cook, brother? Boiled potatoes?"

"She's not so new, brother. We've been married thirteen years."

"Oh, the Irish love boiled potatoes," Ma said.

"Actually, bro, we had boiled hot dogs last night. Ballpark franks."

"I thought so," George said.

"Susie has other talents," I said.

"I read about them in your book," Mil said.

"The lobster's delicious, hon," George said. Everyone ate in silence for a few minutes. Then Dad spoke.

"I read the book." Tears welled up in his eyes. "It was painful to read."

"What about you, brother?" I asked.

My brother looked at me without expression. "I read it. It was a very good book. How's it selling?"

"Not so hot."

"Maybe you should write about things people want to read," George said. "Instead of always writing about yourself."

"Brother! Don't you find me interesting?"

Dad spoke. "George only reads books on philosophy and theology. Isn't that right, son?" George and I both looked at Dad, wondering which of us he was talking to.

"Does anyone want more lobster?" Mil asked. Everyone shook their head, no.

After a few minutes, I said, "You know, Mil, Ma told Susie the secret to being a good wife. Didn't you, Ma?"

"I didn't have to tell her. She's Irish."

"What's that, brother?" George asked.

"Ma told Susie to keep her legs in the air and keep her own bank account," I said.

George snapped at me, "Not in front of the kid, brother."

"What kid?" I smiled at Lois. "What are you, Lois, about twenty-one?"

"Next month," she said.

Dad said, "Patty was always a womanizer." Everyone glanced at him. He was struggling to crack open a lobster claw.

Ma said, "Patty married the perfect wife for him. All Irishers are *puttanas*, isn't that right, Dad?"

George said, "Dad hasn't been feeling himself these days, brother."

"Not that bad," Dad said.

"I don't feel myself these days either, pop," I said. Dad nodded.

"You look like an old man with that white beard," he said.

"George takes Dad to the doctor every week," Ma said.

I looked at my brother and said, "The good son, eh, brother."

George said, "It beats the alternative."

Mil cleared the dishes and brought out dessert. I said, "Not for me, Mil. I think I'll go out for a drink, see if I can't scare up a few of my old drinking buddies."

"Patty's always going someplace," Ma said. "He's never there when you need him."

"I was there when my brother needed me twenty years ago, wasn't I, Ma? I flew up from Florida the next day. You remember, Mil, don't you?" Mil looked away. Ma and Dad glared at me.

George said, "Why don't you take Lois out with you for a drink?"

I looked at Lois. Her face was red. "I'd get arrested," I said.

"Go ahead, Lois," George said. "Go out with your uncle for a drink. You'll get to know him."

Lois looked down at her dessert, still blushing. "I don't think so."

"I don't think Lois wants to get to know her uncle," I said. "I can't blame her."

George smiled. "Oh, I forgot. Her mother forbid her to go out with you, brother. She told me, 'Dad, whatever you do, don't let Lois spend any time with Uncle Pat.'"

"Great!" I said.

# CHAPTER FORTY

I woke the next morning at four in the upstairs guestroom set off from the other bedrooms by a separate staircase. The staircase was so narrow and steep that it was a death trap. I walked down the stairs holding on to the railing. I went into the kitchen and turned on the coffee pot. Beau was waiting for me in his cage. He looked at me and wagged his tail.

"OK, big guy." I let him out of his cage and opened the kitchen door. Beau ran out into the darkness. I followed him to behind the barn where he squatted to piss. "Not like that, big guy," I said. "Watch." I unzipped my fly, raised my leg and pissed. "Like that." Beau looked at me pissing against the side of the barn.

After a while I led Beau back into the kitchen. I sat down with my coffee and Beau lay down at my feet. The house was quiet. I lit a cigar. "Nothing changes, does it, Beau?" He wagged his tail.

My brother woke late in the morning and had his breakfast. The same breakfast he'd had since I could remember. Raisin Bran cereal with milk and strawberries. Buttered wheat toast. A small glass of orange juice. When he was finished, we took Beau for a walk. We walked down the steep driveway to the street and began walking past old colonial houses like George's, except they were smaller. I held Beau's leash as he sniffed the grass. He pulled me this way and that after scents.

"Don't let him drag you around," George said. "Show him who's boss."

"He's just being the big hunter, bro. That's part of the fun for him."

Beau sniffed a bush, then squatted and pissed. George watched him and shook his head. "Damned dog," he said.

"When did you get him neutered?"

"When he was six months."

"I told you to wait a year, until he'd got used to raising his leg." Beau stopped squatting and walked off, jerking me after him.

"The vet said six months," George said.

"Vets don't know shit about dogs, brother, I told you that. You shoulda checked with me."

George looked at me with that blissed-out, ethereal smile I remembered from the sanitarium. "You always know everything, don't you, brother?"

"I know about dogs." Beau jerked me into the grass.

George reached out his hand. "Here, give me that damned leash. You don't even know how to walk a dog." He took the leash and jerked it hard. "Heel!" Beau cowered close to George's legs and followed him. "That's how you train a dog. Show him who's boss."

I walked after my brother and his dog. Every time Beau strayed from George's side, he jerked his leash and Beau pressed himself against George's leg.

When we returned to the house, Mil was making breakfast for Lois. Lois was in the screened porch reading her film book. George and I joined her. We sat on white wrought-iron chairs as the morning sunlight slanted through the screens and fanned out over the slate floor. I lit a cigar. George picked up a copy of the *New Yorker* and showed me an article about Ingmar Bergman.

"I wanted to discuss this with you," he said.

"What's it about?" I asked. Lois, reading her book, ignored us.

"Bergman thinks it's a shame that we tell stories to make a point with people," George said. "He says we can't just tell people the truth because they won't accept it. So we tell them stories."

"By indirections find direction out," I said.

My brother glared at me. "That's not what I meant!" Lois looked up from her book. Her grandfather said, "I'm talking about the duplicitousness of man. How corrupt man is. People can't stand the truth so they tell stories. They make things up. Lies! It's disgusting."

"Stories aren't necessarily lies, brother. Sometimes..."

George called out, "Mil! Where are those boxes of photographs?"

She called back from the kitchen. "Under the table."

George picked up a cardboard box from under the table and began looking through it. He held up a photograph and showed it to Lois. "Look, Lois, your mother jumping at Madison Square Garden." Lois looked at her mother in her S&M riding outfit. "Wasn't she beautiful?" George asked. "You look just like her."

I watched as George pulled out photograph after photograph of his kids and grandkids and showed them to Lois. "Isn't she beautiful?" he asked. "Isn't he handsome?"

Lois was standing behind him now, looking at the photographs over his shoulder. She reached out her hand and took out a photo. A young man with curly, black hair, his arms crossed against his bare chest. He was lean and tanned, yet muscular, too, with a faint smile on his lips.

"Who is this?" Lois asked. "He's so handsome!" She held the photograph up for her grandfather to see.

"That's me, Lois," I said. "I wasn't always an old man with a white beard."

She blushed and put the photo back in the box as if it was on fire.

"Your uncle was always the pretty brother," George said.

"The picture of Dorian Grey," I said. "Everyone gets old, Lois. Even you."

She looked at me strangely, as if to her I was somehow different now. An old man who had once been young, like her. I could see her thinking, what was he like before it all changed, before he changed? Would she change, too? Like him?

I looked at Lois. "Don't worry, Lois," I said. "Not everyone gets angry when they get old." She looked embarrassed that I knew what she was thinking. Then she smiled at me, the faintest of smiles, and looked away.

After breakfast, Mil said she'd drive Lois to the train station. I kissed Lois good-bye on the cheek. "It was good to meet you, finally, Lois."

"Yes," she said. "It was."

George loaned me his BMW for the day. I spent the day driving around to all the places I remembered from my youth, and manhood, until I left Fairfield at forty-two. The house where I was raised. The sidewalk where my brother had had catches with me when I was a boy. The park where I pitched my Little League games. The woods beyond the park where I had taken a girl and we had lain down in the grass and kissed and she let me put my hand on her breasts. The bars, where years later, I had picked up women and had sex with them. The beach where I had met Susan for the first time, and then we'd talked for hours in the bar across from the beach.

I returned to George's house just in time for dinner. He said, "Jeez, brother, I thought you drove back to Florida. What the hell did you do all day?"

"Relived my past life, brother." I told him where I'd gone, but not about the women. "Remember the first time you took me to the big-league diamond? The mound seemed a mile from home plate. I threw the ball to you on three bounces."

"You were only a baby, for chrissakes. Five or six years old. What did you expect? I was always hard on you, pushing you." He smiled. "In a week you could throw the ball all the way to me behind the plate. I said to myself, that's my brother. He always tries hard."

"I owe it all to you, brother."

He flung the back of his hand in the air. "Aw, it was in your nature, brother. You never gave up."

After dinner George and I went into his family room to watch a movie while Mil did the dishes. I said to Beau, "Wanna watch a movie, big guy?" Beau wagged his tail and followed us. He lay down on the rug while George knelt on the rug and searched through his cabinet stacked with DVDs. "Anything you want to see?" he asked. "I copied almost a thousand movies."

"That's illegal, bro. Don't you read that FBI warning before the movie? $250,000 fine and five years in the slammer. They call it copyright theft."

He smiled at me. "That's why I do it."

"Living on the edge, eh, bro?"

"That's what Dad taught us. Ah, here's one. An Italian movie. You'll love it. This is the one I want you to see." He looked over his shoulder at Beau. "What the hell's he doing here? We won't be able to concentrate on the movie with him around."

"I'll keep an eye on him."

George stood up, grabbed Beau by the collar and half-dragged him into the kitchen. I heard Beau's cage door slam shut.

George slipped the DVD into the VCR and clicked on the TV. He sat down on the sofa. I sat beside him on his big easy chair. The movie began. "It's in Italian, brother," he said. "So pay attention to the subtitles."

"Yes, brother."

George was already engrossed in the movie. A naked couple was making love on a bed. The woman was sitting astride the lying man, fucking him slowly. She asked him how he was going to kill her tonight. He said, by slitting her throat. That excited her and she started fucking him harder. The man reached under his pillow, withdrew a sharp knife and slit her throat, blood spurting all over him and the bed. The woman slumped off him onto her back, her eyes fixed open. The man got off the bed and went around the room meticulously planting clues that would lead the police to him, the chief police inspector of the city.

"He wants to prove he can get away with the murder," George said.

We watched in silence. Mil came into the room and stood beside us. "What are you watching, George?" she asked. He was sitting on the edge of the sofa, leaning toward the TV, engrossed in the movie. He didn't say anything. Mil looked at the movie for a few moments, then said, "Again? I'm going to bed. I'll see you in the morning, Patty. The coffee's already made. Just turn it on when you wake up."

Mil went upstairs. I was dozing off. I forced myself awake. "He gets away with it," I said.

"Just watch the goddamned movie!"

At the end of the movie, the chief police inspector did get away with the murder. Nobody would believe such an upstanding citizen, even in the face of overwhelming evidence, could be a crazed murderer.

George sat back on the sofa and said, "Most people would think he's crazy. But that's because he proved he was smarter than everyone else."

I stood up and said, "I'm going to bed, brother. I have to catch an early train."

"Aren't we going to discuss the movie?"

"Not tonight, bro. Maybe tomorrow morning." I went into the kitchen, past Beau, lying with a sad face in his cage. "See you in the morning, big guy," I said.

George called out to me, "Don't forget to wake me. I'll drive you to the train station."

"Right, bro."

I went up the narrow stairs and fell asleep on the bed without taking my clothes off.

I woke the next morning at four, went downstairs with my bag. I saw Mil had set up the coffee pot for me. All I had to do was turn it on. Beau looked at me and whimpered in his cage. I opened his gate and he ran out to the kitchen door. He wagged his tail and looked up at me.

"The coffee can wait, Beau. One last piss call." I opened the door and Beau ran out into the darkness. I followed him to the back of the barn. He was already squatting and pissing. I unzipped my fly and pissed, too, only this time I didn't raise my leg. Beau couldn't help it. "It's not your fault, big guy." Beau looked up at me with a wrinkled brow, still pissing. His hind legs were splayed, his ass almost touching the grass. "My poor brother," I said.

When Beau finished pissing, he ran into the darkness, then came back with a Frisbee in his mouth. We played a game of tug of war for a few seconds until Beau let me pry the Frisbee from his clenched teeth. Then he danced away from me, looking at me expectantly. I tossed the Frisbee high into the darkness. He ran after it. I walked back toward the kitchen. When I got to the door, Beau ran to me with the Frisbee. He let me take it from him. I opened the door, tossed it inside, and Beau ran in after it. I went in and shut the door behind me.

I looked at the coffee pot for a moment, then picked up my bag. "Sorry, Beau. No time." It was a long walk to the train station. But if I left now I could catch the 5:04 to Grand Central, and then an early flight from LaGuardia to Ft. Lauderdale.

I walked down the steep driveway with my bag, past the side of my brother's big, old colonial house in darkness. The kitchen light was on now. I stopped at the bottom of the driveway and lit a cigar. I looked back at my brother's house and saw a small figure, standing outside beside the house in darkness. I waved good-bye to Mildred and turned the corner.

# CHAPTER FORTY-ONE

After Susan and I were married in Florida, we made our new life. Our dogs, our parrot, our friends, the beach, the sun, the bars and clubs and our work in our tiny apartment on the Intracoastal. Susan was an actress, and a writer now. She published stories in *Good Housekeeping*, *Cosmo*, the *New York Times Sunday Magazine*, and a book, *The Immune Spirit*, a memoir about her breast cancer. She wrote in one room of our tiny apartment, and I wrote in another. Whenever I had a question about grammar – Susie had been a grammarian as a high school teacher years before – all I had to do was call out. "Babe! Is blow job one word or two?" She'd call back, "I don't know. I never had to spell it."

As an actress, she occasionally made a few hundred dollars a week in local theater productions. The plays were in strip malls, the patrons sitting on folding chairs. One was in the upstairs lobby of a hotel, with a noisy bar below. The noise got louder and louder as the drinkers got whacked. The prompter in the wings had to shout to the actors on stage to be heard.

She also went to *Miami Vice* auditions and TV commercials for local Ferrari dealers in Coral Gables, south of Miami. One torrentially raining day, Susie dressed in her most provocative high-class hooker outfit so that when she was filmed getting out of a Testarossa, her skirt would hike up to her thighs, flashing her long, tanned legs.

After her mastectomies in Fairfield, Susie lost a lot of weight. So I put her on a high protein diet and a body building routine with weights. She responded quickly. Her arms and legs became muscular, her shoulders and back, too. When we moved to Ft. Lauderdale, she got breast implants from a Cuban plastic surgeon in Miami, covered by her Blue Cross Blue Shield health insurance. She spent a few days a week lying in the sun on the beach in her g-string bikini. She tanned quickly, too. She got a short haircut, and had her hair dyed ash blonde. The guys in our Ft. Lauderdale dirty iron gym called her Spike, because of her spiky do, and because she could squat twice her body weight. She had the body of one of those female Marvel Comics heroines now. So she entered female Hot Bod contests held at beach bars near the ocean. She competed against college girls from the north on Spring Break, and local strippers in their twenties. When the announcer called out her name he said, "You will not believe it, ladies and gentlemen! This lady is fifty years old." She regularly won cash prizes of $250, then a week trip to Barbados, all expenses paid for two, then another to Jamaica. When we went out to dinner, she wore spandex mini dresses that fit her body like sprayed-on paint, and strippers' six-inch stilettos. I called her Baby, only now it wasn't a joke. She was a femme fatale now, but in color, not black and white, in a paradise of palm trees, a blinding sun, pale blue skies, and a blue-green ocean. She bought a pink, tight-fitting T-shirt with gold script letters on her chest, "It Ain't Pretty Being Easy." She was easy now. We had a lot of sex. She was still as enthusiastic as that first time, but now she had also acquired the talents of a seasoned concubine in Kublai Khan's harem. She told me once after sex, "I'll do anything you want, Baby, as long as it's only me and you."

One night we were in a bar in downtown Ft. Lauderdale. I was at the bar alone while Susie, dressed as usual in a pink, spandex minidress like sprayed-on paint and her stripper stiletto heels, was talking to a guy she knew from our gym. A woman came up to me at the bar. She was a gorgeous little tanned brunette, also wearing a sprayed on spandex minidress, with black and brown leopard spots, and stiletto heels. She pointed toward Susie and said, "Is that blond chick your wife?" I said, yes. She leaned close to my ear and whispered, "She's gorgeous. I'll do you if you let me do her." I laughed and said, "Go ask her, see what she says." But she didn't.

I drove her to the Ferrari audition in the Gables in a "pocket Ferrari," our rusted-out, old Alfa Romeo. It broke down on Route 1 in the midst of rush-hour traffic. Susie and I got out of the car in torrential rain to push it toward a gas station. She was wearing her strippers' pumps and a white spandex mini dress that barely covered her ass. She bent over to push the car, her ass in the air. Her mini dress was so drenched with rain that it became transparent and plastered to her body like a second skin. Car horns honked, drivers waved C-notes at her. We got the Alfa fixed at a gas station and then drove to her audition. When we arrived, her hair was matted to her head, her mascara dripping down her cheeks, her lipstick smudged. She looked like one of those stoned models in heroin chic *Vogue* layouts, slumped on the floor of a grunge bar's men's room. We were too late. Everyone had left. Susie looked at her reflection in the dealer's plate-glass window. She said, "All for the best. I look a little too outré, even for Miami."

In our early years in Ft. Lauderdale, before Susie became Spike, we were broke a lot. We had to hustle for money any way we could. I had left *Sports Illustrated* to write novels in the early 1980s. The novels tanked, book contracts dried up, and I had lost my connection to *S.I.* We struggled to meet our nut. Susie cleaned motel room toilets, the only white lady working alongside Haitian maids speaking Creole. She made forty dollars a day, and all the change she could find in the big industrial clothes dryer. We lived off Blue Bird tuna fish, nine cents a can after we cut out Sunday newspaper coupons. If we were flush, we'd go to different bars in town for Happy Hour. We each ordered a dollar beer, ate the Happy Hour hors d'oeuvres for dinner, and left a dollar tip. One day, we stole a T-bone steak from Winn-Dixie. We raced home on our bicycle. I pedaled like Lance Armstrong, looking over my shoulder for the heat. Susie sat on the handlebars, laughing and kicking her long legs like a chorus girl. She clutched that steak to her chest as if it was her baby.

We used our maxed-out credit cards to pay for gas for our Alfa, and other incidentals we needed to live on. We never charged more than $22.99 at one time on those maxed-out cards. In those days, there were no electronic devices for merchants to instantly check a credit card's status. They had to call an 800 number to check it. But if the bill was for less than twenty-three dollars, they didn't bother. The credit card company had to eat all bad charges under twenty-three dollars. Dad would have loved that. One day, however, we screwed up at a liquor store and charged a twenty-five-dollar bottle of vodka on our card. The clerk called the 800 number while a line of customers waited behind us. When he got off the phone he reached under the counter and produced a pair of scissors as big as garden shears. He held up our card for everyone to see, and cut it in half. The customers behind us cheered the clerk, as if he had just machine-gunned Bonnie and Clyde. We slunk out, Susie whispering to me, "The garden shears were a bit much, don't you think?"

Still, every day I wrote at my desk. I wrote story after story, about my baseball career, my family, our life in Florida, even our "pocket Ferrari." They were first-person, slice-of-life stories magazines weren't much interested in then. But in the late 1980s, for some reason, magazines began to buy them. *People, Life, Time, Reader's Digest, TV Guide, Woman's World, Southern Magazine.* I churned out those stories one after another for a few hundred dollars each. The magazines were so pleased with my work they gave me assignments, mostly profiles of famous people. Then, more prestigious magazines like *Gentleman's Quarterly, Playboy,* the *New Yorker,* and the *New York Times Magazine* gave me assignments. Now for five and ten thousand dollars each, big money for us in those days, I was writing cover stories on Wayne Huizenga, of Blockbuster fame, Tom Selleck, Burt Reynolds, and Ted Turner, CNN mogul and owner of the Braves, pre Jane Fonda. Soon, we weren't poor anymore. We bought our steaks now. We took our friends out to dinner, our treat. I left big tips. We bought a dog, and then more dogs. A parrot. In the early 1990s we bought a new car, then our house, with Dad's help. We stiffed Visa, Mastercard, Amex.

I talked to Ma and Dad over the phone a few times a week. I played it fast and light, like an old soft-shoe man in Vaudeville. I told them only good news, never bad. How Stella got knocked up by Nero, and the two puppies they produced. Ma roared with laughter, "A *puttana frigida,* that Stella." I told Dad what stories I was working on, when my next story would appear in what magazine. "I'll send you copies, pop," I said. "You don't have to buy them anymore." He said, "I'm glad things are going well for you, son."

I talked to my brother maybe twice a month. I didn't see him but maybe ten times in the twenty-seven years we lived in Florida. I would come back to Fairfield to stay with him for a day or two while I commuted to New York City to interview an actress or an athlete. He didn't seem to mind our long absences. And when we did talk, over the phone or at his house, I deferred to him. Yes, brother. You're right, brother. I should have known, brother. I think he knew what I was doing, but he never let on. His much younger brother now condescending to him as if he was the child. I think he felt a kind of freedom in our relationship now. He was relieved he no longer had to fulfill his little charade of our brotherhood after all those years. God, how he must have hated the terrible pressure I had put on him since I was a child. How I must have, unwittingly, burdened him with my brotherhood all those years. How he must have hated...no! I will never believe that...how he must have resented me.

After enough years had passed, we made our separate peace. I had caught up to my brother in age, in a way. When he was forty, I was a kid in my twenties. Now I was in my sixties, an old man with white hair and a white beard. My brother was in his late seventies, but still he looked younger than me, with his steel-gray Brillo hair like Ma's. He always looked the same to me, like Dad did. I had caught up to Dad, too. An old man pushing ninety, with old sons in their sixties and seventies. We occupied the same turf in our turf wars now.

One day in the late 1990s, George called to tell me Dad needed triple bypass heart surgery. I said, "He's eighty-eight, for chrissakes, the surgery will kill him!"

George said, "Actually, brother, the doctor said, except for his heart, Dad has the body of a fifty-year-old. If he survives the operation, he'll live another seven years. If he doesn't have the operation, he'll be dead in six months."

"What does Dad think?"

"Well, he talked to the doctor and he asked him what the odds were that he'd survive the operation."

"What'd the doctor say?

"Sixty-forty."

"What'd Dad say?"

"Whose favor?" He paused a second, then said, "The doctor said, 'Sixty-forty, your favor, Mr. Jordan.'"

"What'd Dad say?"

"I'll take those odds any day."

I laughed, then said, "When's he having the operation?"

"That's why I'm calling, brother. Since there's a risk in the opera-tion, the doctor wants his closest blood relation to sign off on it."

"So sign the fucking paper."

George didn't say anything for a moment. Then he said, "You're the only one who can sign it, brother."

So I signed. Dad survived the operation and lived seven more years.

A year or so after his operation, Dad and Ma moved into an assisted living home. Dad adjusted easily. He told me, "I'm used to living on the fly." But Ma didn't like it. She refused to have anything to do with the other old biddies, as she called them. She spent most of her time in their apartment. She refused to eat with the others in the common dining room. So Dad brought her food to her. She ate in her wheelchair. Her legs were swollen and discolored now that she was retaining water. When Ma dozed in her wheelchair, Dad dressed in his Ivy League uniform, and wandered through the complex as if he owned it. The suckers bought his con. The nurses cooed over him, this dapper old man, with his oozing charm, like maple syrup. The other inmates, as Dad called them, relied on Dad for help. How to fill out forms. A halting walk back to their rooms, an old lady holding on to Dad's arm, hobbling, but smiling, too, at faint memories of her first walk down the aisle seventy years ago. When older children of prospective residents visited the home to check it out for their aged parents, the warden trotted out Dad to show them around.

"Just like the carnival," Dad told me. "I'm a shill again." Then he added, "I was born in an institution and I'll go out in one." But that didn't stop him from his life's work. He booked bets on the pay phone in the lobby. He hustled an old Mark, five years younger than him, in pool in the recreation room. "I let him win the first few days," Dad said, "now I'm gonna raise the stakes and drop the ham-mer." Dad was living a parody of his entire life in a fucking old age home. Unbelievable! He always did make the best of any situation, especially the bad ones. He made something positive out of every-thing in his life, which, now, at ninety-one, as always, was an inspi-ration to me. He told me, "Always keep going. You walk through shit until it turns to clover. It always did, for me."

I only visited Ma and Dad one time in their assisted living home. George called me in the summer of 2001. He told me Dad really missed me, and would love to see me. But more importantly, Ma, at ninety-five, was fading fast. "This might be the last time you'll get to see her," he said. "I'll tell her I'm coming for a visit, and you could surprise her."

George met me at Bradley Airport in Hartford and we drove straight to the home. It was situated up on a hill, surrounded by trees and looking down on the scenic Merritt Parkway in Stratford. It was a one-story, red-brick building that looked like a classy motel. Inside, the walls were paneled in wood, the rugs a dark green. There was a working fireplace in the common room. Old men and old ladies were sitting there on sofas and easy chairs, some talking, some sleeping, a few just staring vacantly into their dimly-remembered, distant past.

George led me down a narrow hallway, past doors, until he came to Ma's and Dad's apartment. He knocked on the door, winked at me, and called out, "Ma, it's your favorite sonny boy." I heard Ma's voice, "Dad, it's my George, open the door."

When Dad opened the door and saw me, his eyes teared up. George put a finger to his lips and shook his head. Dad kissed me on the cheek like he and George always did. He looked the same, a little more bent over, but still a sharp-looking old guy. George had told me on the drive from Hartford, "Dad's in great shape, brother. You got great genes." I replied, "And what about Ma? She's ninety-five. You don't have great genes, too?"

George walked ahead of me into their small living room where Ma was sitting in her wheelchair. I walked behind him, Dad behind me. Ma's face lit up when she saw George. Before she could say any-thing, my brother stepped aside to reveal her other son, smiling at her. "Surprise, Ma," I said. Her smile vanished. George said, "It's Patty, Ma." She said, "I know who it is." George said, "Go give your mother a kiss, brother." I went over to Ma, leaned down and kissed

her on the cheek. I said, "You look great, Ma, not a day over seventy."
She looked at me with those black predator's eyes and said, "You look
like an old man." I smiled, "I am an old man, Ma. I'm not little Patty
anymore."

My brother and I sat on their small sofa, side-by-side, facing Ma.
Dad sat on an easy chair across the room. Ma sat sideways to us, in
her wheelchair, staring straight ahead. Her legs were swollen and
discolored, her hair thinning, but she was still my mother, refusing
to look at us with those eyes of animal cunning. No thought, no in-
trospection, just instinct. Like a wolf.

I remembered something that happened after George returned
home from his nervous breakdown. He was still in a very fragile
mental state. One day, one of George's daughters visited Ma for
lunch. After her granddaughter left, Ma discovered that most of her
jewelry was gone from her bathroom jewelry box. She was livid. The
following afternoon, in her apartment, Ma told me that she was going to tell George his daughter stole her jewelry.

I said, "You can't do that, Ma. Forget the fucking jewelry. You tell
George his daughter's a thief, you could send him back to the sanitarium."

She looked at me with those predator eyes and said, "I don't care.
I want my jewelry back."

George said to Ma in her wheelchair, "Patty was dying to see you and
Dad, Ma. He got on the first plane he could."

My mother said nothing.

Dad leaned toward her in his chair and said, "Say hello to your
son, Flo. You haven't seen him in years."

She gave him a look. "I talk to him on the phone." Dad sat back.

"It was a long flight, Ma," George said. "Patty had to change
planes twice. Just to see his mother."

My mother looked at me with barely concealed rage.

Dad said, "Ma made tuna fish sandwiches for lunch. I'll get
them." He got up to get them.

"I only made three," she said.

George said, "Patty can have mine, Ma. I'm not hungry."

"Neither am I, Ma," I said.

There was a long silence. Dad sat back down.

George threw his arm over my shoulder and smiled. "You got your two sonny boys together, Ma. Isn't that great?"

My mother said nothing.

Dad said, "Flo, what's a matter with you? Talk to your son."

George said, "I was telling Patty about when I was a kid living in the tenement with you and Grandma and Aunt Marie. Remember the time you broke the window with your purse? Tell Patty what happened."

"I don't want to talk about it." My mother and I looked at each other.

# CHAPTER FORTY-TWO

My mother lived her life, and left it, exactly as she wanted to. She died at 5 a.m., November 2, 2003, a Sunday. She was ninety-seven. She had gone into St. Vincent's Hospital because she was losing weight. Her doctor performed tests. He came into her room with his clipboard and said, "Mrs. Jordan, there's nothing wrong with you. You don't even have high blood pressure. You could live another five or six years." She said, "I'm tired." He said, "That's because you lost weight. We'll fatten you up in a week and send you home." My mother said, "I don't have a home. I live with strangers."

The nurses brought my mother her meals. She refused to eat them. So her nurses fed her intravenously and watched her throughout the day. She told them stories that made them laugh. Three and four nurses stood around her bed, laughing at her stories about her childhood, her girlhood, her parents, her sisters, her brother, her husband, and her sons. When they left her alone at night, she pulled the feeding tubes out of her arm.

"Her arms were black and blue," my brother said when he called to tell me Ma had died.

I flew from Florida to Connecticut for the church service. My brother and I stood in the back of the old stone Gothic Cathedral of my youth and greeted the other mourners. All of her contemporaries were dead. Her brother and two sisters, her friends, everyone except Dad, who was ninety-three. She was survived by her two sons, our children and grandchildren, and my mother's nieces and nephews. Only a few of my mother's eleven grandchildren and twenty-four great-grandchildren were there. Many of them lived out of state. My brother and I told them it wasn't necessary for them to make the trip. We relieved them of the burden of attending the funeral of a

woman none of them were close to. My mother didn't much countenance children. They were messy, silly, a nuisance. She had no interest in changing their diapers, cooking pastina in butter for them,
teaching them to draw, amusing them as grandmothers do. When
my six-year-old daughter broke her arm so badly that she almost lost
it, Ma didn't visit her in the hospital for days. It was summer, and
Ma liked to go to the beach in the summer. Finally, on a rainy day,
Ma went to the hospital. I showed up twenty minutes later to hear
Ma, sitting beside my sedated daughter's bed, saying to her, "If you're
not interested in talking to Grandma, I might as well leave."

When children grew up, and amused Ma now, she tolerated
them a bit more.

Dad, looking lost and frail, stood behind my brother and me in
the back of the Cathedral. He looked down with his faded blue-gray
eyes at his felt fedora he fingered in his hands. He kept turning the
brim of his fedora around and around as if looking for an imperfec-
tion. My brother and I blocked him from view as we greeted the
mourners. We told them funny stories about Ma. How she hated
to cook. Soup out of a can for George. Fried dough for me. "Never
more than one ingredient," George said. They laughed. No one cried,
except my Down syndrome cousin, Kenneth.

Kenneth was sixty-two, but childish, and old ladyish, too. He had
spent most of his life in the kitchen with his mother and her sisters,
tiny, fierce, dark-skinned women who fussed over and protected him.
When he was born, and the doctor informed my Aunt Marie of his
condition, she screamed and went into shock. All her hair fell out, and
never grew back. She always wore henna-colored wigs. The doctor
suggested she put her son into a home for such children, which might
better care for him. But Aunt Marie refused. She raised Kenneth as if
he was an animal. If he spilled his milk or wet his pants, she beat him
with a strap. Over the years, Kenneth was trained to function in this
world at an elemental level. He learned to read and write, add and
subtract. He became a baseball and basketball fan. He kept his own
box scores of those games. He would show them to me, and say, "See,
Cousin Patty. Mickey Mantle made two hits last night. He's batting
.356.9." One summer, in his teens, his parents took him on a cruise

to Europe. Kenneth spent his time on that ship reading magazines. One day in the middle of the Atlantic Ocean, he brought a copy of *Life* magazine to his mother. He showed her an article about Down syndrome children. "That's me, isn't it?" he said.

In his adult years, Kenneth got a job as a bank courier in downtown Bridgeport. He would carry documents in a leather briefcase, walking down Main Street from one bank to another. People got to know him. They smiled and waved. He ate his lunch always in the same little diner off Main Street. When the bill came, he bent over and examined it as if it was the Dead Sea Scrolls. And for him, maybe it was, all those numbers. Satisfied the bill was correct, he calculated the gratuity on his fingers, always 10 percent. He counted out the coins from his rubber sow's purse and left them by his dish. The waitress took away his dish, pocketed the coins, and thanked him with a smile.

After Kenneth's mother and father died, my father used to drive him to work every morning and pick him up at night. Kenneth paid Dad fifty dollars a week for his efforts. His parents had left him millions to support himself, with the aid of a live-in nurse, and my father's help.

One winter morning, Dad's Volkswagen Beetle skidded in the snow and dented a parked car on Main Street. Neither Dad nor Kenneth was hurt. Kenneth, beside him, said, "You hit a car, Uncle Pat." Dad said, "It's nothing, Kenneth, we're all right." Dad got out of his Beetle and left a note on the parked car's windshield. The note read, "Sorry."

That night, Kenneth called Dad and told him he didn't want him to drive him to work anymore. "You're too old," Kenneth said. Dad was in his eighties then, but still vigorous. More to the point, Dad and Ma would miss that fifty dollars a week. When Dad got off the phone, he told Ma that Kenneth had fired him. Dad said, "Fired by a retard." Then he cursed "that bearded bastard on a cross who deserved his own crucifixion." Dad did not often curse, but when he did, it was always the same curse, as if he had a personal relationship with our Savior, who had betrayed him.

Now, Kenneth came up to me in the back of the church where I stood with George and Dad. Tears streamed down his hairless cheeks. He threw his arms around me, wailing like an hysterical woman in an orgy of grief I was not sure he felt, or understood.

The story of how his parents got those millions of dollars to leave to Kenneth was one never spoken of in my family. But I remember it. I was six, asleep in my upstairs bedroom one night when I was jolted awake by my mother's animal-like shrieks from the kitchen, like a wolf with its leg caught in a steel trap. Then she began to cry, pitifully, the only time I ever heard my mother cry. Through her tears I heard her say, "But how could you, Marie? Your own brother and sister!"

"I deserved it," Marie said. "I took care of Ma when she was dying. Look at you. You have your beautiful son. Patty can take care of himself someday. Who's going to take care of my son?"

I learned over the years, in bits and pieces, that as Grandma Diamond lay dying of cancer, Aunt Marie did take care of her. As the youngest, she was the only sibling still living in the tenement with her mother, and Marie's new husband and son. When Grandma's pain increased, the nurses gave her more and more morphine. Marie waited until the morphine had disoriented Grandma, then Marie put a revised will in front of her and told her to sign it. That will had been drawn up by Aunt Josephine's husband, my Uncle Ken, whose law career had been saved by my father's intercession. That will left three quarters of Grandma's estate, a few hundred thousand dollars, to Marie, one quarter to Josephine, and nothing to my mother or Uncle Ben. Marie's husband, my Uncle Pat, was a stockbroker at A.M. Kidder. He invested their inheritance in stocks, and over the years he turned it into millions of dollars.

My brother and I and Dad walked down the aisle to our seats in the front row closest to the altar. George wore a gray suit from J. Press, Dad wore his Ivy League uniform. I wore a creased and cracked, black leather sport jacket, jeans, and work boots, which I often wore when my feet were swollen from arthritis. Dad slid into the row first, then me, then my brother on the aisle. Everyone else sat behind us. We waited for the priest to come out to the altar and begin Mass. The three of us sat in silence, staring at the altar. Behind us we heard muffled voices.

I looked for my mother's coffin on the altar, but it wasn't there. I leaned toward my brother and said, "Where's Ma?" Still staring at the altar, he said, "She was cremated." I didn't know that. Nobody told me. I wanted to ask my brother why she was cremated, where, when, and where were her ashes. But I didn't. I just kept staring at the altar wondering where my mother was.

A bell rang and everyone stood. A priest in white robes came out of the sacristy onto the altar. He had blue eyes and a full, red beard like a warrior from *Braveheart*. He began Mass in English. My brother and I shared a missal, but lost our place. We mumbled responses. Behind us, the other mourners mumbled responses. Dad was silent, staring at the altar. I leaned toward my brother and whispered, "No altar boys." George nodded. Another bell rang. Some of the mourners sat, others kneeled, then the ones who sat kneeled, too. Throughout Mass we all sat and stood and kneeled out of sync. Finally the priest read the gospel, and then went to the pulpit to speak. Everyone sat.

The priest began talking about my mother. He said she was beloved by everyone who knew her. He said that her life, like every life, was like an ocean. It swept on to shore, then receded. I whispered to George, "What does that mean?" He shrugged. The priest was smiling now as he said we'd all remember "happy times and laughing times and bright and sunny days with Florence. Her echo would always be whispering softly down the ways." My brother leaned toward me and said in a hushed voice, "Whispering softly? Ma?"

When the priest finished talking about our mother, my brother and I slid out of the pew and went up to the pulpit. My brother would speak first. I stood behind him. I looked at my brother's back as he took a typewritten piece of white paper from his inside jacket pocket. He unfolded it, put on his reading glasses, and began to read in his droning voice, without inflection. For the next fifteen minutes, he held up slides, many of which I had never seen before.

He read my mother's full name. I didn't know her middle name was June. He said our grandfather was a prize fighter. I knew that. But I didn't know that my grandmother was "a beauty from Brooklyn," who was born in the United States, not Italy, in the 1880s. I did know she was a businesswoman who sold bootleg wine during Prohibition and paid the Irish cop on the beat to look the other way.

My brother said our mother was "a beauty, too," like her mother. Which was a stretch. Ma had a strong, big-nosed, mannish face, which, with age, would be described as handsome. She had a man's strong will, too, my brother said. I knew that. And a perceptive mind, quick wit, and unflinching honesty. When he visited her in the hospital the day before she died, she introduced him to the nurses as "My handsome son." When the nurses left, George asked her why she always told people he was handsome. She said, "You were my son. What the hell else could I say?" The mourners' muffled laughter drifted up from the pews. What my brother didn't mention was that Ma always said I was "the pretty son."

Then my brother told the story of our parents' "great romance." He didn't mention his own natural father. He said our mother was the first and only woman Dad would ever love. I knew that. Dad was younger than Ma. I knew that. All the men in my family married women older than themselves. Mil was two years older than George, Susan was two years older than me, and both of my sons married women five years older than themselves. George said Dad mooned around Ma like a lovesick cow for years before she consented to marry him. I didn't know that. I thought they married when George was a child, not a nine-year-old boy. "My father waited patiently until my mother turned his way," George said. "It was a long wooing."

Then my brother talked about what it was like to be an Italian when he was a boy. How Italian Americans had a thing about their names in those days. His wife, Mildred, had changed her name from Carmela. I never knew that. His grandparents' last name was DiMenna, but they changed it to Diamond. I knew that. Dad's last name was Giordano, but he changed it to Jordan a few days before his son was born. "He wanted his son to have an American name,"

George said. I knew that. But I had thought Dad had changed his name long before I was born.

"Dad went before a judge to change his name," George said. "The judge told him it would cost seven dollars. Dad said he didn't have seven dollars. The judge was already late for his golf game so he changed Dad's name for nothing. He never found out that Dad had almost a thousand dollars in his pocket that day." The mourners laughed. I never knew that story.

George said, "Dad always loved the con." The mourners laughed again. I knew that.

My brother concluded his talk with a reference again to our mother's indomitable will. He looked out at all her relatives seated in the pews and said, "a part of her is in all of us, and my brother." I thought it odd that, up until that moment, all my brother's reminiscences of my mother and father and him had to do with their life before I was born.

My brother left the altar and sat down in his pew. I moved to the pulpit and took out four pieces of note paper on which I had written my reminiscences of my mother. I put on my reading glasses and looked out over them all, my cousins and nieces and nephews, whom I hadn't seen in twenty years. The men had dark hair tinged with silver. The women had dyed jet-black hair that I remembered from my youth. The women were darker skinned than the men, and not so handsome with their black eyes and big noses. I saw my cousin who was on her sixth marriage. "I'm still trying to get it right, Patty," she told me. I saw George's daughter whom my mother had accused of stealing her jewelry. I saw my cousin whom I used to play with as a boy. She and I were always getting in trouble, instigated by me. When we were eleven, I convinced her to drive off with her mother's car. "Why me?" she asked. I said, "Because you're taller than me." We drove the car around the block. I gave her instructions as her co-pilot. "Faster, faster!" and then, "Watch out for the car coming at us." When we came back down the street toward her house, we saw her mother, my Aunt Josephine, standing on the sidewalk, her fists planted on her hips.

I saw Kenneth in the pew by himself. When we were kids, he and my car thief cousin and I would play cards together on Aunt Josephine's screened porch. One day, Ken made a foolish throw of the cards. I said, "That was stupid, Kenneth." His mother flew into the porch in a rage. She screamed at me, "Don't ever call my son stupid!" My mother followed her into the porch. She glared at her younger sister with her black eyes, and snapped, "Don't you talk that way to my son. He doesn't know."

I looked for my male cousin who had served a year and a day in the Danbury Federal prison for stock fraud, but I couldn't find him. The Feds furloughed him on weekends so he could visit his wife. On weekdays he played tennis on the Club Fed courts, where he perfected his backhand. When he was released he gained notoriety as a local country club tennis champion.

I saw my father and brother looking up at me, waiting. I began to talk.

I talked about how my mother was always trying to make a man of me. When I cried over some little thing she told me to stop crying and be a man. I was five the first time she said that. I waited for the mourners to laugh. They didn't. So I told them about the neighborhood bully who made me cry and how Ma pushed me out of the house and wouldn't let me back in until I got even. When I did, and the bully was crying now, Ma and I laughed crocodile tears in the kitchen. Nothing.

I switched gears and told the mourners about the Woodfield girls my mother told me were good girls. Nothing. I looked at my notes and decided not to tell the mourners about Ma's sex lesson to me. "Don't buy a girl a hamburger and try to squeeze it out of her afterwards."

I fiddled with my notes until I came to something I was sure they would smile at. I told them Ma never raised a hand to me, although she had reason to often enough, except one time. I was fourteen, a big kid. Ma was a little person, barely five feet tall. I did something that angered her, I don't remember what. Everything I did seemed to piss her off when I was a kid. So she got a broom and chased me around the house, from room to room, swatting the broom at me, and missing, which made her more furious. She finally trapped me in the kitchen. But she was breathing heavily now. I said, "Catch your breath, Ma. Here." I put a stool in front of her and said, "Stand on this so you can reach me, Ma." I helped her step up onto the stool, like a Prince helping a Princess up to her throne. She wobbled a bit on the stool, then smacked me on the back with the broom. It broke in half. I laughed, "That didn't even hurt." Her face flushed in anger, and then she burst out laughing. Resigned, she said, "You're too big to hit now. I should have beat you like a rug when you were younger." Now the mourners laughed.

I didn't tell the mourners that Ma was always a tough audience. I had to work my ass off to make her laugh. And she worked just as hard not to laugh with me. Not because Ma had no sense of humor, she was a funny old girl, and not because I wasn't a funny son, I was. But because, I think, Ma saw laughter, with me, as a kind of surrender that betrayed her oldest son.

I turned over my notes, but I had misplaced the last page. I stood there like a confused old man, looking for the last page, trying to remember how I was going to end my talk. Then I remembered the only time I was ever cruel to my mother. We were all sitting around George's dining room table, me, Dad, George, and his granddaughter, Lois. We were eating and drinking while George told a story about Ma, how beautiful she had been as a girl. "She still is beautiful, isn't that right, brother?" he said. I laughed and said, "Even Ma will admit she was never a beauty, right, Ma?" The table went silent. I looked at my mother. An old woman in her eighties. I saw the humiliation on her reddened face. It didn't shame me then. I thought I was being funny. But remembering it, now that she was dead, it shamed me like nothing else I ever did in my life.

I was too ashamed to tell the mourners that story.

The Church was silent, everyone waiting. Finally, I said, "Everything I learned about being a man I learned from my mother." I looked up and saw Dad and George. I went on "...and from my father and my brother."

I left the altar and went down to the pew. My brother stepped out into the aisle to let me in. He put his arms around me and kissed me on the cheek.

# CHAPTER FORTY-THREE

After Mass, we all drove to my brother's house. It was a cold, damp day. I drove past the small Dutch colonial house where I had lived for forty years, first with my parents, then with my wife and five children. I drove past the park where I'd played baseball, and the grammar school I'd gone to, and the drug store where, as a boy, I'd spent hours sitting on a soda fountain stool, sipping my chocolate milk shake while reading stories in sports magazines about my baseball heroes. Then I came to the winding driveway that led up a hill to an old colonial house with its plaque on the front door.

Inside, the house was already packed with people. Everyone was eating Italian pastries and drinking and talking and laughing. I could barely move through the kitchen to the bar in the hallway. I poured myself some bourbon and went into the dining room that never changed. The six-foot walk-in fireplace, Abe and George Washington on the walls. That round dining room table groaning under the weight of all that food.

My relatives came up to me to express condolences, not with tears, but with smiles. They all had funny stories to tell about my mother, which, if she were alive, she wouldn't have found funny. My cousin, my co-conspirator, childhood car thief, introduced me to her daughter whom I had never met, and her daughter's husband, who was Japanese. He bowed as he shook my hand. I told him and his wife about the time my cousin and I stole her mother's car. They laughed, and then moved off. I was alone with my cousin. She was tall, thin, and dark-skinned, with black hair. She had been a nurse for almost forty years. I thanked her for caring for my mother in her last days. Her eyes teared up and she said, "I wished I could have done more for her. She'd done so much for me... She was like a mother to me." She wiped her eyes and smiled at me, "But you knew that." But I didn't know that. She went on, "Aunt Flo was so warm and alive and funny. You knew my mother. How cold she was. I used to fantasize that if only Flo had been my mother."

"Aunt Joe never liked me much," I said. "I don't blame her. She thought I was a bad influence on you."

My cousin laughed. "You were! I loved it!"

"Remember the baseball?" I asked. When we were ten, we used to play baseball in the street in front of her house. I gave her a glove and told her to catch the balls I hit. I hit baseballs over her head. She chased them down the street or into the neighbor's back yard. She snuck in, grabbed the ball out of a rose garden, and ran back to the street. Out of breath, she said, "When do I get a chance to hit, Patty?"

"Soon."

One time I hit a high fly ball. She circled under the ball, put the glove up in front of her eyes, and caught the ball on her lip. Blood splattered everywhere. We ran to her house. When her mother saw the blood, she screamed at me, "You've disfigured my daughter!"

My cousin laughed. "Actually, my lip was a little fatter." She gave me a sly smile. "It went better with the rest of me when I got older."

I remembered when we were fourteen, sitting together in the backseat of her mother's car, while her mother drove and my mother sat beside her sister. "They were discussing your breasts," I said. My cousin laughed, "Oh, please, don't remind me. It was humiliating."

My mother was saying, "Her breasts are getting fuller."

Aunt Josephine said, "Not too full, I hope."

My mother said, "Why not? The fuller the better."

I remembered something else that happened when we were fourteen. But I was too embarrassed to bring it up. The time my cousin caught me staring at her breasts while we were watching television. She gave me a knowing smile.

My cousin must have known what I was thinking. She said, "You know, I would have done anything for you when we were kids." She looked at me. "I still would, Patty. I wanted to be like you so much. You were always so alive. When I was ten my mother caught me in the bathroom, standing over the toilet, peeing. She screamed at me,

'What are you doing? Sit down on the toilet like a girl's supposed to.' I said, 'Patty stands up to pee. I can, too.'" We both laughed so loud that people in George's dining room stared at us.

My cousin said, "My mother was such a prude. But Aunt Flo was never prudish about sex." I knew that. Then she smiled to herself at some distant memory.

"What?" I asked.

She said, "I was just thinking. When I was eighteen Flo was more my girlfriend than some old Auntie. Remember, at the time, the drinking age in Connecticut was twenty-one. So all the high school kids drove to Portchester, New York, where the drinking age was eighteen. When Flo found out what my girlfriends and I did every weekend, she insisted that she go with us. My girlfriends loved that, because she was so funny and cool. It didn't hurt either that when we got to the liquor store, she gave us forty bucks to pay for the booze. Then she insisted she drive back while my girlfriends and I passed around a bottle of scotch and sang dirty songs." She paused a moment, frowning, then said, "One of my girlfriends said to me, 'Your poor aunt, she must be so lonely to hang out with teenaged girls on the weekend.' I was furious. I couldn't believe how stupid that girl was. I said, 'You think she comes to hang out with four teenaged girls? She comes to protect us, you idiot.'"

My cousin smiled at me, "And she did it so off-handedly that those girls never knew. But I knew... Your mother was a pip, Patty." Another thing I didn't know.

I said, "Yeah, well, Ma wasn't a pip with me, cuz."

My cousin flapped a hand at me, as if to dismiss a child. "Oh, Patty, don't be foolish. Auntie Flo was always talking about you. 'Patty did this and Patty did that.'" She smiled. "My girlfriends would listen to her talk about how handsome you were and what a great baseball pitcher you were when she was driving us to Portchester. My girlfriends were salivating. They'd whisper to me, 'When are we gonna meet your handsome cousin?'"

"Why didn't I meet them, cuz?"

"Because I decided they weren't good enough for you, Patty." Then she said, "When you went to Florida to live, you know, your parents missed you so much. So I stopped at their apartment every day. I loved talking to your mother and father. They were like my parents."

I said, "You were lucky, cuz. You had two sets of parents."

She looked at me. "No, I didn't. I couldn't stand my parents. Your parents were my mother and father."

My other cousin, the serial matrimonialist, came over to us. She told me I looked older than she remembered. I told her she looked the same, at fifty-seven, with her jet-black hair. She ran her hands through her hair, "Genes," she said, and laughed. I asked her about her new husband, number six. She said, "He's a keeper, Patty." Then she added, "I'm tired being the Liz Taylor of Fairfield." We all laughed. My two cousins drifted off.

Kenneth came up to me. He threw his arms around my neck and hugged me. He said, "I loved Auntie Flo so much. She was like a mother to me after my mother died. And Uncle Pat, too, was always like a father to me." I pulled his arms away from my neck and walked away. I went into my brother's wood-paneled den. The room was crowded with people sitting on his overstuffed chairs and sofas and loveseat. My father was sitting on a small wing chair, drinking scotch. He was talking to one of his great-granddaughters. I sat across from him beside my brother. I asked my brother about his grandson, Tony. He was a minor league player with the Dodgers, as I had been with the Braves years before. My brother used to keep a huge black-and-white photograph of me, at eighteen, in a Milwaukee Braves' uniform, in his law office. It was taken at County Stadium in Milwaukee. Whitlow Wyatt, the Braves' pitching coach, was to my right, but my face was turned to my left toward Warren Spahn, the greatest left-handed pitcher ever. Spahn was saying something to me while I looked at him with my amused smile.

When George moved into his home office, that picture was too big for his wall so he put it in the attic. Now, all he wanted to talk about was his grandson Tony's career. Which always annoyed me. Tony, inadvertently, had been the cause of my brief estrangement from my father a few years ago. I kept asking Dad to come visit

Susie and me in Florida for years. He always had an excuse why he couldn't come. A few years back, he said he couldn't make the trip because he couldn't leave Ma. "She's getting old, son," he said. I said, "Then get a live-in nurse for her and you come down for a few days." He said, "Oh, I could never do that."

A week later I called Ma to see how she was. A strange woman answered the phone. "Who are you?" I asked. She said, "Your mother's nurse." I asked her where my father was. She told me he had gone to Omaha, Nebraska, to see his great-grandson play baseball. She said, "His great-grandson's father sent his Learjet for your father, and flew him to Nebraska." The nurse chuckled. "He had a stewardess all to himself. Your father was quite impressed. 'They treated me like a King,' he told me."

My brother, beside me, was still talking about Tony. I nodded as if I was listening. But I was looking across at my father. He was staring at me while George talked. Dad's eyes were red-rimmed. Suddenly Dad said loudly to me, "You look like a bum. Don't you have decent shoes?"

George stopped talking and looked at Dad. Before I could say anything, my brother said, "Give the kid a break, Dad. He came all this way." My brother always called me the kid, no matter how old I got.

My father stood up, lurched forward as if to fall. I stood up and caught him by his elbow. I led him to the hall bathroom and waited outside. Then I led him back to his chair. He slumped down, his head hanging almost to his chest. He muttered something.

"What was that, Dad?" I asked.

He said, more forcefully, "What am I going to do without her?"

"You'll be all right, Dad," I said.

He looked at me with tears in his eyes. "I miss you, son. When will you come back to see me again?"

"Soon," I lied.

# CHAPTER FORTY-FOUR

Two years after my mother died, my father finally visited me and Susan in Florida. He was ninety-five. The visit was my brother's idea. "To connect with Dad one last time," he said.

I went to the airport early in the afternoon to meet Dad. I got a pass that let me meet him at the gate. George told me to get Dad a wheelchair. I said, "He's too vigorous for that. It'll embarrass him." George said, "No. He likes the attention." I pushed the empty wheelchair down to the gate and waited. When his flight arrived, I got as close to the tunnel that led to the plane as I could. I eyeballed the passengers emerging from the tunnel. I asked one of the passengers if he remembered an old man on the flight. "He's bald, with a white brush mustache and blue-gray eyes. He's wearing a navy blazer and gray slacks." The man smiled, and said, "You're the writer. I sat next to him. He talked my ear off about you the entire flight."

"That's him."

Finally Dad came hobbling out of the tunnel. He was clutching a bag in one hand and in the other, a paperback book. He looked the same as always. His uniform, those eyes, his con.

"Curly!" I said. He looked up and smiled at me. We kissed. Then I said, "I got you a wheelchair. George's idea. But I told him you wouldn't need it."

"I'd like it," Dad said in a weak voice. I wondered, was he really as frail as he was acting? Or was he just auditioning a new con? The curse of a con man's son. You trust no one.

I took his bag and settled him in the wheelchair. I began pushing him through the crowded airport. He arranged the paperback book on his lap so that its cover showed, something by Camus. A new twist for Dad, I thought, the Existential French. He made his bones on the Greeks years ago. Plato, Socrates, Aristotle. He memorized bits and pieces he would quote, "An unexamined life is not worth living." It impressed the suckers while he stole their money.

People smiled down at the old man with the book. *Il Professore* with his dutiful son, also an old man in his sixties with his white hair and beard.

I leaned over Dad and said, "How does it feel to be ninety-five, pop?"

"Not like I felt at eighty-five."

I helped him out of the wheelchair at the escalator and pushed it aside. I held him by the elbow as we descended. At the bottom, we walked a few feet through the baggage claim and then through the sliding doors and we were outside in the hot, humid Florida sunshine. The noise and the traffic were disorienting. I leaned over and said, "Do you want to sit here, Dad, while I get the car?"

"No. I can walk."

A sheriff's deputy stopped traffic so Dad and I could cross the street to the parking garage. It was dark and cool in the garage. I sat him down on a bench near the elevator. "I have to hunt for the car, Dad," I said. "If I'm not back in an hour, call the cops." He didn't laugh or smile. He just put a hand on my arm and said, "Don't leave me here, son." I said, "Don't worry, Dad, I won't lose you."

As I walked toward the car at the far end of the garage, I called Susie on my cell phone. She said, "How is he?"

"I can't tell yet."

"What does that mean?"

"He either got old, or he got a new con."

When we pulled up in front of our Key West bungalow with the tin roof, I said to Dad, "This is your house, Dad. We wouldn't have it if it wasn't for you." He said, "It's a pretty little house. I'm glad I could do it for you, son."

Susie greeted Dad at the front door with a kiss. "We missed you," she said. He smiled, "I missed my beautiful daughter-in-law, too." She said, "Wait here, Dad, until I put the dogs out back." She was afraid our six dogs would greet Dad effusively, as they did all our guests, by putting their front paws on him and knocking him down.

"That's all right," Dad said. "I want to see the orphan." He meant Matthew, our rescue dog from the mountains of western North Carolina. He was a Golden Retriever-Spaniel mix. We called him a Retraniel, our designer dog. Our other five dogs were thoroughbred Shiba Inus, short, muscular Japanese hunting dogs, close descendants of wolves.

The first time we brought Matthew to our vet in Ft. Lauderdale, he held Matthew's snout and looked him close in the eye. The vet said, "Do you realize how lucky you are? How fucking lucky you are?" Matthew did. He never did a thing wrong in all the days of his life. All he asked for in that life was to be close to us and be fed twice a day, which made him deliriously happy, unlike our more neurotic Shibas with their conflicting moods. They were aloof, stubborn, needy, playful. When we fed Matthew he looked up at us as if to say, "Oh, you're feeding me. You must be God." When we fed our Shibas they looked up at us as if to say, "Oh, you're feeding me. I must be God."

Dad had never met Matthew. He knew him only by the photos I sent him. But he identified with Matthew from the first moment he heard Matthew's story. "An orphan like me," Dad said.

Matthew was a con like Dad, too. He ran out of the North Carolina woods with his two brothers one night and up onto the front porch of our vacation cabin. They were scraggly, starving, flea-and-tick infested puppies no more than twelve weeks old. We could see the outline of their ribs. Matthew's brothers wolfed down the food we gave them, then ran back into the woods. Matthew stayed. He tried to climb onto our laps. He licked our hands. He lay on his back with his legs spread, his pink belly and tiny balls exposed. Who could resist Matthew's con? So we adopted him. The Shibas were wise to him, however, his eagerness to ingratiate himself with them. They played him off, ignored him, growled at him, this interloper. But Matthew was indomitable. He had patience for the long con. Like Dad always said, "You walk through shit until you get to clover." Matthew wore down our Shibas' stubborn defenses. Finally they surrendered, exhausted from trying to beat him off. After a few months, they accepted him into the pack.

After I told Dad Matthew's story, that's all Dad wanted to talk about on the phone. "How's my fellow bastard?" he'd ask. I told him Matthew stories. When I had none to tell, I made them up.

Susan opened the front door wide and Dad stepped into the house. Our dogs came running. The Shibas sniffed Dad's shoes and pants, pawed him a bit, then lost interest and went outside to the backyard. Matthew stood on his hind legs and put his front paws on Dad. He whimpered and wagged his plumy tail as if he'd been waiting for Dad all his life. Dad giggled like a child. "See! He loves me!" I didn't tell Dad that that was Matthew's con. He loved everyone who entered our house.

We finally got Dad seated at the dining room table. Matthew draped his front paws over Dad's knees. He nuzzled his snout against Dad's chest and stared up at Dad with his huge, round chocolate eyes filled with such love and affection and instant devotion that Dad was almost moved to tears. Matthew knew a Mark when he saw one.

"Enough, Matthew," Susie said. "Leave Dad alone."

"Leave him, Susan," Dad said. "He loves me." He petted Matthew's floppy ears.

I made Dad a Tanqueray martini and brought it to him. "You remembered, son," he said. I got myself a glass of bourbon. Dad and I sipped our drinks. Matthew lay at Dad's feet. Dad smiled down at him, "He won't leave me." Susie brought Dad a plate of marinated olives and peppers, a wedge of Asiago and crusty ciabatta bread. Matthew perked up. Dad ate the olives and purred to himself, "Mmmmm, delicious." He took a bite of Asiago. A small piece fell to the floor. Matthew licked it up.

I put Dad's bag in the tiny guest room while Susie set the table for an early dinner. I heated up the sausage, onions, and peppers I'd cooked all morning. I served it to Dad with some spaghetti, garlic bread, and a glass of red wine. Dad ate methodically, silently. When he finished, he said, "I'm tired. I think I'll go to sleep."

"Do you want to take a bath first, Dad?" Susie said.

"I don't think so." He went into the guest room and closed the door. Susie started clearing the table.

"So far, so good," she said.

"So far."

Dad didn't sleep long. He came out of the guest room at six o'clock. I asked him how he was feeling? "Fine," he said. I said, "You feel rested enough to go to Miami with me? I'm supposed to read from one of my books at a well-known bookstore called Books and Books. You might get a kick out of it." I told him two of my friends he had met during his last visit, Phil, the Booby Trap owner, and Sol, the smuggler, and also my closest friend, Peter, my lawyer, and his father, Peter Sr., would meet us there. "Peter's a member of your club," I said. "He's an orphan, too. And his adoptive father is a gambler. Not like you, just small time. But you'll like him. He's a sweet man, pushing ninety. He's a war hero. He was wounded on Normandy Beach."

"I think I'd like that," Dad said.

Susie stayed home with the dogs. At the door, as Dad and I were leaving, she said, "The boys' night out. Have fun."

Books and Books was an old-timey independent bookstore. Wooden shelves along the walls overflowing with books, tables piled high with books, and a small open space for authors' readings. All the folding chairs in the open space were occupied by strangers and my friends. I re-introduced Dad to Sol and Phil, and then introduced him to Peter and his father, a slight, little man. Peter Junior stood up and gave Dad his chair alongside his father. Dad said, "That's not necessary, son." Peter Junior said, "Yes, it is, Mr. Jordan."

I went to the lectern and opened my book to a passage I was going to read. It was about Dad. His colorful life. All the things he taught me. The debt I owe him. I looked out over the audience and saw Dad and Peter Senior talking to each other. Peter Junior was standing behind them, smiling at me. He pointed down at the two old men and nodded.

After I finished reading the passage about Dad, the audience applauded. I thanked the audience and then said, "And the man who was the greatest inspiration in my life is with us tonight. Dad, stand up." My father struggled to his feet, with the help of Peter Sr.'s hand on his elbow. The audience gave Dad enthusiastic applause. He was blushing.

Strangers came up to me to tell me how much they had loved my book. They asked me to sign copies they had brought with them.

Some people brought their books to Dad and asked him to sign them, too. Dad and I signed books for about twenty minutes until all the strangers left and only my friends and Dad were waiting for me.

We walked outside into the darkness and down the sidewalk toward a bar. Dad and Peter Sr. walked ahead of us, deep in conversation. Peter Junior, Sol, Phil, and I walked together.

Phil pointed to the two old men in front of us. "Look at that," he said. Dad and Peter Sr. were holding hands to support each other as they hobbled along. Phil shook his head, and said, "Man, I want to get old like those two guys."

In the bar we sat around a big table near the wall and ordered drinks. I was exhausted. I was in a hurry to get Dad home, but he and Peter Sr. were still talking. Phil was sitting alongside them, eavesdropping. At one point Peter Jr. produced a syringe with insulin and gave his father his diabetes shot. Phil said, "Save some of that for me." Everybody laughed.

An hour later, I stood up and said, "Guys, I gotta get the old man home. He's been up since 5 a.m. traveling."

Phil smiled at me, and said, "You can't leave yet. These two old guys have been talking for hours and they aren't up to 1930 yet."

Dad and I got home after midnight. Before he went to his guest room to sleep, he said, "I had a wonderful night, son."

"I'm glad, Dad." I kissed him good night.

Susie was asleep in our bedroom with the dogs, behind the closed door. I lay on the couch in the Florida room in case Dad woke, disoriented, not knowing where he was. I watched TV for an hour. I kept glancing toward the guest room until I fell asleep.

"Patty! You awake?" I opened my eyes to an old ghost hovering over me. His stale old man's breath inches from my face.

"Dad! Jesus! It's 2 a.m. What are you doing up?"

"I woke up. I want another martini."

I got up and made Dad a martini. I poured myself a bourbon. We sat at the dining room table across from each other in the darkness, our faces illuminated only by the moonlight shining through the window. We sipped our drinks.

Dad said, "I was never a good father to you, son."

"What are you talking about, Dad? You were the best."

"I didn't have the time. You came too late. I was tired after raising your brother."

"Dad, everything I am, the good stuff, anyway, I owe to you."

"Some things, maybe, but most you did yourself."

"You taught me things I never forgot. Never quit. Make your nut for your family. Give it all away to make people happy. Only a fool or a child believes in perfect justice." I didn't tell him what I'd always thought. If there had been perfect justice in this world, Dad would have had a mother and a father.

"I never did anything with you when you were a kid."

"What do ya mean? You took me to the Sea Grill with Ma. I was six years old, eating a two-pound lobster and flirting with strippers." I thought he'd laugh, but he didn't.

He said, "Aw, that was grown-up stuff. I mean, kid's stuff, like the circus."

"That shit's overrated, Dad. Cotton candy and clowns. I'll take what you gave me any day of the week."

"My only excuse was I didn't know how to be a father. I played it by ear. Sometimes I got it right. Sometimes..." He shrugged.

"I always admired you, Dad. Despite the orphanage, you were never bitter."

He looked up at me with his faded, blue-gray eyes and said, sharply now, "I had no one to be bitter at."

I felt tears in my eyes. I changed the subject. "How's it going at the assisted living place?"

"Aw, I'm surrounded by old people. They're always complaining. Some of them, they lost their marbles." He smiled. "This one Haitian nurse, Desiree, she calls me her chere. She loves me. Whenever someone comes to the place to check it out, she introduces them to me. Like I'm an ambassador. But she always tells me ahead of time so I can dress in my good clothes."

"Your Ivy League con."

"You remember, huh." Then he said, "I was in their newsletter." He looked at me. "You're not the only one, you know."

"I know. What were you in the newsletter for?"

"There was this old lady there that liked me. She was OK to talk to. The wardens there saw us together a lot. They asked us if we wanted to get married. It would be a first for the place. They could put it in the *Bridgeport Post*."

I laughed. "How old was she?"

"She was a kid, eighty-six. But she was all for it."

"And you?"

"I dunno. I told them there was only one woman for me, and she's gone."

We talked and drank until the early morning. I could hear Susie stirring in her bed, listening. I reminded Dad of the cruelest thing I had ever done to him. When I was ten, Davie Perkins's father would take all the neighborhood kids to the park to play baseball with them. When I asked Dad one day to go to the park to have a catch with me, he said, "I'm not a kid. Go play with your friends." I blurted out, "I wish you were like Davie Perkins's father."

"I hated myself for that, Dad. I could see in your eyes I'd hurt your feelings."

"Maybe," he said. "But you were right. I was selfish. I should have done more things with you."

"But you did. Remember when I was going for my master's degree at Trinity in Hartford? You drove up with me, an hour and a half each way, just to keep me company. You sat in the students' lounge before class. All the students thought you were a professor. Then you went to class with me." I laughed. "You took notes on T.S. Eliot." After class I introduced my professor to my father. The professor asked Dad if he was a professor, too. I said, "My father's a famous classics *professore* in Italia." He bought it. Academics were easy Marks.

"I loved that day, too," Dad said. "I felt like a student. But I didn't do it for you. I did it for me."

Finally, Dad went to his little guest room to sleep. I lay back on the sofa, but I couldn't fall asleep.

Susie woke before Dad and came into the kitchen where I was making Dad's breakfast. When Dad came out of the guestroom, Matthew ran to him and wagged his tail. Dad giggled, "My fellow orphan missed me." The Shibas were in the backyard pissing and chasing the possums that were walking on top of our privacy fence. Only our old Shiba girl, Kiri, stayed inside. She was blind, diabetic, and epileptic. Kiri slept under the dining room table while we ate breakfast. Matthew lay alongside Dad's chair, waiting for him to drop some toast crumbs, or even better, bits of bacon.

After breakfast Susie washed the dishes at the sink. She called over her shoulder, "There are towels in the bathroom, Dad, if you want to take a bath."

"I don't think so."

Susan glanced at me. I shrugged. Dad was petting Matthew at his feet. I heard Kiri whimper under the table. She was having an epileptic seizure. She stiffened and her eyes rolled back into her head. I got under the table with her and held her. I stroked her forehead and whispered to her, "Shhh, it'll be all right." Dad was talking to Matthew.

Kiri's fit lasted a few minutes and then she came out of it. She stood up, wobbly. I noticed she'd peed on herself. I got some paper towels and wiped her off, then wiped up the puddle on the floor.

Dad looked down at me with disgust. "Doesn't she know enough to go outside?" I explained about her epilepsy, her diabetes, her blindness. "She's an old girl, Dad, sixteen." I smiled. "Older than you."

He said, "I want to go outside for a while." He got his Camus book and went into our backyard that was as lush as a tropical rain forest. I saw through the Florida room window Dad lying down on the chaise lounge under the shade of a carrotwood tree. Matthew lay beside him. The other dogs were snorffling through the liriope. Dad lay there, the book on his lap, staring off as if thinking, or remembering.

"Isn't he ever going to take a bath?" Susie asked.

"I think he's embarrassed. He won't be able to get in and out of the tub."

"You can help him."

"That's what'll embarrass him."

"That's ridiculous. You're his son, for God's sake." But I was more than just a son. I was his only blood relative he'd ever known. Susie looked at me and said, "That was nice last night. You and your father talking."

# CHAPTER FORTY-FIVE

Late that morning, I drove Dad to West Palm Beach where Tony was scheduled to start at shortstop for the Dodgers in a spring training game. Tony, my brother's grandson, was pushing thirty. This would be his last chance to make the Dodgers after nine years in the minors. I had never seen Tony play. I only knew what my brother told me about him. "He hit two home runs last night in Omaha," George said. But George never told me when Tony went through a 2-for-32 slump.

Dad sat alongside me in my 1989 Taurus SHO that I had cared for, lovingly, for over sixteen years. He looked at the leather seats and through the windshield at the new black paint job. He said, "You always took care of your things, son. You were never wasteful."

"I still use the same thirty-five-year-old manual typewriter."

"I never took care of things. I thought they were disposable. Something broke, I told your mother, 'Call the man.'"

"I like old things. Susie's two years older than me." I thought he'd laugh, but he didn't.

"Your mother was five years older than me. I wanted a wife and a mother." I glanced at him. He wore a navy windbreaker with "Los Angeles Dodgers" written in white script across the front, and a Dodgers' baseball cap. Beth had given them to him before he'd left for Florida.

We drove north on I-95 in the late morning sunlight. Dad said, "Tony's a good kid."

"I'm looking forward to seeing him play."

"He's a good kid."

"He's almost thirty, Dad."

"He's a handsome kid."

"I know." I had been a handsome kid, once. Dad, too.

"Tony's crazy about me. He thinks I'm the greatest."

"You are."

"He's always saying how smart I am. He tells everyone that his great-grandfather is the smartest."

"You are the smartest, Dad. I learned everything from you."

He looked at me. "I was talking about Tony. It's not always about you."

Harley and Beth were waiting for us in front of the stadium. There were people all around them, waiting for tickets, going through the turnstiles. I dropped Dad off and he went over to Beth and Harley. I parked the car and went back to them. Harley was wearing his Dodgers' polo shirt. Beth was heavily made up, as she always was. She had big, Midwestern, blond hair and wore lots of gold jewelry and diamonds. Harley was a handsome man with short, silver hair like Paul Newman. Harley had the tickets, so we followed him through the turnstile and up the stadium steps to the top row of seats along the first base line. I sat between Harley and Beth. Dad sat beside Beth.

"There he is!" said Harley. "Number 28." The Dodgers were doing calisthenics in right field before the game. I picked out Tony in his tight-fitting uniform. He was a medium-sized young man, muscular, and as handsome as a male model. Harley said, "He looks great in his uniform, doesn't he, Pat?" I didn't say anything. I thought he was talking to Dad. But Dad was sitting beside Beth, the book in his lap, staring out at the field with that distant look of his.

Harley looked at me. I said, "Yeah, great."

"Wait till you see him hit, Pat. He murders fastballs." I glanced at the centerfield scoreboard to see who was pitching for the Marlins this afternoon. Josh Beckett and his 98-mph fastball.

I said, "There are fastballs and there are fastballs, Harley." He looked at me as if confused. When I pitched in the minor leagues, I had Beckett's fastball. One night as I walked out to the mound to start a game, one of my fellow pitchers in the dugout called out, "You can't give Jim Hicks fastballs. Jim Hicks murders fastballs." I glanced over my shoulder and said, "He murders your fastballs, maybe. But the sunuvabitch won't murder mine." I struck out Jim Hicks four times that game. I threw him nothing but fastballs.

Harley had never played much sports. He'd gone into his family's window business right out of college, and now, in his mid-fifties, he had a Learjet. Each summer he and Beth would rent an apartment wherever Tony was playing, and stay there all summer. They were already looking for an apartment in L.A. for this coming season. Now for spring training, they were living in Vero Beach, where the Dodgers trained. After this game, they would bring Dad back with them to Vero, where he'd stay with them for a few days so he could be with his great-grandson.

Before the game began, I went to the concession stand to buy beers and peanuts for everyone. Harley came with me. While I waited in line, he said, "Dad's the greatest."

"Who?"

"Dad." He meant my father.

I paid for the beer and peanuts and we went back to our seats. I watched the game for a few innings. I tried to talk to Harley but he was distracted by his son on the field. So I talked to Beth. She asked me questions about Beckett. I told her if Tony could hit Beckett's fastball "then he's a big leaguer."

"You should know, Uncle Pat."

I looked across at Dad. He was staring out at the field as if he was not seeing it, but seeing something else beyond it that only he could see.

Tony struck out twice, swinging through Beckett's 98-mph fastball. He had one fielding chance at shortstop. He charged a groundball, almost getting his feet tangled up, then lobbed the ball to first base barely in time to get the runner. At the beginning of the fifth inning I stood up and said, "I've got to be getting back to Susie and the dogs."

Dad said, "You and those damned dogs."

I left him with Beth and Harley.

Four days later, in a driving rainstorm, I met Beth at a motel parking lot in West Palm to pick up Dad. I held an umbrella over Dad as he changed cars. I went back to Beth sitting in the driver's seat of her Mercedes. "How was he?" I asked.

"Fine. But I couldn't get him to take a shower."

"We couldn't either." Then I said, "You gonna be all right driving back?"

"Don't worry, Uncle Pat. But first I'm going shopping in Palm Beach."

I drove slowly with Dad in the driving rain, past construction on I-95. My air conditioner wasn't working so the windshield steamed up quickly. I had to wipe it off with my handkerchief.

"Use the defroster, for chrissakes," Dad said.

"It doesn't work."

"Can't you afford a decent car?"

We drove in silence for a while. Then Dad said, "Look at these." He pointed to his shoes. "Beth and Harley bought them for me. They cost over $200."

"They're nice."

"They treat me like a King." I didn't say anything. Dad stared ahead in silence. Then he said, "What'd you think of the kid?"

"He's OK."

"He looks like a big leaguer in his uniform."

"Yeah."

"He's got a great body for a ball player."

I didn't say anything.

"He's gonna make the Dodgers this year." I shrugged. He said, "Can't you say anything?"

"What do you want me to say?"

"You saw the kid. You should know."

"You want to know what I think?"

"I asked you, didn't I?"

"He doesn't have any game, Dad."

"What?"

I stared straight ahead through the rain. Finally, I said, "He can't play, pop. He's got a slow bat, no arm, and lousy footwork at short."

"How do you know such things?"

"I played. Remember? With Joe Torre and Phil Niekro and Ron Hunt."

"Yeah, but you never made it. You weren't good enough. All you know how to do is criticize." He glared across at me. "He's my great-grandson, for chrissakes!"

"No, he isn't."

"Why do you always have to be like that?"

We drove in silence the rest of the way.

When Dad entered our house, Matthew greeted him effusively. Dad snapped at him, "Get down!" Matthew sat down and looked up at Dad. Dad went into the guest room and closed the door. Matthew looked up at me as if to say, "What did I do?" How do you explain to a dog that Dad's charm was his con to get you to let down your guard? Then he attacked.

"What happened?" asked Susie.

"Not now." I poured myself a bourbon. When Dad finally came out of his room, I said, "You want a martini, pop?"

"You drinking already? You drink too damned much."

Susie said, "He doesn't drink that much, Dad."

Dad smiled at her. "Oh, aren't you the good wife? Defending your husband. I wouldn't want to cross you."

"Then don't cross me," Susie said.

Dad giggled like a mischievous child. "Oh, boy, you're a hard one. Hard on an old man, aren't you?"

"Really?"

Dad wasn't smiling now. He said, almost with admiration, "I can't get over on you, can I?"

"No. Any more than you could get over on your son."

I said, "For chrissakes, Dad, do you have to play your fucking games?"

He grinned at me with his eyebrows raised. "What games? I don't know what you're talking about."

"Have it your way." Dad always thought his con was his strength. And maybe it was in some things. But he never realized, in the things that mattered, his con was his weakness.

We ate dinner in silence. Susie washed the dishes and went to bed with the dogs. Dad and I stayed up, sitting at the dining room table.

"I'll have that martini, now, son."

I made his martini and then another bourbon for me. I sat down in the rocking chair a few feet from him in the darkened room.

"I'm sorry I got mad at you over Tony, son," Dad said. "You always tell the truth. People think that makes you a bad kid. But I try to defend you. I tell them, 'He's just too quick.'"

"Thanks."

Dad sipped his drink. "I was just protecting your brother. Tony means so much to him." Dad looked at me. "I always deprived you of affection and gave it to George."

"I know."

"He needed it more. He was never equipped like you. Even your mother knew. The poor bastard! What did he have?"

"He had you. And Ma. And me."

"He always tried hard. But he wasn't smart. He was like his father."

"That wasn't my fault, Dad."

Dad looked at me with a cold anger, as he had that night in Florida, on our little apartment deck on a canal, when he realized I had conned him in pool at the Mis-Cue Lounge. He said, "It was your fault. You stole everything."

I was silent for a moment. Then I said, "I didn't steal anything, Dad. I was just a kid. I didn't know."

Dad said, "Yes, you did. You stole all the gifts I should have had." He looked down at his hands on the table. Then he said, "That's why I resented you all these years."

The next morning I drove Dad to the airport before Susie came out of the bedroom. He was silent as I drove, staring out the window. Who knows what old men are thinking?

We went up the escalator. I told Dad to wait there while I got his wheelchair. I returned with my pass and the wheelchair and settled him in it. He arranged his book on his lap, cover up. I pushed him through security and then to his gate. I went over to the airline employee at the counter. I said to her, "Could you keep an eye on my father until his flight boards? The old guy in the wheelchair. I have to get home."

"Certainly," she said.

I went over to Dad. "Your flight will board in a few minutes, Dad. I have to get home. The girl at the counter will take care of you."

"That's all right, son. Get home to your wife and dogs." He grabbed my hand and squeezed it hard.

"What's this?" I asked when he released my hand.

"A few C-notes. I won't need them."

"Thanks, Dad." I took those C-notes as he had taught me. But also because I knew it was the only way my father could show me his love. I kissed him good-bye and walked back toward the escalator. I glanced back and saw Dad talking to the airline woman. She was smiling down at him. She picked up his book and looked at it. She said something to him.

Driving home, I realized Dad's visit with us was for less than a full day. We were a pit stop for his real visit to Beth, Harley, and Tony.

The next day, Dad called from Connecticut. "How's the dog, son?"

"Matthew misses you, Dad."

"No. I mean the one who got sick under the table."

"Oh, Kiri. She's fine. Listen, Dad, I can't talk now. I'm on another line, business. I'll call you back." But I didn't.

# CHAPTER FORTY-SIX

I never spoke to Dad again. Those three C-notes were my inheritance from him. Among other things. He died five days after he had left us in Florida. He was ninety-five. One of my brother's daughters was in St. Vincent's Hospital in Bridgeport, where I had been born, sitting alongside Dad's bed while he drifted in and out of consciousness. Early in the morning he woke and sat up in bed. He said, "Patty! I have to talk to my son, Patty!" Those were his last words. My brother called at five in the morning to tell me, "Dad died this morning, brother." I said, "Oh, God!" My brother said, "I'm sorry, brother."

Susie was still sleeping. I didn't want to wake her so I went outside into our small garage. I shut the door behind me.

When I returned to the house, Susie was up, making coffee. She saw my puffy, reddened face and said, "Your father."

After Dad died, George and I talked to each other on the phone twice a week. Like old men, we talked about the past. Mostly about Dad. Things I remembered, things George remembered, like the CR&L bus and the cops.

In the 1940s, Dad spent most of his time gambling at the Venice Athletic Club. "Fellow athletes," George said. "Their most athletic physical activity was throwing dice against a wall and dealing from a deck of cards." The police vice squad raided the Venice A.C. regular as clockwork. So the gamblers paid an old Mustache Pete to sit in a chair outside, reading *La Nazione* and smoking his Toscano cigar. When Pete saw the cop cars speeding down the street, forcing the big CR&L buses to move aside, he hustled to the front door and called out, "*Polizia! Polizia!*" The cops in their dark blue uniforms pounded on the club's wooden door with their nightsticks until finally someone opened it. When the cops burst in, they found a dozen or so men dozing in easy chairs, sipping espresso, listening to a baseball game on the radio, all of them looking up startled at the *polizia*. They offered the *polizia* an espresso.

A few weeks later, the cop cars sped down the street, the buses moved aside, Pete shouted at the door, the cops ran at the door, this time with a battering ram that splintered it to pieces. They arrested everyone inside, except my father. Detective Ford grabbed him by the elbow and steered him out the back door. "Beat it, Patsy. You don't belong with these bums."

A month later the cop cars sped down the street. Mustache Pete didn't budge from his chair. He just kept reading his *La Nazione*. The cops charged past him toward the door with their battering ram. The battering ram hit the new four-inch-thick steel door with a metallic clang. The cops bounced backwards, tumbling onto the sidewalk like the Keystone cops.

After that, the denizens of the Venice A.C. no longer feared police raids. They got cocky, and careless. They left the big metal door unlocked and put Pete out front on his chair again so that when he shouted out, "*Polizia!*" they just turned a lock on the door and kept gambling.

More than a month passed. No cop cars. Just the usual CR&L bus that stopped on the corner, a few feet from the Venice A.C. One day the CR&L bus lumbered down the street and stopped at the corner to let passengers out. A few men dressed as day laborers. Two men in banker's three-piece suits. A sporty-looking wise guy in his wop suit with the big lapels and his pointy-toed, black, patent leather shoes. While the laborers and the guys in banker's suits loitered on the sidewalk talking to Mustache Pete, the wop walked up to the door of the club, and opened it. Before he stepped inside, he held the door open for the men on the sidewalk. They walked casually into the club and arrested everyone.

I told my brother about the time I was walking down the sidewalk alongside Main Street in Bridgeport with Dad. I was forty at the time. Dad was telling me how the New York mob used Bridgeport as a minor league training camp for young thugs. I asked him why he never joined the mob. He said, "And be owned by them? Three a.m. calls to do their bidding? You've got to be kidding. I was a freelance. They respected that and left me alone." Just then a dapper wop in a short leather jacket and black pants came walking toward us. He greeted Dad effusively. Dad introduced me to Frank. Frank smiled and said, "The baseball player. Your pop always talked about you." I said, "That was in another lifetime." He said, "But still you did it once. I wished my son had been an athlete." He patted me on the shoulder and walked off.

I said to Dad, "Who was that guy, pop? Seems like a nice guy."

"You think so? Maybe you could pitch batting practice to him some day. He carries a Louisville slugger in the backseat of his Caddy. I was in the car with him one afternoon, right here driving down Main Street. Suddenly he jams on the brakes, jumps out, grabs a guy off the sidewalk and pushes him into the back seat. 'You drive, Patsy,' he says. So I slide over and start driving." Dad glanced at me. "Frank says, 'Drive,' you drive. I hear the sound of someone gagging so I look in the rearview mirror. Frank's got the barrel of a .38 in the guy's mouth, and he's rattling it around, all the guy's teeth flying out like piano keys. Lips, they called the guy after that."

"Jesus! What'd the poor bastard do to piss Frank off?"

"He was a slow pay, maybe. Maybe he made a wisecrack about Frank's son being a hop head and it got back to Frank. Or maybe he didn't do anything at all. Frank's crazy. He's a contract killer for New York. On the side, he imports heroin for the *melanzana*. For his son, too. God's punishment."

"A dangerous guy to know, Dad."

Dad shrugged, and said, "Not for me. Frank was the guy respected me for being a freelance. He wouldn't let anybody touch me. I had carte blanche in Bridgeport as long as Frank was around. I cheat a guy in cards, he goes to Frank, wants satisfaction. Frank laughs at him, 'You play with Patsy you should know better. He never dealt a straight hand in his life.'"

A few weeks later I opened the front page of the *Bridgeport Post* and saw a photo of a telephone booth on Main Street. The phone booth glass was shattered all over the street, the sidewalk, the body of a man slumped like a rag doll at the bottom of the booth, his body oozing blood through bullet holes. The story with the photo said that Frank Piccolo, Gambino Crime Family Capo, was machine-gunned by rival mobsters because he was encroaching on their turf.

"I knew one of the guys rumored to have killed Frank," I told George. "I was in high school, driving in Stratford with a girl, when somebody rear-ended my car at a stoplight. I get out of the car and this humungous fat guy, 400 pounds, gets out of his car, steam coming out from under its crumpled hood. He comes waddling at me like a crazed circus freak, yelling, 'My fucking car, you cocksucker!' The girl screams at me, 'Get in the car! Get in the car!' I jump in, and we speed off. The girl is so shaken up, she makes me drive her home. She gets out of the car, leans over, and says through the window, 'You're a nice guy and all, but please don't ever call me again?' I say, 'Why not? What'd I do?' She says, 'You'll find out,' and goes into the house and slams the door.

"That night I told Dad about the accident and the fat guy and the girl. He said, 'Smart girl.' Then he said, 'The fat guy is Fat Franny. He's a made man. He won't let this rest. I'll make a call.' So he made a call and it all went away. It wasn't until after Frank Piccolo was killed, supposedly by Fat Franny and his brother Gus, that Dad told me Frank was the guy he called."

George said, "Dad protected his sons. He had no fear."

I said, "He was always there for us." I told George about the thirty Gs Dad had given me to buy the Florida house. "Cash in a FedEx envelope, for chrissakes," I said.

George laughed. "I didn't know about the FedEx, but I knew Dad always did prefer cash. I knew about the thirty Gs, though."

"He told me. He said you signed off on it."

"You needed it. I never resented he gave it to you and not me."

"I think he figured you got four years at Georgetown and two years law school paid for. He was just evening the score."

"My father, George Senior, paid for that, not Dad."

"Who do you think shamed George Senior to make him pay?" I asked. "It was Dad. He went to him, hat in hand, and told him he'd never asked him for a cent for you, but now he was asking. It was a question of the rest of your life."

"I never knew that. Dad never told me."

"Why would he? He wanted you to feel good about your father, at least once in your life."

It dawned on me at that moment that Dad had told me a lot of things he'd never told George. Over the years I'd tell George things Dad had taught me: only a fool or a child believes in perfect justice, an accident is always your fault, you fuck Amex but never the working man, you get the cash you never give it up, get it done any way you can, and don't get caught. I'd just assumed he'd told George the same things when George was growing up. But George would just look at me and say, "Dad never told me that."

From my earliest years, Dad was educating me on the sly with all the lessons he'd learned from his life, "you keep walking through shit until it turns to clover." He kept his education of me from Ma and George. I think he felt Ma would consider it a betrayal of her and George if she discovered Dad was favoring me with his life's lessons, and not George. I can only surmise what Dad's reasons were for teaching me in private. Maybe because I was his son, and George wasn't. Maybe he felt George wasn't equipped to handle the things Dad taught me. Whatever Dad's reasons were, he expected me to understand what he was doing. I did, but only after Dad was gone.

After I told George it was Dad who had shamed his natural father into paying for his Georgetown education, George went silent. Finally, he said, "I miss Dad so much. I miss him every damned day."

"Me, too."

Three years ago, when George was eighty-eight, he called to tell me he was dying. "I need a triple bypass, brother. Like Dad." He coughed a little.

I said, "Then get it. Dad lived seven more years."

"I'm not Dad. What's the point?"

"Don't be a fucking mule."

"I haven't seen you in years, brother. Why don't you come home to visit your brother one last time?"

"Brother, I visited you a year ago, remember?" But he didn't remember. Maybe because on that visit I was lost in the throng of well-
wishers, who'd come to Fairfield University on a night in November
2015, to honor him as The Father of Fairfield University Basketball.
George had been the head coach at that Jesuit institution from 1958
to 1968, and was the school's athletic director from 1962 to 1971.

That night at the Fairfield U. gym, hundreds of people filled the
seats of the gym before an exhibition game where George was first
honored with a bronze relief in the lobby. Then, while he and his
family, and over one hundred former players and friends, stood on
the court, it was announced, to George's surprise, that the gym had
been renamed, The George R. Bisacca Basketball Court.

I was in the bleachers, watching my brother get his award he
so much deserved. But I couldn't help but wonder why the Jesuits
honored him with this award so late in his life, forty-four years after
the school had fired him as its athletic director. Then, during the ceremony, the master of ceremonies announced that, coinciding with
the naming of the gym after my brother, the school had also created
a fund called The George R. Bisacca Fund for Men's Basketball that
was funded by the generous support from his family.

After my brother called to tell me he was dying, I flew back to
Fairfield in the fall of 2016 to visit him one last time. He looked the
same. A big, vigorous, homely man. He'd lost his cough.

We sat at his kitchen table while Mil stirred the sauce at the
stove. She looked the same, too, with her jet-black, dyed hair. I said,
"Am I the only one in this fucking family who looks old?"

Mil laughed. "You're still incorrigible, Patty."

"You gonna make him get the bypass, Mil?"

She looked at me. "I haven't been able to make him do anything
in sixty-seven years. You make him get it, Patty. He'll listen to you
now that you're an old man." She laughed and went back to her
sauce.

George said, "Actually, I went for another opinion, brother. The
second guy said I don't need it. 'It won't kill you,' he said. 'But you
won't live past hundred without a by-pass.'"

"And when did you get this second opinion, brother?"

"A few weeks before I called you." He was smiling at me.

"You sunuvabitch."

"I wanted to see my brother."

"You conned me."

My brother said, "Somebody's got to fill the old man's shoes."

Three days later, George drove me back to Hartford Airport for my flight home. He stopped his BMW at the Delta terminal and got out. He took my bag out of his trunk and handed it to me. Then he reached into his jacket pocket and took out an envelope. He pressed it into my hand and said, "A little something for my brother."

"What's this?"

"It's only five grand." He smiled. "I was going to put the cash in a FedEx envelope and send it to you. But you fell for my con, so here it is."

He threw his arms around me and we kissed as all the men in our family did.

I looked at the envelope with the cash my brother had given me, as Dad had so many times before him. Then I stuffed it in my carry bag. I mean, I got it. I sure as hell wasn't gonna give it up. I am, after all, a con man's son, like my brother.

# End of Part Three

# EPILOGUE

Through all of 2017, up to May 2018, my brother and I talked on the phone every day. If there was a sports game on TV that night, we talked sometimes fifteen or twenty times a night. I didn't have any of the sports cable channels, but George had them all. So he'd call me during the action and give me a play-by-play account. During the World Series, he'd say, in a sportscaster's portentous voice, "Runner on first and third, game tied, seventh inning, the pitcher's in trouble." Then his voice would change to my brother's voice, and he'd say, "What should he throw in this situation, brother?" So I told him.

"Something that breaks down on the first pitch. Slider, curve, sinker. Get him to hit a groundball. The batter will be tense, anxious, probably looking for high heat. Quick to pull the trigger."

George became the sportscaster again, his voice intoning, "The pitcher goes into his motion, delivers. An overhand curveball. The batter hits a groundball to second, the second baseman underhands it to the shortstop, who tags second, leaps to avoid the runner, and fires the ball to first. *Double play!* Inning over." Still the sportscaster, my brother says, "*My brother knows!*"

If it was a college or NBA basketball game, it would be me asking my brother what a player would do in a given situation. He'd say, "LeBron's gonna drive to the hoop, muscle the ball in, maybe get a foul, too." And when LeBron did what my brother said he'd do, I'd say, "My brother knows."

Sometimes I'd fall asleep before a game was over. When I woke up the next morning, I'd see a missed call on my phone. When I checked it, I'd hear George's annoyed voice, "Brother, you fell asleep on me! You're missing the action! *Wake up!*"

When my brother called me during the day, or at night, and caught me off guard, I answered the phone annoyed at this intrusion into my worries over my writing, money, Susie's health, my health, all of which I always hid from my brother. For George, I was always the upbeat brother, hyper, excited, profane, the kid, laughing without a care in the world.

"Brother!" he said, startled, if he heard my subdued voice. "What's wrong?"

"Nothing, brother. I'm just tired. I didn't sleep last night."

"Are you sure? You're not lying to me? Do you need anything?"

"Yeah, sleep. I was up all night watching movies till 3 a.m."

"Are you sure? Is it money? Do you need money?"

I faked a laugh, "Yeah, send me a pound of C-notes in a FedEx envelope."

"I'll do it," he said.

"Jesus, brother! I was kidding. You're such a literal fuck." I had never talked like that to my brother. But now that we were so close, I could be myself, up to a point.

"You telling me the truth?"

"Yes, for chrissakes! Give me a fucking break... Now, why did you call just when I had a gun in my mouth?"

Finally, he laughed.

When we finished talking, we signed off as we always did. George said, "I love you, brother." I replied, "I love you, too, brother."

In April 2018, George called to tell me he'd made plans to visit me and Susie in Abbeville, our tiny, upstate South Carolina town that billed itself as The Birthplace and Deathbed of the Confederacy.

"You can introduce me to some of your Klan buddies, brother," he said.

"We'll burn a cross for you, bro," I said.

George lived in Fairfield County, one of the wealthiest and whitest counties in the country: mostly WASPs, and striving ethnics like my brother, and expat New Yorkers who commuted to work in New York City, thirty-seven miles west. One of the few Black families in Fairfield was that of Meadowlark Lemon, the wealthy Harlem Globetrotter star.

My little South Carolina town of 4800 was 60 percent Black. The mayor and five of the nine city council members were Black. The former county sheriff was Black. Half of my friends were Black. The grocery stores and pharmacies I shopped in were staffed by Blacks. Half the guys in my gym were Black. My next-door neighbor and his wife were Black. Like most of the small, poor towns of the Old South, today Abbeville had seemingly shed its racist past, yet still retained the graciousness of the Old South.

I told George to book his flight into Charlotte, North Carolina, a nonstop flight for him, rather than Greenville, South Carolina, which would make him layover in Charlotte for an hour before catching a commuter flight.

"How long a drive is it for you to Greenville?" he asked.

"An hour."

"How long a drive to Charlotte?"

"A little longer."

"You're lying."

"I'm not lying! It's less than two hours." It was a three-hour drive.

"I don't want my brother doing all that driving," he said. "I'll fly to Greenville."

My brother booked his flight to Charlotte, with a connection to Greenville, for May 4, the day before the Kentucky Derby, a big celebration in our town. The local accountant and his wife always hosted a Derby Day party with lots of food and booze and betting. The accountant, wearing a green eye shade like Bob Cratchit, sat at his desk in front of his computer, calculator, and money counting machine, while his guests lined up to place their bets. There were a few businessmen, ex-military, high school coaches, cops, working men, a few Blacks, and Yankees. But mostly the bettors were the town's more genteel ladies of a certain age. They wore flowered dresses and the kind of fancy hats you see at the weddings of British Royalty. They wore short white gloves, too, with a fistful of C-notes in their gloved hands.

"Too bad Dad can't make it," I said to George. "He could past post the accountant."

George said, "Why don't you get one of your Florida gangster friends to rob the joint?"

"This is the South, brother, not Fairfield. Everybody packs heat, including the doyennes. It could get messy, all those old ladies with bad eyesight, blasting away with their nine millimeters, like *Reservoir Dogs*."

And then my brother got sick. It began with a cough. "A cold," he said. "It's freezing up here."

But the coughing got worse. I'd call to check up on him and he'd cough, wheeze, struggle for breath. "It's nothing," he'd say, then cough some more. A real cough this time. Finally, he went to the hospital for a checkup. I called him a few times to hear what the results were, but he never answered. So I called his oldest daughter, Beth.

"I'm at the hospital now, Uncle Pat," she said. "He's in an oxygen tent. He has pneumonia. It doesn't look good." My brother was too sick to talk to me, she said. "But the moment he feels just a little better I'll have him call."

I waited for his call for two or three days. Finally, on the fourth day, he called. I heard him gasping for breath, his voice weak. "I don't think I'm gonna make Derby Day, brother. Maybe next year. I'm sorry. But I'm gonna send you a little something instead." He began wheezing again, then coughing.

Two days later I got a FedEx letter envelope from him. A white envelope inside, no cash, just a check. And a note, "Hope this helps, brother." His script was still strong, bold letters written with a fountain pen with a broad point. It was the Mont Blanc, 24 karat gold-nibbed pen I had given him forty years ago. I had bought it on a whim for $375, a lot of money for me then. But I never used it much. I was too afraid of losing it on the road during a magazine assignment. So I gave it to my brother, who used it every day.

I called Beth and asked her if George could talk. She said, "He's right here, Uncle Pat."

George got on the phone and said, "Did you get the FedEx, brother?" I could tell he was forcing himself not to sound weak.

I said, "Yes, you saved us, brother. Susie and I can relax now about our old age."

"Understood."

"I miss you, brother."

He said, "I love you, brother."

"I love you, too, brother." Then he hung up. He died the next day.

Dad always preached to us, "You get the cash, you never give it up." I never had any problem keeping the cash. But this one time, I would have given it up, all of it, if I could have had my brother in my life for another year, another month, another week, another day, another hour. I wondered, would that have made Dad happy? More to the point, would it have made Ma happy?

A few days later, Susie and I went to the Derby Party. It was crowded and noisy, everyone talking, laughing, drinking, eating, standing in line to lay down their bets. Dave Bacon, my drinking buddy from Boston, asked me, "Where's your brother?" I looked for Susie. She was talking to the accountant's wife.

I smiled at Dave and said, "Something came up, Pancetta. Last minute. He couldn't make it." Pancetta bought it. "Maybe next year," he said, and stepped up to lay down his bet. He was a short, round, little guy with white hair, like one of Santa's elves. Pancetta was the Italian word for bacon.

I watched the accountant count his C-notes. I got a glass of bourbon and went outside to smoke my cigar. I sat on a deck chair in their beautifully manicured little garden. It was a sunny day, the sky a cloudless blue. I sipped my bourbon, neat, Jim Beam Black, the brand my brother always had waiting for me when I visited him in Fairfield. I lit my cigar, took a puff, and looked up to the blue sky. I said out loud, "Brother, post time in five minutes. Ask Dad who he likes in the Derby?"

Three years have passed since my brother died. At first, I mourned my brother's passing according to the admonitions of Ecclesiasticus

38:16. Lots of bitter weeping, most fervent wailing, and deep grief. Then, with time, my grief subsided, and I was "comforted in (my) sorrow." My brother's face grew fainter in my memory, his voice receded into the silence of the past, as it had with Mom and Dad. But I kept his messages to me on my cell. I played them back only once. It was too painful. But I couldn't delete them.

Yesterday Susie found an old black-and-white photograph of my brother in our attic. It was a team photo of his 1945 Prep basketball teammates when he was seventeen. Serious looking teenaged boys in their red and white uniforms with high-top, black leather shoes. No smiles, gaunt faces all cheekbones and angles, and rawboned bodies. They looked more like men than boys, the way immigrant boys looked in those days. The first row of boys was seated on folding chairs. Their hairy legs were identically crossed at their ankles. Emil Garafolo, with his lush Italian lips and curly, black hair. Mickey McBride with his long, dour, pale face, jug ears, and half-lidded eyes. Eddie Dailey, with his mean, threatening, pale-blue eyes that I remembered from all the micks I knew at Prep.

The second row of boys was standing behind the seated boys. They were equally grim-faced like their coach, Tom Murphy, with his unruly, black hair and unshaven melon jaw, like a thug from a Mickey Spillane novel. My brother, the tallest player in that row, was standing alongside of his coach. My brother was smiling! His big, sweet, guileless smile was spread across his homely face. The smile of an innocent boy I had never known. That picture made me weep anew, despite the admonitions of Ecclesiasticus. "A grief-stricken heart can undermine your strength...respect his memory and do not fret for him once his spirit has departed. He is at peace."

My brother may have been at peace, and my mother and my father, too. But I wasn't.

There was so much I didn't know about my brother, and my mother and my father, and the lives they lived together before I was born. I knew them only as they were when they were all so much older than I, fixed in their selves. Why did they keep their past from me? Because their past was a bond that united them, and they didn't want me to intrude on it? Or because their past was so painful for them that they wanted to spare me of it? The latter, I think, now that they're gone. Keeping their past from me was their gift that freed me to live a different life than they had lived.

I understand it all now, too late, in my old age, the last living member of a family I have always loved, but never knew.

# The End

*The author's brother, George, at 17 years old, second from left, standing, as a high school basketball player with his teammates.*

*The author at one with his mother.*

*The author's brother, George, standing. Mildred, the author's sister-in-law, and the author's father.*

*The author, standing. The author's mother, and the author's second wife, Susan, the Irisher.*

# ABOUT THE AUTHOR

Pat Jordan has made his living as a writer since 1963. He presently lives in a small town in upstate South Carolina with his wife of 42 years, Susan, a writer and former stage actress. They live with two dogs, a house cat, a ménage of feral cats, and a parrot named Florence, after his mother, also a tough old bird. His father, born Pasquale Michele Giordano, was the most profound influence on his life.

# ABOUT THE PUBLISHER

The Sager Group was founded in 1984. In 2012 it was chartered as a multimedia content brand, with the intent of empowering those who create art—an umbrella beneath which makers can pursue, and profit from, their craft directly, without gatekeepers. TSG publishes books; ministers to artists and provides modest grants; and produces documentary, feature, and commercial films. By harnessing the means of production, The Sager Group helps artists help themselves. For more information, please see www.TheSagerGroup.net.

# MORE BOOKS FROM THE SAGER GROUP

*The Swamp: Deceit and Corruption in the CIA*
*An Elizabeth Petrov Thriller (Book 1)*
by Jeff Grant

*Chains of Nobility: Brotherhood of the Mamluks (Book 1-3)*
by Brad Graft

*Meeting Mozart: A Novel Drawn from the Secret Diaries of Lorenzo Da Ponte*
by Howard Jay Smith

*Death Came Swiftly: Novel About the Tay Bridge Disaster of 1879*
by Bill Abrams

*A Boy and His Dog in Hell: And Other Stories*
by Mike Sager

*Miss Havilland: A Novel*
by Gay Daly

*The Orphan's Daughter: A Novel*
by Jan Cherubin

*Lifeboat No. 8: Surviving the Titanic*
by Elizabeth Kaye

*Hunting Marlon Brando: A True Story*
by Mike Sager

See our entire library at TheSagerGroup.net

Artifex Te Adiuva

CPSIA information can be obtained
at www.ICGtesting.com
Printed in the USA
LVHW112017210622
721767LV00016B/410/J